WORLDMAKING AFTER EMPIRE

Worldmaking after Empire

THE RISE AND FALL OF
SELF-DETERMINATION

Adom Getachew

PRINCETON UNIVERSITY PRESS

PRINCETON & OXFORD

Published by Princeton University Press
41 William Street, Princeton, New Jersey 08540
6 Oxford Street, Woodstock, Oxfordshire OX20 1TR

press.princeton.edu

Library of Congress Control Number: 2018939876
First paperback printing, 2020
Paperback ISBN: 978-0-691-20234-1
Cloth ISBN: 978-0-691-17915-5

British Library Cataloging-in-Publication Data is available

Editorial: Rob Tempio and Matt Rohal
Production Editorial: Ellen Foos
Cover Design: Layla MacRory
Cover art: Frank Bowling, *Barticaborn 1,* 1968 © Frank Bowling. All rights reserved,
DACS / ARS, NY 2018. Image courtesy of the Rose Art Museum, Brandeis University, MA.
Photography: Charles Mayer
Production: Erin Suydam
Copyeditor: Kathleen Kageff

This book has been composed in Miller

For My Parents

Yesemwork Bekele and Getachew Teferra

CONTENTS

ACKNOWLEDGMENTS

SINCE EMBARKING ON THIS PROJECT, I have looked forward to this moment when I can acknowledge the debts I have happily incurred along the way and thank the institutions, teachers, colleagues, friends, and family for the many ways they have made this book possible. The generous support of the Ford Foundation as well as Yale University's MacMillan Center for International and Area Studies, International Security Studies program, and Department of African American Studies provided grants for the research for this book. A visiting summer fellowship at University of London's Institute for Commonwealth Studies supported archival research in London and Oxford. A one-year Provost's Career Enhancement Postdoctoral Scholarship at the University of Chicago afforded me essential time to revise the manuscript. Additionally, a book workshop grant provided through the Center for International Social Science Research at the University of Chicago funded a daylong workshop dedicated to discussing a draft of the manuscript.

I am grateful to my teachers at the University of Virginia and Yale University whose classrooms and mentorship created the conditions in which I could pursue this project. At Virginia, the example and encouragement of Lawrie Balfour, Robert Fatton, Claudrena Harold, and Corey D. B. Walker opened up the possibility of pursuing graduate school, and I thank them for planting the seed early. At Yale, where this book began life as a dissertation, I was glad to have found inspiring teachers and dedicated advisors who pushed my thinking, gave me the space to find my question, and offered unwavering support once I landed on this topic. Seyla Benhabib's guidance and perceptive questions helped me clarify the theoretical stakes of this project. Hazel Carby pushed me to reimagine the category of black political thought and to consider the present political stakes of historical narratives. Karuna Mantena patiently read multiple versions of each chapter, and our many conversations have profoundly shaped my own thinking about decolonization, postcolonial politics, and political theory. I am deeply grateful to count her as a friend, mentor, and colleague. Andrew March was an avid supporter of this project and encouraged me throughout my time at Yale. As an external reader, Bryan Garsten's fresh perspective on the project raised critical questions that shaped the ways I conceived the transition from dissertation to book.

This project draws on archival research in Barbados, Ghana, Switzerland, Trinidad, and the United Kingdom. I am grateful to Jeffrey Ahlman, who shared his collection directories for the Public Records and Archives Administration and the George Padmore Research Library on African Affairs in Ghana. At each of my research sites, I benefited from knowledgeable librarians, archivists, and staff. I thank Lorraine Nero and Aisha Baptiste at the University of West Indies–St. Augustine, James Nabah at the George Padmore Library, Philip Murphy and Alegria Perez at the Institute of Commonwealth Studies in London, and Jacques Oberson and Colin Wells at the United Nations Library in Geneva.

My friends and colleagues from Yale's African American Studies and Political Science departments sustained me through the research and writing of this book. I thank Dana Asbury, Alyssa Battistoni, Jalylah Burrell, Charles Decker, Blake Emerson, Aaron Greenberg, Chris Johnson, Jamicia Lackey, Jennifer Leath, Travis Pantin, Celia Paris, Hari Ramesh, Joshua Simon, and Dawn Teele for their camaraderie. At a crucial moment of transition, conversations with Stefan Eich helped me see the shape of the book. Anna Jurkevics and Erin Pineda read versions of the manuscript at every stage, and their own projects have shaped my thinking in countless ways. With her incisive wit and wisdom, Shatema Threadcraft has helped me navigate the ups and downs of this project. Over the last decade, Brandon Terry has been a fellow traveler in this journey who sharpens my thinking, reminds me of the ethical stakes of this work, and provides many moments of comedic relief. From the inception of this project to the very last days of writing and revising, Anurag Sinha's generous friendship, calming presence, and enthusiasm for this project were a constant source of encouragement.

The ideas and arguments in this book have benefited from constructive comments when presented at the Political Theory, African Studies, and Human Rights workshops at the University of Chicago, Harvard University's Charles Warren Center for American History, the University of Minnesota Political Theory Colloquium, the "Post-colonialism, Critical Theory, and Democracy" conference hosted by the journal *Constellations*, the Carter G. Woodson Institute for African-American and African Studies and the Political Theory Colloquium at the University of Virginia, the "After Nation and Empire" conference at the University of Illinois–Chicago, Cornell University's Politics, Sandwiches, and Comments (PSAC) Workshop, the Political Philosophy Colloquium at Princeton University, and the Political Philosophy Seminar at the London School of Economics.

Finishing this project at the University of Chicago has been richly rewarding. My colleagues in political science—Cathy Cohen, Michael Dawson, Patchen Markell, John McCormick, Sankar Muthu, Jennifer Pitts, Lisa Wedeen, and Linda Zerilli—have graciously welcomed me into the department and generously provided feedback on parts of this manuscript. Jennifer has been an untiring mentor who, over the last three years, has read and commented on multiple versions of the chapters included here. I am indebted to her for her patience and thoughtful suggestions. I am glad to have joined the department with Demetra Kasimis. Our conversations have inspired my thinking and deepened our friendship. The dissertation projects of and conversations with Emma Mackinnon and Tejas Parasher have enriched my understanding of human rights and anticolonialism as well as the distinctive dilemmas of popular sovereignty in the postcolonial world. I am grateful to the undergraduate and graduate students whose enthusiasm and dedication in my courses have energized me. I appreciate Urvi Kumbhat, who provided invaluable research assistance and editing support in the last year of writing and revising. The interdisciplinary and politically engaged world I found at the Center for the Study of Race, Politics, and Culture has been an important second home to me. I thank Dara Epison and Tracye Matthews for all the ways they welcomed me into the space and for their support in organizing the "Racing the International" series during the 2016–17 academic year. I am grateful for Cathy Cohen's and Michael Dawson's leadership at the center and to Adrienne Brown, Jessica Swanston Baker, Eve Ewing, Alfredo Gonzalez, Yanilda María González, Marcus Lee, Erin Pineda, Danielle Roper, and Christopher Taylor for making the center a vibrant intellectual community.

During an intense and exciting book manuscript workshop, Chiara Cordelli, Manu Goswami, Patchen Markell, John McCormick, Jeannie Morefield, Sam Moyn, Sankar Muthu, Emily Osborn, Jennifer Pitts, Christopher Taylor, and Jim Wilson provided incisive criticism and perceptive comments that helped me clarify the central arguments and theoretical interventions. I am grateful to Aziz Rana, who could not attend the workshop, but generously read the full manuscript and provided detailed feedback. I owe a special debt of gratitude to Jeannie Morefield and Sam Moyn, who also served as reviewers for Princeton University Press. I thank my editor Rob Tempio for enthusiastically embracing this project. At the press, Matt Rohal, Ellen Foos, and the rest of the production team have expertly and efficiently shepherded the book through the publication process. Kathleen Kageff and Amy Sherman provided invaluable support as copy editors while Thomas Broughton-Willett prepared the index.

I wrote and revised much of this book at a moment of renewed excitement and political possibility in the academic labor movement. For all the ways they inspired me to imagine a democratic and egalitarian academy and to work toward the realization of that vision, I am deeply grateful to my comrades of the Graduate Employees and Student Organization/UNITE HERE Local 33: Alyssa Battistoni, Jeffrey Boyd, Charles Decker, Lena Eckert-Erdheim, Aaron Greenberg, Stephanie Greenlea, Kelly Goodman, Sarah Haley, Chris McGowan, Lukas Moe, Hari Ramesh, Anita Seth, Joshua Stanley, Gabriel Winant, and Lindsay Zafir. In Chicago, Cathy Cohen and Beth Richie as well as Barbara Ransby and Peter Sporn have modeled what politically engaged scholarship might mean in this city. I thank them for the ways they have generously opened their political worlds to me.

I am grateful to my large extended family—Almaz Dubale, Kidist Seleshi, Solomon Kemaw, Banchu Mossa, Elias Kemaw, Teferi Kemaw, Teddy Kemaw, Fantu Teferra, Tilahun Fresenbent, Kassahun Zenebe, Melat Mekonnen, Berhanu Abegaz Gashe, and Teguest Guerma for their constant support and encouragement. Semrete Eyesus generously welcomed me into her family when I was in the midst of my research trip to Trinidad and feeling the isolation that comes with archival work. I am deeply appreciative of Amber Roberts, Geraldine Pierre-Haile, Alda Boateng, and Starlynne Gornail, who ensured that many adventures were had while I researched and wrote this book. My sister, Aleshadye Getachew, and brother, Sofonias Getachew, are ardent champions of all my projects and have enriched this and every other journey with laughter and love. They gently remind me to take life a little less seriously and have offered the needed detours and diversions along the way.

This book is dedicated to my parents, Yesemwork Bekele and Getachew Teferra, who are the coauthors of all my endeavors. Over twenty years ago, they made the fateful decision to leave the world they knew and loved in search of a better one for me. I am deeply humbled by their sacrifices and perseverance. They have been unwearied companions on this project, and their love is my greatest source of strength and inspiration. My debt to them is inexpressible, but I hope that in some small measure this book captures their generosity of spirit and sense of justice.

WORLDMAKING AFTER EMPIRE

Introduction

AT MIDNIGHT ON MARCH 6, 1957, Kwame Nkrumah took to the stage in Accra to announce the independence of the Gold Coast, renamed Ghana in homage to the ancient West African empire. In his speech, Nkrumah declared that 1957 marked the birth of a new Africa "ready to fight its own battles and show that after all the black man is capable of managing his own affairs." In his view, the decade-long struggle for Ghanaian independence was only one battle in the broader struggle for African emancipation. "Our independence," Nkrumah famously maintained, "is meaningless unless it is linked up with the total liberation of the African continent."[1] This connection between Ghana's independence and African emancipation not only looked forward to the formation of new African states but also envisioned national independence as the first step in constituting a Pan-African federation and transforming the international order.

Half a century removed from Ghanaian independence and as we reckon with the failures and limits of the postcolonial state, it is easy to miss the revolutionary implications and global reverberations of that March night in 1957. From our vantage point, the transition from empire to nation in the twentieth century appears inevitable. And while the universalization of the nation-state marked an important triumph over European imperialism, it has also come to represent a political form incapable of realizing the ideals of a democratic, egalitarian, and anti-imperial future. In contrast, for those in the audience in Accra that night and observers across the world, the world historical significance of the first sub-Saharan colony to gain independence was palpable. Within the Black Atlantic world, the independence of the fourth black state after Haiti, Liberia, and Ethiopia was

[1]

especially momentous. Nkrumah's audience that night included Martin Luther King Jr., Coretta Scott King, A. Philip Randolph, Ralph Bunche, and Congressman Adam Clayton Powell.[2] The Trinidadian Marxist George Padmore and St. Lucian economist W. Arthur Lewis attended as members of Nkrumah's administration, while nationalists from across the continent including Julius Nyerere of Tanzania also participated in the Independence Day celebrations. Barred from traveling to Ghana because the United States had revoked his passport, W.E.B. Du Bois wrote a public letter to Nkrumah and the Ghanaian people congratulating them on their hard-won independence and urging the new state to take up the mantle of the Pan-African movement that he had helped to foster since the turn of the twentieth century.[3] For these figures, Ghanaian independence, arriving just months after the successful conclusion of the Montgomery bus boycott, constituted the beginnings of a struggle for racial equality across the world.

This book studies the global projects of decolonization black Anglophone anticolonial critics and nationalists spearheaded in the three decades after the end of the Second World War. Drawing on the political thought of Nnamdi Azikiwe, W.E.B. Du Bois, Michael Manley, Kwame Nkrumah, Julius Nyerere, George Padmore, and Eric Williams, I argue that decolonization was a project of reordering the world that sought to create a domination-free and egalitarian international order. Against the standard view of decolonization as a moment of nation-building in which the anticolonial demand for self-determination culminated in the rejection of alien rule and the formation of nation-states, I recast anticolonial nationalism as *worldmaking*. The central actors of this study reinvented self-determination reaching beyond its association with the nation to insist that the achievement of this ideal required juridical, political, and economic institutions in the international realm that would secure nondomination. Central to this claim was an expansive account of empire that situated alien rule within international structures of unequal integration and racial hierarchy. On this view, empire was a form of domination that exceeded the bilateral relations of colonizer and colonized. As a result, it required a similarly global anticolonial counterpoint that would undo the hierarchies that facilitated domination.

In three different projects—the institutionalization of a right to self-determination at the United Nations, the formation of regional federations, and the demand for a New International Economic Order—anticolonial nationalists sought to overcome the legal and material manifestations of unequal integration and inaugurate a postimperial world. Attending to these global ambitions of anticolonial nationalism offers opportunities to revisit and rethink the critique of nationalism as parochial and anti-universal. Rather than foreclosing internationalism, the effort to achieve national independence propelled a rethinking of state sovereignty, inspired a far-reaching reconstitution of the postwar international order, and grounded the twentieth century's most ambitious vision of global redistribution. In casting anticolonial nationalists as worldmakers rather than solely nation builders, I illustrate that the age of decolonization anticipated and reconfigured our contemporary questions about international political and economic justice.

In the background of this book's thesis that anticolonial nationalism was a project of worldmaking is the history of European imperialism as itself a world-constituting force that violently inaugurated an unprecedented era of globality. Beginning in 1492, European conquest and colonization coupled with native dispossession and genocide, the forced migration of twelve million African slaves over three centuries, and the circulation of commodities linked the Atlantic world and transformed the conditions of economic and political life in each node of the triangular trade. This first moment of imperial globalization reverberated beyond the Atlantic as European expansion extended to Asia and then Africa, producing new dislocations and transformations.[4] By the height of imperialism at the turn of the twentieth century, Europe's political and economic entanglements with the rest of the world constituted a novel era of world politics that made it impossible to think domestic politics in isolation from the ever-widening global interactions.[5] The contradictions and tensions between the nineteenth-century rise of the democratic nation-state within Europe as well as in the settler colonies and the scale and scope of imperial expansion were a central preoccupation of European intellectuals who offered a series of ideological and institutional sutures for the divides between nation and empire.[6]

The first antisystemic worldmaking project emerged in this context with the founding of the International Workingmen's Association in 1864.[7] Both the *Communist Manifesto* and Karl Marx's *Capital* situated the rise of capitalist production and its creation of a world market in imperial expansion.[8] "The dawn of the era of capitalist production," Marx argued, was to be found in "the discovery of gold and silver in America, the extirpation, enslavement and entombment in mines of the indigenous populations of that continent, the beginnings of the conquest and plunder of India, and the conversion of Africa into a preserve for the commercial hunting of blackskins."[9] Through this violent domination, the European bourgeoisie sought to create "a world after its own image" and in turn produced the conditions of its own overcoming.[10] In linking together disparate political parties and trade unions against the growing consolidation of an international system of nation-states, the First International envisioned a global emancipation of labor that would remake the world.

Beginning at the turn of the twentieth century, anti-imperialists of the colonized world radicalized this Marxist critique of empire's political economy. They argued that Europe's effort to produce "a world after its own image" through imperial expansion was always a chimera that belied colonial dependencies and inequalities. Imperial integration did not create one world but instead entailed racialized differentiation.[11] After the Bolshevik revolution, and working within and beyond the Third International, interwar anti-imperialists mobilized this critique to envision a reordering of the world that transcended imperial inequality and anticipated anti-imperial and often antistatist futures.[12] Operating through transnational networks, internationalists experimented with political forms beyond and below the nation-state. They offered visions of a world after empire that ranged from Marcus Garvey's transnational black nation organized through the Universal Negro Improvement Association to Padmore's International Trade Union Committee of Negro Workers, an arm of the Third International that fashioned black workers as the vanguard of the struggle against imperialism and capitalism.[13]

The worldmakers in this study traveled the circuits of interwar anti-imperial internationalisms. However, they arrived on the political stage at a moment after the fall of the Third International and when the midcentury collapse of empires coincided with the triumph of the nation-state.[14] These conditions set limits on the range of political possibilities for anticolonial worldmaking. However, the emergence of the nation-state as the normative unit of the international order also provided occasion to rethink the conditions in which a system of states might overcome imperial hierarchy and domination. In this context, nationalists argued that in the absence of legal, political, and economic institutions that realized an international principle of nondomination, the domestic politics of postcolonial states were constantly vulnerable to external encroachment and intervention. Worldmaking was thus envisioned as the correlate to nation-building, and self-determination stood at their nexus. In its domestic face, self-determination entailed a democratic politics of postcolonial citizenship through which the postcolonial state secured economic development and redistribution. In its international face, self-determination created the external conditions for this domestic politics by transforming conditions of international hierarchy that facilitated dependence and domination. This book demonstrates that instead of marking the collapse of internationalism and the closure of alternative conceptions of a world after empire, anticolonial nationalism in the age of decolonization continued to confront the legacies of imperial hierarchy with a demand for the radical reconstitution of the international order.

The Worlds of Pan-Africanism

To understand this history of anticolonial worldmaking, we need to grasp the worlds of Pan-Africanism that the central characters of this study inhabited. As Anglophone Black Atlantic intellectuals, Nnamdi Azikiwe, W.E.B. Du Bois, Michael Manley, Kwame Nkrumah, Julius Nyerere, George Padmore, and Eric Williams were interlocutors beginning in the interwar period. While I focus on Anglophone thinkers, it should be noted that interwar black internationalism transcended imperial boundaries and gave rise to political collaboration and intellectual exchange between British and French colonial subjects.[15] In fact, during the 1920s and 1930s, Francophone figures like Aimé Césaire, Paulette Nardal, and Léopold Senghor had spearheaded much of this collaboration, but the suppression of black intellectuals in Paris, which intensified during the German occupation, significantly eroded Francophone internationalist circles.[16] By 1945, London rather than Paris was at the center of black internationalism. Moreover, the postwar project of a transnational French federation, which occupied figures like Césaire and Senghor, created divergent trajectories of decolonization in the Francophone world.[17]

While the Anglophone world emerged as the central site of black internationalism by the end of World War II, anticolonial worldmaking was not limited to the central characters of this book. Broader political formations such as the Bandung Conference and the Non-aligned Movement also advanced the project of constituting a postimperial world order. Organized around the rubrics of Afro-Asian solidarity and the Third World, these formations played a central role in securing a right to self-determination and envisioning a New International Economic Order.[18] But if anticolonial worldmaking captures in this sense a broader set of political solidarities, it took a distinctive trajectory in the Black Atlantic, where imagining a world after empire drew on an anticolonial critique that began from the foundational role of New World slavery in the making of the modern world and traced the ways its legacies were constitutive of racial hierarchy in the international order.

The global legacies of slavery and emancipation were already central to the framing of the first Pan-African Congress, held in 1900, where W.E.B. Du Bois had famously announced, "The problem of the twentieth century is the problem of the color line."[19] In this formulation, he linked the modes of racial domination in postemancipation societies that the Jim Crow color line epitomized with the new era of imperial expansion in the late nineteenth century. During the interwar period, a new generation of black internationalists extended Du Bois's critique. Crisscrossing the Atlantic, this cohort of anticolonial nationalists was deeply influenced by their experiences of travel, education abroad, and encounter with fellow colonial subjects. Through literary, institutional, and political circuits, they offered a rethinking of the history of transatlantic slavery, formulated their critique of empire as enslavement, and articulated early conceptions of anticolonial worldmaking.

Capturing the worldliness of his generation's political and intellectual formation, Eric Williams retrospectively wrote that the nationalist party he had founded, the People's National Movement of Trinidad, "is part of the world movement against colonialism . . . [that emerged from] the very colonials who formed part of the university generation of the thirties, who saw the rise of Hitler, the rape of Ethiopia, the trampling of Spanish democracy, and who heard the Oxford Union refuse to fight for King and Country."[20] Born in Trinidad in 1911, Williams had won the island scholarship to study at Oxford University. He received his BA in history in 1935 and completed a dissertation on the economic history of slavery and abolition in 1938. Later published as *Capitalism and Slavery*, Williams's dissertation was inspired by C.L.R. James, who was his secondary school teacher and had also moved to the United Kingdom, where he wrote and published *The Black Jacobins*. The seminal history of the Haitian Revolution explicitly linked the nineteenth-century struggle against slavery in the Americas with the impending anti-imperial revolutions in Africa. Together with Du Bois's *Black Reconstruction* (1935), these texts illuminated the constitutive role of the transatlantic slave trade and slavery in North Atlantic modernity.

Williams moved from Oxford to Howard University in 1939, where he joined the political science faculty. At the "Negro Oxford," he participated in debates about the structuring role of white supremacy in the international order with Ralph Bunche, Alain Locke, Rayford Logan, and Merze Tate.[21] Howard and other black colleges and universities functioned as key nodes in black internationalist networks by supporting the research agendas of scholars like Williams, educating a generation of nationalists, and connecting African and Caribbean students and intellectuals to an African American public sphere.[22] The Nigerian nationalist Nnamdi Azikiwe first enrolled at Howard and took courses with Alain Locke, before completing his degree at Lincoln University in 1930.[23] In his first book, *Liberia in World Politics*, Azikiwe extended the explorations of international racial hierarchy pioneered at Howard by examining modes of imperialism that exceeded alien rule.[24] When Azikiwe returned to West Africa, he started a number of newspapers in Accra and Lagos that were modeled on African American newspapers and provided a new forum for West African nationalists.

In Accra, Azikiwe met Kwame Nkrumah, at the time a student at the Achimota Teacher's College, and encouraged him to study at Lincoln. Nkrumah followed Azikiwe's path to the United States in 1935, stopping in the United Kingdom to secure a visa. Echoing Williams's reflections on the significance of the 1930s, Nkrumah notes in his autobiography that as he arrived in London, he heard news of Italy's invasion of Ethiopia and describes feeling "as if the whole of London had suddenly declared war on me personally."[25] While he did not know it at the time, the 1935 invasion had been a catalyst for black internationalists in London. George Padmore, who resigned from the Third International in 1933, turned toward an explicitly Pan-African politics in this period, while C.L.R. James offered a more radical critique of the League of Nations as a racially hierarchical organization. Together, Padmore and James formed the International African Friends of Abyssinia to organize support for Ethiopia, and later the International African Service Bureau with a broader aim of coordinating Pan-Africanism in the United Kingdom. During this period, Padmore wrote *How Britain Rules Africa* (1936), where he deployed the term "colonial fascism" to describe the British Empire and highlight the limits of European antifascism.[26] The following year, he published *Africa and World Peace*, which traced the ways in which imperial competition and rivalry were once again leading to world war.[27]

By the mid-1930s, black internationalists had rewritten the history of New World slavery and had honed their critique of unequal integration and international racial hierarchy. But at this moment they remained largely undecided about the institutional forms of a postimperial world. The contours of the worldmaking projects described in this study would take shape only over the next decade. Between 1935 and 1945, Nkrumah was in the United States studying at Lincoln and the University of Pennsylvania. These ten years were some of his richest intellectually and politically.[28] He participated in African student groups, where he sharpened his ideas about African unity; was connected with left-leaning political organizations; encountered the writings of Marcus Garvey, which he described as the most influential texts on his political thinking; and joined local branches of Garvey's Universal Negro Improvement Association.[29] It was in this context that Nkrumah began to articulate a demand for national independence and translated Garvey's black nationalism into a vision of Pan-African federation.

Having moved to the United States to join the Trotskyist Socialist Workers Party in 1938, James met Nkrumah and facilitated his entry into the black internationalist circles in London with an introduction to Padmore. When Nkrumah arrived in London in 1945, they organized the Fifth Pan-African Congress and began a political and intellectual relationship that lasted until Padmore's death in 1959. At the congress and in their publications over the next decade, they developed an account of decolonization in which national self-determination was the first step toward African union and international federation.[30] After Ghana's independence, they hosted the Conference of Independent African States and All People's African Conference in 1958, the first Pan-African gatherings on the continent. Through these meetings of independent African states and liberation movements, they set the groundwork for Pan-African federation and supported a new generation of anticolonial nationalists.

The 1930s university generation, which included Azikiwe, Nkrumah, Padmore, and Williams, shaped the first phase of anticolonial worldmaking in the age of decolonization. They deployed the new histories of slavery to critique empire as a form of enslavement, institutionalized the right to self-determination at the United Nations, achieved national independence, and worked to realize regional federation in Africa and the Caribbean. A second generation of anticolonial worldmakers represented here by Michael Manley and Julius Nyerere responded to the limits of this first moment and articulated a new project of worldmaking. Born in the 1920s, both Manley and Nyerere were too young to travel the black internationalist circuits of the interwar period, and they came of age when the promises of communist internationalism had dissipated.[31] While they did not share the formative experiences of the 1930s generation, they witnessed and supported the early moments of anticolonial worldmaking. Manley campaigned for Williams's West Indian Federation while a student at the London School of Economics, and Nyerere directly participated in the debates about African union.

When these projects failed, Nyerere and Manley returned to the question of imperialism's hierarchical worldmaking and the distortions it created in postcolonial societies to reimagine a world after empire. At the center of this second phase of worldmaking was an effort to rethink socialism for these conditions and reestablish economic equality as the central ideal of a postimperial world. In doing so, Manley and Nyerere, educated at the London School of Economics and the University of Edinburgh respectively, drew on Fabian socialism and, in particular, the writings of Harold Laski.[32] Interlocutors since their days in the United Kingdom, Manley's and Nyerere's distinctive socialist projects, coupled with their efforts to institutionalize the New International Economic Order, marked the final and most ambitious phase of anticolonial worldmaking.

Organization of the Book

In excavating the projects of anticolonial worldmaking that constituted central episodes of self-determination's rise and fall, this book draws on extensive research in African, West Indian, and European archives. The animating motivation of this recovery is to contribute to a history of the present by rethinking decolonization. Narratives that equate decolonization with the transition from empire to nation-state understand postcolonial state formation as one episode in a recurring and generic set of questions about political founding, constitutionalism, and popular sovereignty. These narratives also constitute the implicit historical backdrop for normative theorists concerned with international economic and political justice. In illuminating the multiplicity of political projects that decolonization entailed, this book attends to the specificity of postcolonial sovereignty and seeks to reorient the questions we ask about international justice. It highlights the ways that the experience of colonial domination and international hierarchy gave distinctive shape to debates about sovereignty and state formation and recenters the enduring legacies of European imperialism in our present.

Distilling the main theoretical interventions from the historical excavation and reconstruction central to this book, chapter 1 sketches a political theory of decolonization that rethinks how anticolonial nationalism posed the problem of empire to expand our sense of its aims and trajectories. Drawing on recent histories of international law as well as the political thought of Black Atlantic worldmakers, I reconceive empire as processes of unequal international integration that took an increasingly racialized form in the late nineteenth and early twentieth centuries. Confronted with a racialized international order, anticolonial nationalists turned to projects of worldmaking that would secure the conditions of international nondomination. When we examine the worldmaking aspirations of anticolonial nationalism, we can move beyond the preoccupation with nationalism's illiberalism and parochialism to consider the specificity of the animating questions, aims, and contradictions of anticolonial nationalism. I argue that attention to the specificity of political projects that emerged out of the legacy of imperialism also provides a postcolonial approach to contemporary cosmopolitanism. Drawing on the conceptual and political innovations of anticolonial worldmaking, a postcolonial cosmopolitanism entails a critical diagnosis of the persistence of empire and a normative orientation that retains the anti-imperial aspiration for a domination-free international order.

Chapter 2 examines the institutionalization of empire as unequal integration in the League of Nations. Recasting the Wilsonian moment as a counterrevolutionary episode, I argue that Woodrow Wilson and Jan Smuts excised the revolutionary implications of the Bolshevik right to self-determination and repurposed the principle to preserve racial hierarchy in the new international organization. In this appropriation, which drew on Edmund Burke's critique of the Jacobins as well as their disavowal of the democratic possibilities entailed in nineteenth-century emancipation, Wilson and Smuts effectively remade self-determination as a racially differentiated principle, which was fully compatible with imperial rule. I chart the implications of their account of self-determination by examining Ethiopia's and Liberia's membership in the international organization. The membership of these two African states is often viewed as an example of the first expansion of international society. However, I argue that rather than protecting their sovereign equality, the inclusion of Ethiopia and Liberia created the conditions of their domination through a burdened and racialized membership where obligations were onerous and rights limited. In setting the stage for the history of anticolonial worldmaking, this chapter establishes the problem of empire as racialized international hierarchy and destabilizes the idea that the universal principle of self-determination had Wilsonian origins.

Chapter 3 moves from the League of Nations to the United Nations, where anticolonial nationalists staged their reinvention of self-determination, transforming a secondary principle included in the United Nation Charter into a human right. Through the political thought of Nnamdi Azikiwe, W.E.B. Du Bois, Kwame Nkrumah, and George Padmore, I illustrate that this reinvention drew on a distinctive account of empire as enslavement. In this expansive critique, anticolonial nationalists began with the arbitrary power and exploitation that structured the relationship of the colonizer and colonized and traced the ways in which this colonial domination reverberated in the international sphere. They framed their answer to this problem of empire as a wholesale transformation of domestic and international politics understood as combined projects of nation-building and worldmaking. The right to self-determination marked the first step of this transformation. Through its guarantees of independence and equality, it secured the formal conditions of international nondomination necessary for the domestic exercise of self-government. The emergence of a right to self-determination is often read as an expansion of an already existing principle in which anticolonial nationalists universalize a Westphalian regime of sovereignty. In contrast to this standard account, I argue that the anticolonial account of self-determination marked a radical break from the Eurocentric model of international society and established nondomination as a central ideal of a postimperial world order. Rather than tether the idea of independent and equal states to the legacy of Westphalia, we should identify this vision of international order with an anti-imperialism that went beyond the demand for the inclusion of new states to imagine an egalitarian world order.

Chapter 4 recovers the largely forgotten projects of regional federation in the West Indies and Africa that anticolonial nationalists pursued alongside their reinvention of self-determination. In returning to the centrality of the federal imaginary to anticolonial nationalists, I demonstrate that alternatives to the nation-state persisted at the height of decolonization. For federalists like Kwame Nkrumah and Eric Williams, freedom from alien rule did not sufficiently guarantee nondomination as powerful states, international organizations, and private actors exploited relations of economic dependence to indirectly secure political compulsion. The postcolonial predicament of de jure independence and de facto dependence, captured in Nkrumah's thesis of neocolonialism, made domestic self-government vulnerable to external encroachment. I reconstruct how Nkrumah and Williams positioned the United States as a model of postcolonial federation to make the case that regional federations could overcome the postcolonial predicament by creating larger, more diverse domestic markets, organizing collective development plans, ensuring regional redistribution, and providing for regional security. If in the formulation of a right to self-determination nondomination was to be secured by creating juridical defenses against domination, federations secured nondomination by creating new political and economic linkages between postcolonial states, which would gradually erode the relations of dependence and domination that subordinated them in the international sphere. In its federal phase, anticolonial worldmaking envisioned dispersing and delegating sovereignty beyond the nation-state. I trace the ways that this model of regional federation gave way to forms of functional integration that bolstered the nation-state as critics rejected Nkrumah's and Williams's proposals for centralized federal states. While short-lived, the federal moment in the Black Atlantic draws attention to the ways that a critique of international hierarchy and the effort to secure national self-determination prompted far-reaching institutional experimentation that attended to both the political and economic dimensions of international nondomination.

Chapter 5 analyzes the ways that anticolonial nationalists responded to an intensified postcolonial predicament with their most ambitious project of worldmaking—the New International Economic Order (NIEO). After the failure of regional federation, postcolonial states, which were largely producers of raw materials, experienced a significant decline in their terms of trade that threatened economic development and revealed once more the ways the postcolonial nation-building remained vulnerable to external forces. I illustrate that when confronted with the limits of the development economics Nkrumah and Williams had embraced, Michael Manley and Julius Nyerere articulated a new political economy of self-determination by returning to the ways in which unequal economic integration engendered a distorted postcolonial economy and produced a damaging international division of labor. Analogizing this international division of labor to domestic class politics, they engaged in a distinctive politicization of the global economy that framed postcolonial states as the working class; fashioned Third World solidarity as a form of international class politics; and demanded redistribution on the basis that the global south had in fact produced the wealth of the global north. Drawn from this account of the global economy, the NIEO constituted a welfare world that sought to enhance the bargaining power of postcolonial states, democratize decision-making, and achieve international redistribution. I argue that at the center of this welfare world was a radical recasting of sovereign equality as a demand for an equitable share of the world's wealth. The NIEO envisioned this expansive account of sovereign equality as the economic component of international nondomination. The view that sovereign equality had material implications marked anticolonial nationalists' biggest departure from the postwar international legal order and was quickly rejected and displaced in the neoliberal counterrevolution of the 1970s.

Finally, the epilogue charts the fall of self-determination and illustrates that the collapse of anticolonial worldmaking continues to structure our contemporary moment. Picking up in the immediate aftermath of the

NIEO, I locate self-determination's fall in two developments—the increasingly critical orientation of Western (especially American) intellectuals and politicians toward the right to self-determination as well as the diminution of international institutions like the United Nations where anticolonial nationalists had staged their worldmaking. Together the normative erosion of self-determination and marginalization of the UN set the stage for the resurgence of international hierarchy and a newly unrestrained American imperialism. At the same time, the critical resources of anticolonial nationalism appeared to be exhausted as the institutional form of the postcolonial state fell short of its democratic and egalitarian aspirations and anticolonial worldmaking retreated into a minimalist defense of the state. But while we live in the aftermath of self-determination's fall and no longer inhabit the political and ideological contexts that gave shape to the visions of a domination-free international order that anticolonial worldmakers pursued, the task of building a world after empire remains ours as much as it was theirs.

CHAPTER ONE

A Political Theory
of Decolonization

JUST THREE YEARS after Ghana's achievement of independence, seventeen African states joined the United Nations, marking the high point of decolonization in the Black Atlantic world. In what would come to be called the year of Africa, the newly constituted African bloc in the United Nations successfully led the effort to secure passage of General Assembly resolution 1514, titled "Declaration on the Granting of Independence to Colonial Countries and Peoples." The declaration described foreign rule as a violation of human rights, reiterated the right to self-determination, and called for the immediate end of all forms of colonial rule.[1] Resolution 1514 offered a complete repudiation of foreign rule and rejected any prerequisites for the attainment of independence. Soon after its passage, the resolution formed the basis of a new committee with broad powers to investigate colonial rule and hear petitions from colonial subjects, making colonial rule subject to international scrutiny and to the demands for self-determination.[2]

While 1960 marked a radical rupture in the history of modern international society, it has largely been subsumed in a standard account of decolonization where the transition from empire to nation and the expansion of international society to include new states is a seamless and inevitable development. This account of decolonization is premised on the view that anticolonial nationalists appropriated the language of self-determination from the liberal internationalist tradition of Woodrow Wilson in order to secure independence from alien rule. In adopting the language of liberal self-determination, the nationalists of the colonized world are thought to have mimicked the existing institutional forms of the nation-state. And while decolonization is credited with universalizing this state system, its nationalist and statist premises are viewed as anachronistic in a postnational and increasingly cosmopolitan world order.

Recasting anticolonial nationalism as worldmaking disrupts the central assumptions of this standard account. First, it expands the account of empire beyond alien rule by illustrating the ways black anticolonial critics theorized empire as a structure of international racial hierarchy. Drawing on W.E.B. Du Bois's famous diagnosis that the "problem of the twentieth century is the problem of the color line," the central characters of this book drew critical attention to the enduring legacy of racial hierarchy and slavery in the making of modern international society. Second, in response to the political dilemmas international racial hierarchy posed, anticolonial nationalists in Africa and the Caribbean insisted that self-determination required a combination of nation-building and worldmaking. Their vision of a postimperial world order prompted nationalists to create international institutions that could secure the conditions of nondomination. This claim that national independence required international institutions was a key insight of the anticolonial account of self-determination. Finally, recovering their global aspirations highlights the persistence of international hierarchy and outlines new directions for contemporary debates about global political and economic justice. Together, the expanded account of empire, the rethinking of anticolonial nationalism, and the theorization of a postcolonial cosmopolitanism constitute elements of a political theory of decolonization.

Beyond Empire as Alien Rule

As postcolonial states worked to pass resolution 1514 in 1960, historians, philosophers, and political scientists offered their first interpretations of the unprecedented process of decolonization. That same year, the Oxford philosopher John Plamenatz published *On Alien Rule and Self-Government*, while, across the Atlantic, the Harvard political scientist Rupert Emerson published *From Empire to Nation*.[3] Emerson and Plamenatz sought to explain how "alien rule" suddenly became illegitimate in the twentieth century, and they found their answer in the global diffusion of Western ideals. The delegitimation of alien rule in the mid-twentieth century, Plamenatz argued, was itself a product of the gradual Westernization of the world. European imperial expansion fueled the spread of principles like self-determination, democracy, and freedom and made possible anticolonial nationalists' critique of alien rule.[4] Emerson concurred, arguing that "through global conquest the dominant Western powers worked to reshape the world in their own image and thus roused against themselves the forces of nationalism which are both the bitterest enemies of imperialism and, perversely, its finest fruit."[5]

Key tenets of these early interpretations—the emphasis on alien rule, the inattention to the international conditions and context of imperialism, the identification of decolonization with the globalization of the nation-state, and the expansion of international society—continue to shape our understanding of the collapse of territorial empires. From international relations to normative political theory, the recurring emphasis on alien rule conceives of empire as a bilateral relationship between metropole and colony. On this view, empire is a "a system of interaction between two political entities, one of which, the dominant metropole, exerts political control over the internal and external policy—the effective sovereignty—of the other, subordinate periphery."[6] Involuntary subjection, nonreciprocity, and inequality characterize this relationship between the colonized and colonizer.[7] The international component to alien rule is understood as exclusion of the colony from international society.[8] Such exclusion differentiates alien rule from other forms of international hegemony that emerge within a rule-bound international order.[9] As a result, the international order is conceived as a dual structure that grants metropolitan states membership as sovereign equals and excludes colonies outside of its boundaries. With this bilateral account of imperial domination and a bifurcated view of international society, the alien rule thesis understands self-determination as a double move of overcoming alien rule and achieving inclusion in international society. Empire comes to an end when formerly excluded colonies enter international society as full members, and central to this inclusion is the universalization of the nation-state as the accepted institutional form of self-determination.[10] Twentieth-century decolonization is thus viewed as the culmination of a long history in which the nation-state is progressively globalized and becomes the counterpoint to empire.[11]

While the empire-to-nation narrative appears to capture the transformations of the international order in the mid-twentieth century, this account of decolonization also obscures the more far-reaching efforts to remake rather than expand international society. Characterizing decolonization as a process of diffusion, in which a "gradual Westernization" of the world took place, blunts anticolonial nationalism's radical challenge to the four-century-long project of European imperial expansion. Like British prime minister Harold Macmillan's evocative phrase "the wind of change," the diffusion narrative naturalizes decolonization, rendering it an irresistible development that necessarily follows from empire.[12] Indeed, well before the rapid decline of the British Empire, interwar metropolitan intellectuals and elites coined and adopted the term *decolonization* to reconcile their imperial past and present with what they believed was an inevitable postimperial future.[13] In this early articulation, decolonization was pictured as already immanent within the project of empire and did not signal imperial defeat. Decolonization thus "worked to absorb and deflect the phenomenon it ostensibly described."[14]

Rather than a seamless and inevitable transition from empire to nation, anticolonial nationalists refigured decolonization as a radical rupture—one that required a wholesale transformation of the colonized and a reconstitution of the international order. For Kwame Nkrumah, decolonization was not a wind blowing over the African continent but instead a "hurricane of change . . . [that is] razing to the ground the many bastions of colonialism."[15] From this perspective, "independence means much more than merely being free to fly our own flag and to play our own national anthem. It becomes a reality only in a revolutionary framework."[16] Nkrumah's vision of decolonization as revolution was directed toward undoing the dependencies that colonial domination left behind. Dependence structured the condition of formerly colonized subjects as well as the relationship between the former colony and the international order. According to Nkrumah, a people "long subjected to foreign domination" become habituated to their dependence.[17] The nationalist movement and postcolonial state would combat the economic, political, and moral-psychological forms of colonial dependence through an expansive politics of postcolonial citizenship.[18] This nation-building project, however, was insufficient in a context where dependence also characterized the new nation's condition in the international order. The hoisting of national flags and singing of national anthems—the mere transfer of power—left intact the economic and political position of new states. Decolonization understood as a revolutionary project thus required remaking the international order that sustained relations of dependence and domination. Nation-building was to be situated and realized through worldmaking.

Nkrumah's concern with the persistence of domination in the international sphere points to the ways that anticolonial accounts of empire extended beyond alien rule and homed in on the problem of international hierarchy. Anticolonial nationalists argued that a bifurcated system with sovereign and equal members and excluded colonies did not characterize the international order. Instead, colonies and peripheral states were internal to international society but appeared in that space as unequal and subordinated members. For instance, the colonization of Africa in the late nineteenth century was facilitated through international treaties and conferences. In those contexts, African states and political communities were endowed with an international personality that had made possible their domination. Viewed from this perspective, colonization was not experienced as exclusion from but as unequal integration into international society.

Unequal integration conceives of international society as an internally differentiated space that includes sovereign states, quasisovereigns, and colonies, which are organized through relations of hierarchy. The hierarchical ordering of international society ensured that non-European states were not afforded the full rights of membership in international society. The distribution of rights and obligations was such that non-European states and colonies were encumbered with onerous obligations and had only limited or conditional rights. In highlighting the ways that unequal integration is embedded in the formal institutions of international society, this account of hierarchy departs from theories that emphasize how dominant states exercise economic and military authority over states.[19] Distinct from hegemony, unequal integration as a constitutive practice of international law produces differential legal and political standing in international society. This unequal international standing functioned as the enabling background of European imperialism. It coincided with and facilitated political and economic domination.

The concept of unequal integration is drawn from recent histories of international law and international relations that have highlighted the centrality of empire in the constitution of these disciplines. While both fields are concerned with an international order composed of sovereign and equal states, key figures in the history of international thought, such as Francisco de Vitoria and Hugo Grotius, took up the colonial encounter as a primary site for theorizing international politics. As Antony Anghie has argued, the sovereignty doctrine, the central concept of international law, "emerged out of the colonial encounter."[20] Rather than view international law as first articulated among European states and later expanded, Anghie highlights the ways that unequal integration was always at the center of modern international society. And while unequal integration took a variety of forms during Europe's long history of imperial domination, the incorporation of non-European societies in the law of nations and the mobilization of treaties to usurp resources and sovereignty emerged in the early colonial encounter and remained prevalent in the twentieth century.

The early colonial encounter in the Americas forced European jurists to reckon with the possible limits of the law of nations. In addressing the question of whether the law of nations applied to the New World peoples, Vitoria offered an equivocal answer that would be foundational for subsequent debates in international law. On the one hand, he confirmed the universality of the law of nations and found it to be binding for Native Americans owing to their capacity for reason. However, their political and cultural practices were simultaneously marked as violations of the law of nations, which required disciplining and transformation. According to Anghie, the application of the law of nations to Native Americans created a discrepancy between "the ontologically 'universal' Indian and the socially, historically, 'particular' Indian [which is then] remedied by the imposition of sanctions which effect the necessary transformation."[21] In this early encounter, Native Americans are both included within the ambit of international law and found to be deviating from its prescriptions. The result was a partial and burdened form of inclusion—partial because it did not entail equal membership and burdened because Native Americans could be legible only as criminal actors who violated the law. As a result, the obligations and duties of their inclusion would be more pronounced than their rights.

This partial and burdened membership in international society did not stem from exclusion but instead depended on recognizing the international personality of non-European societies. More often than not, international treaties and alliances with local authorities, rather than outright conquest, were central to the making of European empires. While Europeans largely rejected alliances with non-Christians until the seventeenth century, this prohibition on treaties with infidels was gradually dropped in the course of imperial expansion in the Americas and Asia. Grotius's justification of Dutch treaties with East Indian rulers in a struggle against Portugal was central to this reversal.[22] According to Richard Tuck, once Grotius's permissive attitude became commonplace in the seventeenth century, "Europeans were morally freed to become fully involved in the complex politics of the Indies," marking a transition from an empire of "purely commercial relations" to a more interventionist project.[23]

Even in the nineteenth century, when international society was at its most exclusionary, marking its boundaries through the standard of civilization, colonial treaties "presupposed a common legal universe to which both parties adhered."[24] While the standard of civilization denied non-European societies sovereign membership in international society, key figures in the development of nineteenth-century international law argued that treaties and other legal relations with nonsovereign states made sense only because these states "are in some way or another International

Persons and subjects of International Law."[25] International society was thus governed by a "logic of exclusion-inclusion," in which non-European nations were excluded from the full rights of membership but remained subject to the obligations of inclusion.[26] Partial recognition of this kind granted legal personality to non-European peoples, but it was a recognition that afforded native subjects the right only to dispossess of themselves.[27] Thus, as Anghie concludes, "the native is granted personality in order to be bound."[28]

From this perspective, imperial domination structured modern international society and was internal to the very development of the legal regimes that came to govern international relations. These processes of unequal integration engendered legal and political hierarchy within the boundaries of international society. By the height of European imperialism, international hierarchy had become entrenched and stabilized through appeals to racial difference. To be clear, ideas of difference were always constitutive of unequal integration. What Anghie calls a "dynamic of difference" worked to generate "a gap between two cultures, demarcating one as 'universal' and civilized and the other as 'particular' and uncivilized," and helped to justify empire as a civilizing project.[29] In the late nineteenth and early twentieth centuries, this difference came to be formulated in terms of race. It was this transformation that prompted W.E.B. Du Bois to conclude that "the problem of the twentieth century is the problem of the color-line,—the relation of the darker to the lighter races of men in Asia and Africa, in America and the islands of the sea."[30] While often associated with the Jim Crow US South, in Du Bois's thinking the color line was an international phenomenon of which segregation and racial domination in the United States were only a domestic iteration.

This global color line emerged out of concurrent political and ideological processes during the nineteenth century—the legacies of emancipation in the Americas, imperial expansion in Africa, and a growing racial identification among Europeans and their settler counterparts. Beginning with the Haitian Revolution and culminating in Brazil in 1888, the nineteenth century was the age of emancipation as chattel slavery was gradually abolished in the Americas. But in almost each case, emancipation, which promised citizenship and inclusion, gave way to new forms of coerced labor and exclusion from political membership. From colonial Jamaica to the United States, experiments in extending citizenship to former slaves abruptly ended in new structures of racialized political and economic domination. This transformation coincided with an increasingly unsympathetic view toward black subjects, as accounts that emphasized the intransigence of savagery and barbarism among subject peoples displaced discourses that conceived of former slaves as capable of civilization and reform. In this context, colonial resistance such as the 1865 Morant Bay Rebellion in Jamaica came to be viewed as confirmation of the incapacity of colonial subjects for liberal reform. Former slaves thus shouldered the burden of responsibility for the failure of such reforms.[31]

By the end of the nineteenth century, this racialized dynamic of difference produced a more ambivalent and circumspect orientation to the idea of empire as a civilizing mission. If liberal advocates of empire envisioned imperial rule as a temporary mechanism for ensuring progress, skepticism that such progress was in fact possible owing to the intransigence of the colonized propelled a more minimalist and conservative view of empire that prioritized order and the conservation of native societies.[32] Organized through the theory and practice of indirect rule, this model of empire was central to imperial expansion in Africa, where the racial logics of postemancipation societies would be exported. In this context, the "Negro Question," associated with the American South, was increasingly viewed as part and parcel of a distinctive transnational problem of how to rule large black populations.[33] Linking the condition of postemancipation societies in the Americas with new African colonies, imperial regimes globalized Jim Crow.[34] Seen in this light, Du Bois's comment on the global color line in 1900 was not only an empirical description of a world in which Europe was dominant but also a reference to how a set of ideologies and practices of racial domination, emerging out of the experience of New World slavery, were internationalized.

If the debates that emerged from emancipation in the Americas and imperial expansion in Africa constituted one site where a naturalized and stubborn picture of race and racial difference emerged, a second and parallel impulse toward a racialized international hierarchy could be found in the new self-conscious understanding of Europeans and their settler counterparts as white. The emergence of a conservative defense of empire in the dependencies occurred alongside advancement toward self-government in settler colonies like Australia, Canada, New Zealand, and South Africa. Invocations of whiteness and Anglo-Saxon inheritance justified the demands for greater self-government on behalf of settlers, prompted immigration restrictions and segregationist practices, and provided a source of racial unity in transnational projects like Greater Britain and Anglo-American union.[35] According to Du Bois, the emergence of whiteness was tied to the making of a global Jim Crow. He argued, "The discovery of personal whiteness among the world's peoples is a very modern thing—a nineteenth and twentieth century matter."[36] At once personal and transnational, this new racial consciousness sought to forestall imperial loss and decline by consolidating a white world order, flattening racial distinctions between the "darker races," and reinforcing the global color line.[37]

Global white supremacy was briefly challenged and then entrenched at the end of World War I. On the one hand, what Du Bois called the "dark world" questioned the self-proclaimed superiority of the white world. The violent war and the devastation it wrought made Europe's claims of civilization untenable by calling into question the utility of scientific and technological progress in the context of Europe's perceived moral bankruptcy.[38] As Europe's claims to global preeminence were questioned, Japan introduced a racial equality clause at the 1919 Versailles Conference with the hope that it would be included in the League of Nations Covenant. Yet this clause was rejected and racial hierarchy affirmed as an organizing structure of the newly formed League of Nations.[39] Arthur Balfour, who represented Britain at the conference, voiced the dominant view of race in the international order, arguing that "it was true in a certain sense that all men of a particular nation were created equal; but not that a man in Central Africa was created equal to a European."[40]

Rethinking the Critique of Anticolonial Nationalism

With international hierarchy preserved in the League of Nations during the interwar years, black intellectuals and anticolonial critics reconsidered the problem of empire and articulated their dual project of nation-building and worldmaking. The experiences of the three independent black states—Haiti, Liberia, and Ethiopia—figured centrally in this effort. The 1915 American invasion and occupation of Haiti, informal empire in Liberia, and the Italian intervention in Ethiopia presaged the limits of freedom from alien rule.[41] From the interwar years, anticolonial nationalists gleaned the insight that imperialism "knows no law beyond its own interests" and concluded that in the pursuit of these interests, empire was institutionally flexible.[42] Alien rule itself ranged from the crown colony and protectorate to the mandate, and empire could also accommodate itself to the loss of direct control by deploying the international structures of unequal integration.[43] In each of these cases, however, empire was a structure of domination in which external actors could exercise arbitrary power over colonies and peripheral states.

Because this mode of imperial domination extended beyond alien rule, decolonization could not be limited to securing independence from the colonial master. Instead, it had to overcome the background conditions of unequal integration and international hierarchy that facilitated domination. Anticolonial worldmaking—the project of overcoming international hierarchy and constituting a postimperial world—took the form of securing international nondomination. In using the republican language of nondomination to characterize this project, I aim to highlight the ways anticolonial worldmaking responded to the relations of domination and dependence that exceeded the formal guarantees of nonintervention. For anticolonial nationalists, domination did not always come in the form of direct control or intervention from an alien power. Instead, they argued that even if the international order secured full membership and sovereign equality to all states, relations of economic dependence and inequalities of political power between states would continue to create the conditions in which postcolonial states would be subject to the arbitrary wills of powerful states and other international actors.

This anxiety was at the heart of Nkrumah's definition of neocolonialism in which external actors exploited the economic dependence that outlived alien rule.[44] Like the republican critique of freedom as noninterference, Nkrumah argued that the mere absence of direct political control was an insufficient guarantee of postcolonial freedom. Relations of dependence gave external actors the capacity for arbitrary interference. This ensured that rather than embodying the democratic decision-making of citizens, the postcolonial state followed the dictates of "neo-colonialist masters."[45] In this context, actions that appeared to be the free legislative decisions of an independent state were in fact the result of dependence on other states, private actors, or international organizations. Articulating a tight link between the problem of external domination and the capacity to exercise self-rule, Nkrumah argued that international hierarchy impinged on postcolonial citizenship and self-government. In keeping with the long tradition of republican political thought, he situated independence in a state free from internal and external domination.[46] The interlocked nature of citizenship, domestic institutions, and international relations required creating an international order free from domination.

Anticolonial worldmaking offered a number of strategies to mitigate, circumvent, and undo the hierarchies that facilitated domination. First, through the right to self-determination, anticolonial nationalists strengthened the legal barriers against foreign intervention and encroachment. Through an expansive account of sovereign equality as equal legislative power and a redefinition of nonintervention that went beyond prohibiting military interventions, anticolonial nationalists sought to contain and limit domination through legal instruments. Second, in the constitution of regional federations in the West Indies and Africa, anticolonial nationalists sought to evade the economic dependence inherent in the global economy by organizing regional institutions that were egalitarian and redistributive. Rather than a direct challenge to international hierarchy, federation was an attempt at a partial exit and insulation from the dependencies that facilitated domination. Finally, through the New International Economic Order, anticolonial nationalists directly challenged the economic hierarchies of the international realm. Laying claim to the expansive account of sovereign equality articulated in the right to self-determination, they envisioned an egalitarian welfare world that would be democratic and redistributive. In this final project, nondomination was refigured as a radical form of international equality.

Each of these projects offered a different strategy for achieving non-domination, but they were all envisioned as creating the necessary international conditions for postcolonial nation-building. Anticolonial world-making was viewed not as an alternative to or rejection of nationalism but instead as a necessary vehicle for securing national independence. Central to this combination of nation-building and worldmaking was the view that the global project of European empire had radically transformed the economic and political conditions of the modern world in ways that required a similarly global anticolonial project. In its strongest formulation, this argument suggested that the newly independent states were entirely constituted through international political and economic entanglements that could not be escaped or ignored. For instance, Eric Williams and Michael Manley both traced the ways that the Caribbean island states emerged from the institution of colonial plantations. With native peoples and ways of life eradicated in the process of colonization, the Caribbean was reconstituted through the transatlantic slave trade, Indian and Chinese indenture, and colonial trade. As a result, the Caribbean itself was a global formation and could not be disaggregated from the international political and economic relations in which it was embedded. This extreme form of extraversion necessarily required moving beyond national insularity.[47]

If this account emphasized the specificity of the postcolonial state's entrapment in global forces, a second argument described the dilemmas anticolonial nationalists faced as an iteration of a more generic predicament. Alongside his account of the plantation's distinctive legacies for the Caribbean, Manley argued that international entanglements of trade, capital flows, and financialization, as well as the emergence of transnational private actors, threatened to undermine not only postcolonial independence but also the capacity of all states to steer and regulate their national economies. Anticolonial nationalists argued that twentieth-century globalization was the extension of an imperial economy, which had consequences for all states. While the burdens of globalization were unevenly distributed and distinctively experienced because of a history of unequal integration, this position framed the postcolonial dilemmas that prompted a combination of nationalism and internationalism as part of a more universal experience of national states situated in a global economy.[48]

This anticolonial combination of nationalism and internationalism, articulated at the height of decolonization, extended and departed from interwar anti-imperial projects.[49] While interwar nationalists such as Marcus Garvey envisioned a deterritorial and transnational mode of belonging that mirrored the imperial geographies of the period, the combination of nationalism and internationalism that Nkrumah and others articulated was increasingly tethered to the territorial form of the nation-state. Thus the worldmaking of decolonization should be understood as an internationalism of the nation-state. But even in this phase, where anticolonial nationalism was bound to the institutional form of the nation-state, its vision of the world order went far beyond demanding an inclusion in and expansion of an existing international society. Instead, the pursuit of international nondomination entailed a thoroughgoing reinvention of the legal, political, and economic structures of the international order. The postimperial world order was not only more expansive and inclusive but also grounded on the ideal of creating an international society free from domination.

The novelty and significance of this vision can be appreciated only when we take seriously its challenge to the world order that preceded anticolonial worldmaking. The narrative of decolonization as an expansion of existing international society assumes that while colonies were excluded, the principles of equality and nonintervention governed the "Westphalian" state system and adequately protected sovereign member states from domination. The account of empire as international racial hierarchy recasts the three-century period associated with a Westphalian regime as an era of unequal integration and hierarchy.[50] Anticolonial worldmaking provided a far-reaching challenge to the Eurocentric character of this international order. Even when anticolonial nationalists appropriated key principles, such as self-determination and sovereign equality, they redefined and reinvented their meaning. For instance, anticolonial self-determination always included economic as well as political independence. Moreover, sovereign equality was not limited to a juridical claim but required the redistribution of legislative and economic power. This vision went far beyond the existing terms of the Westphalian world order. Moreover, as we shall see in the epilogue, the international order that followed anticolonial worldmaking not only rejected this reinvention but also undermined the international institutions central to the anticolonial project.

These worldmaking ambitions provide occasion to rethink the critique of anticolonial nationalism specifically, and nationalism more broadly. As we saw, the alien rule thesis, with its view of decolonization as the diffusion of the nation-state, positions anticolonial nationalists as agents of expansion who appropriated Western ideals of self-government. This globalization is largely celebrated as the realization of the universal ambitions of Western modernity but often also raises concerns that the appropriation of Western ideals is either premature or inapplicable in non-Western societies. Thus while Plamenatz and Emerson celebrated decolonization as a gradual Westernization of the world, they also worried that institutional and sociological deficiencies among formerly colonized people made them "ill-prepared to make [the nation-state] work."[51] Viewed here as a "derivative discourse," anticolonial nationalism was an artificial imposition on societies whose political realities seemed far removed from the conditions that gave rise to the nation-state.[52] As a result, nationalists in the decolonizing world could not reproduce the original and normative form of the democratic nation-state said to be instantiated in the Western world. This positing of anticolonial nationalism as a bad imitation or unfaithful copy can conceive of the divergent trajectories of postcolonial politics only as a series of deviations from European institutions and norms.[53]

Writing at the same time as Emerson and Plamenatz, the historian Elie Kedourie gave the sharpest articulation of this critique and situated the deviations of anticolonial nationalism within an account of the inherently pathological character of nationalism. In this seminal argument, Kedourie identified nationalism with a dangerous romantic fantasy that naturalized the nation and falsely equated the realization of the national principle with political liberty and just government.[54] Given the ways in which nationalism was an artificial export to Africa and Asia, the postcolonial context brought these generic tendencies of nationalism into sharp relief. According to Kedourie, Westernized elites mobilized nationalism to capture the state, and, in doing so, they supplanted traditional forms of social organization. Nationalism, in turn, invested this new political class with "extraordinary power to sway and dominate" the masses.[55] The result, Kedourie concluded, was a new form of Oriental despotism.[56] Decolonization thus sharply illustrated that "nationalism and liberalism far from being twins are really antagonistic principles."[57]

The thrust of Kedourie's critique—that the particularistic attachments nationalism inspires and the universal ambitions of liberalism are incompatible—persists among contemporary political theorists. Faced with the coemergence of nationalism and the democratic state in the nineteenth and twentieth centuries, political theorists often seek to distinguish good from bad nationalism.[58] For instance, Jürgen Habermas has argued that nationalism is "Janus-faced" because it combines a civic-republican account of citizenship with a narrative of ethnic membership predicated on claims of history, language, and ancestry. This "tension between the universalism of an egalitarian legal community and the particularism of a community united by historical destiny is built into the very concept of the national state."[59] While for Habermas nationalism's ambivalence can be contained if republican citizenship is prioritized over its ethnonationalist counterpart, Margaret Canovan and Joan Cocks argue that the dilemmas of nationalism cannot be easily circumvented.[60] The virtues of nationalism—"strong communal feeling, a sense of cultural distinctiveness, the love of a particular landscape, pride in shared historical accomplishments, a collective political agency"—cannot be disentangled from "the vices of a suspicion of critics inside the community, a contempt for foreigners outside, a drive to dispossess aliens and conquer new territory, a self-mystified relation to the past, a collective political bellicosity."[61]

The rethinking of anticolonial nationalism offered in this book does not seek to resolve this dilemma but instead aims to recharacterize its coordinates. This effort takes inspiration from Partha Chatterjee's early interventions, which rejected the conceptualization of anticolonial nationalism as an imitation doomed for failure. In Chatterjee's account, subsuming the question of anticolonial nationalism under the generic problem of the relationship between nationalism and liberalism or conscripting it in the effort to identify good or bad nationalisms failed to reckon in any sustained way with the animating questions that shaped the trajectories of anticolonial nationalism.[62] Charting a different approach, Chatterjee called for attending to the "autonomy of nationalist discourse."[63] This turn to autonomy was not a call to identify an authenticity unsullied by Western ideals and practices, but an effort to capture the specificity of anticolonial nationalism. Indeed, for Chatterjee, a central element of anticolonial nationalism's specificity was its imposed relationship to Western modernity and the ways that anticolonial nationalists both challenged and accepted its terms.[64] This approach highlights the ways that nationalists in the colonial world were responding to particular political, economic, and cultural conundrums that require reconstruction on their own terms.

Moreover, rather than tracing the failures, pitfalls, and reversals of anticolonial nationalism to endemic features of nationalism, this account understands them as emerging from historically produced contradictions and dilemmas.

By attending to the animating role the problem of international hierarchy played in anticolonial thought and excavating the worldmaking projects it inspired, this book recovers the universal aspirations of anticolonial nationalism. Neither mere mimicry nor dangerous parochialism, anticolonial nationalism envisioned a world where democratic, modernizing, and redistributive national states were situated in thick international institutions designed to realize the principle of nondomination. While distinct from the liberal universalism to which nationalism is frequently opposed, we find here another universalism propelled by the effort to institutionalize the international conditions of self-government. In this project of worldmaking, rather than foreclosing solidarities beyond the nation-state, the quest to secure national independence propelled robust visions of internationalism. The road to a universal postimperial world order was in and through rather than over and against the nation.

But to argue that nationalism contained a universal project is neither an effort to romanticize anticolonial nationalism nor an attempt to rescue it from critique and return it to a pedestal. Instead, by enriching our understanding of the multiple registers through which decolonization was conceived, we will be better positioned to assess its failures and limitations.[65] First, as I have intimated above, the relationship between nation-building and worldmaking took different and at times contradictory forms in the three strategies of worldmaking. While the right to self-determination sought to mobilize internationalism to strengthen and defend the precarious sovereignty of postcolonial states, the projects of regional federation and the New International Economic Order envisioned international institutions that would meaningfully transcend the nation-state. The regional federations especially required delegating sovereign prerogatives to a new political authority. These two approaches—reinforcing and dispersing sovereignty—remained part of the anticolonial project throughout the period covered in this study, but the former increasingly dominated the orientation of postcolonial states in the international sphere. Preoccupied with military interventions of the Cold War (exemplified in cases such as the Congo and Vietnam), frustrated with the ways that the existing structures of international institutions proved inimical to the transformation anticolonial worldmaking entailed, and increasingly anxious about domestic discontent, anticolonial nationalists articulated an internationalism that defended and zealously protected the postcolonial state. In doing so, they gradually gave up on the prospects of a more radical reimagining of the relationship between the national and international.[66]

Second, the postcolonial dilemmas that had propelled the expansive projects of anticolonial worldmaking appeared to also narrow the possibilities for domestic dissent. Anticolonial nationalists turned to worldmaking because they were keenly aware that national independence in a hierarchical world order was a precarious achievement. This preoccupation with the unstable character of postcolonial independence motivated their projects of regional federation and international economic redistribution. At the same time, concerns about instability also fueled suspicion of domestic dissent and motivated anticolonial nationalists to take an increasingly hostile and punitive stance toward domestic political opposition.[67] In the context of perceived state weakness, dissent and opposition came to represent instability and subversion, which sanctioned state repression. With the more ambitious worldmaking projects waning on the international stage, nationalists deployed the more minimalist version of internationalism in which the international order merely secured the rights of the nation-state to shield these repressive practices from international scrutiny.

Under the weight of these internal contradictions and the rise of external challenges, the anticolonial vision of decolonization was in crisis by the late 1970s. On the one hand, authoritarianism, secession, and humanitarian crises called into question the equation of anticolonial nation-building with democratic self-government, the protection of human rights, and a more egalitarian distribution of wealth. On the other hand, the growing indebtedness of postcolonial states, fissures within the global coalition of new states, and a reassertion of American hegemony contributed to the decline of the anticolonial project of reordering the world. Both the nation-building and worldmaking aspirations of anticolonial nationalism were thus destabilized. Self-determination, the ideal that had linked the domestic and international faces of decolonization, was also undermined as a result of these crises. If, at the end of the Second World War, self-determination had inspired a vision of an egalitarian world that guaranteed the condition of international nondomination in which popular sovereignty could be exercised, four decades later, its moral and political purchase appeared hollowed out. Critics exploited these pitfalls of the anticolonial project to argue that the entire effort at worldmaking was morally bankrupt. In the anticolonial defense of the right to self-determination and demand for international equality, North Atlantic statesmen and intellectuals detected a hypocritical mobilization of the ideals of liberty and equality to legitimize otherwise illegitimate postcolonial states. With this critique in hand, they set the stage for a counterrevolution that would reject and displace the short-lived experiment in making a postimperial world order.

While the internal limits and crisis of anticolonial nationalism contributed to the decline and displacement of its vision of a domination-free international order, the story of self-determination's rise and fall is not characterized by inevitability. Moreover, to read the collapse of anticolonial worldmaking as a sign of the congenital defects of nationalism is to elide the range of global visions it made possible and to forgo the difficult task of delineating the contingent historical trajectories that led to this decline and have constituted our postcolonial present. This study of anticolonial worldmaking is a contribution to this effort. Rethinking the animating questions and political aims of anticolonial nationalism on its own terms provides resources for critically evaluating the contemporary predicaments of postcolonial sovereignty. Our ability to assess and conceptualize these predicaments depends on setting aside an account of postcolonial politics as deviations from a European model and instead theorizing the specificity of political projects that emerged from the legacy of imperialism.

Toward a Postcolonial Cosmopolitanism

Theorizing from the specificity of the postcolonial condition also offers critical resources in normative debates about sovereignty and the international order. Against the backdrop of self-determination's fall, political theorists and philosophers reframed their questions about justice and legitimacy from a global perspective. Historically, these disciplines viewed the domestic sphere and particularly the "sovereign state as the consummation of political experience and activity" and thus limited normative theorizing to questions of domestic politics.[68] However, beginning in the 1970s and in a more sustained fashion after the end of the Cold War, the global turn in political theory questioned this disaggregation of the domestic and international and subjected the international to normative theorizing. Fueling this body of work was a confrontation with the nation-state's empirical and normative limits. On the one hand, the stylized self-sufficient state, which served as the backdrop for John Rawls's *A Theory of Justice*, appeared entirely out of sync with the growing interdependence wrought by economic globalization. In his early critique of Rawls's assumptions about self-sufficient states, Charles Beitz drew on the growing role of multinational corporations and transnational capital flows to argue that "international economic cooperation creates a new basis for international morality."[69] For Beitz and the field of global justice that emerged in the wake of this intervention, this account of economic globalization made it possible to theorize redistributive obligations beyond the state.

By the end of the Cold War, the growing layers of international legal, political, and economic interdependence also opened up new possibilities for rethinking the political institutions of the international order. In this context, a "fortress-like conception of state sovereignty," which historically gave states a monopoly on internal political and economic decision-making, was giving way to international institutions and particularly international human rights law that sought to limit and tame state action.[70] According to Habermas, these developments signaled a growing transformation of "international law as a law of *states* into cosmopolitan law as a law of *individuals*."[71] In this context, Habermas and others have examined the prospects for a constitutionalization of international law that does not aim at the formation of a world state, but disaggregates sovereignty such that the limited functions of securing peace and protecting human rights are lodged in a supranational institution while intermediary and regional institutions address arenas of growing interdependence such as economic and environmental policy.[72]

While the field of cosmopolitan political theory includes debates that range from global distributional justice to the constitutionalization of regional and international organizations, a central assumption of this perspective is that we now occupy a post-Westphalian world order. On this view, an international order governed by the principles of state sovereignty, equality, and nonintervention can be dated to the 1648 Treaty of Westphalia and was progressively expanded and extended in the course of the nineteenth and twentieth centuries. As noted above, decolonization is often viewed as the culmination of this process. At the same time, this moment of its universalization is said to coincide with economic and political transformations that chipped away at the normative model of the "self-determining sovereign national state."[73] Thus, while decolonization made the Westphalian model universal, it quickly became "an anachronism."[74]

This invocation of "Westphalian sovereignty" is often taken to be a conceptual construct rather than a lived reality. But even when this is acknowledged, the division of Westphalian and post-Westphalian elides the continuities between our international past and present by obscuring the ways in which empire was and continues to be constitutive of international society. An expansive view of empire as a practice and structure of unequal integration rather than simply alien rule highlights the deep continuities between the Westphalian and post-Westphalian world orders. For instance, far from being unprecedented, contemporary economic globalization should be situated within a long history of an imperial global economy. The "density, the speed, and the impact of the global flows" that emerged from the first colonial encounters in the Americas were already planetary in the fifteenth century and restructured political and economic relations within and beyond the Atlantic world.[75] This economic integration often took the form of a "non-colonial imperialism" that secured economic access and domination through indirect forms of coercion.[76] Contemporary conditions—such as the outsized power of private corporations, the role of international institutions in ensuring the unfettered movement of capital, and the inequalities this era of globalization has generated—build on these imperial foundations and reproduce the logics of unequal integration.

And as was the case prior to decolonization, relations of economic dependence and inequality are often coupled with legal and political modes of unequal membership in international society. While decolonization is associated with the extension of formal rights to all states, legal handicaps written into the process of decolonization set limits on the sovereignty of postcolonial states.[77] Thus, even at the moment associated with the culmination of Westphalian sovereignty, juridical equality was aspirational rather than fully realized. More recently, international lawyers and scholars of international relations have abandoned even the normative and aspirational commitment to sovereign equality, arguing for a return to modes of conditional and limited membership for states deemed outlaws, failed, or rogue.[78] The explicit defense of a hierarchically organized international order coincides with the growing power of institutions like the UN Security Council and the unilateralism of the United States.[79] Rather than view the international order through the dichotomy of Westphalian and post-Westphalian, we should understand it as an imperial world order that was challenged by projects of anticolonial worldmaking and was reconstituted.

The persistence of unequal integration and hierarchy calls for a postcolonial cosmopolitanism that recenters the problem of empire. Drawing on the critique of international hierarchy and the anticolonial efforts to build a world after empire, which are reconstructed in the following pages, this model of cosmopolitanism is less aimed at the limits of the nation-state and more concerned with the ways that relations of hierarchy continue to create differentiated modes of sovereignty and reproduce domination in the international sphere. As described above, hierarchy designates not

hegemony, but processes of integration and interaction that produce unevenly distributed rights, obligations, and burdens. These processes of
unequal integration are structural and embedded in the institutional arrangements of the international order. They create the international conditions of ongoing imperial domination.

With its critical and diagnostic orientation focused on the present configurations of international hierarchy, the normative and utopian core of
a postcolonial cosmopolitanism remains the principle of nondomination
at the center of anticolonial worldmaking.[80] Nondomination recasts the
current configurations of international hierarchy as infringements on
collective projects of self-government. This approach contrasts with an
account of the injustices of the international sphere that is primarily concerned with the violation of individual human rights. While international
human rights protections have provided important resources in challenging international hierarchy and can be combined with collective claims for
self-government, on their own they offer a limited account of the wrongs
involved.[81] For instance, the expansive claims of private corporations not
only undermine individual human rights but also threaten the capacity
of self-government insofar as corporate prerogatives erode guarantees secured through state constitutions and national legislation. An emphasis
on nondomination thus broadens our account of the injustices that unequal integration and international hierarchy engender. Moreover, as the
examples of anticolonial worldmaking suggest, realizing the international
condition of nondomination necessary to self-government can extend beyond a defense of the state to include more demanding internationalisms.

In this dual focus on hierarchy and nondomination, a postcolonial
cosmopolitanism offers a more circumspect approach to the antistatist
orientation of the cosmopolitan turn in political theory. In championing
the equal moral worth of persons against the morally arbitrary nature of
nation-states, cosmopolitan theorists have advocated taming the state
through international law and have expanded the reach of our political
and moral obligations. However, this privileging and prioritization of the
moral worth of individuals coincides with the normative diminution of
collective claims to sovereignty and self-determination, which have historically served to restrain imperialism. As Jean Cohen has argued, in
"prematurely drop[ping] the concept of sovereignty" and "assum[ing]
that a constitutional cosmopolitan legal order already exists which has or
should replace international law," cosmopolitans risk "becoming apolo-
gists for neo-imperial projects."[82] Viewing sovereignty as primarily an impediment to securing the rights of individuals provides cover for imperial

practices cynically masked as humanitarian efforts and leaves insufficient normative resources to distinguish and critique imperial and hierarchical curtailments of sovereignty.

This is not an argument for retreating into a defensive sovereigntist position, which cannot provide adequate critical and normative resources to address the contemporary dilemmas of the international order, and it should be clear that the postcolonial approach outlined here does not offer an exhaustive theory of the international order. But in returning to the problem of empire, it provides a readjustment of what we take to be the central conundrums and predicaments of international politics. Moreover, it reminds us that claims of sovereignty and sovereign equality not only have preserved the state against claims of international justice by creating a hermetic seal but also have served as the foundation of anti-imperial visions of international justice. These principles provide bulwarks against hierarchy and resources for resisting domination in the international sphere, while also making possible ambitious visions of the international redistribution of political and economic power.

Although this postcolonial cosmopolitanism remains open to the state as an institution that provides normative and political resources against international hierarchy, it is not premised on the ideal of an international order organized as a law of peoples. In response to the field of global justice that emerged in light of his *Theory of Justice*, Rawls turned to the international realm in *The Law of Peoples*. His account of the international sphere treats states as separately constituted entities whose characterization as liberal, decent, burdened, and outlaw can be deduced from their domestic features. Governed by the principles of equality and nonintervention, his Society of People includes a minimal duty to "assist other peoples living under unfavorable conditions that prevent their having a just or decent political and social regime."[83] Rawls views the realm of international politics as a second-order problem that states enter after their domestic constitutions are settled. Absent from this account is a central insight of the postcolonial approach, which focuses on the ways international contexts of unequal integration shape domestic political conditions. The domestic consequences of this context are particularly pronounced for postcolonial states that emerged from the colonial encounter and experienced "dependent state formation."[84] The aggression of outlaw societies and the unfavorable conditions burdened societies experience are inseparable from the process of international unequal integration. As a result, powerful states and the international institutions in which they are dominant "bear a portion of the responsibility for the authoritarianism, the disorder and weakened state capacity" that the categories *outlaw* and *burdened* designate.[85]

Without attention to the ways in which international hierarchies directly and indirectly affect domestic politics, Rawls's law of peoples contains only a limited principle of nonintervention to guard against external encroachment. Philip Pettit expands this Rawlsian model by turning from the principle of noninterference to nondomination. According to Pettit, alien control is not limited to "active interference" but can take the form of "invigilation and/or intimidation" and can be exercised by other states, private actors, and public international bodies.[86] To overcome these modes of domination, "a pre-condition of equalized power must be realized" before a republican law of peoples can be fully instituted. The emphasis on domination and an attention to the ways in which international conditions impinge on domestic freedom brings the republican law of peoples closer to the postcolonial cosmopolitanism described here. According to Pettit, "no matter how free a people is on the inside—no matter how far individual citizens control their states—a people can only be free insofar as an outside condition is satisfied too."[87] But while Pettit acknowledges this relationship between domestic and international freedom, he retains Rawls's view that the conditions of burdened and outlaw societies—what he calls "ineffective and non-representative states"—are largely internal to the states in question. The ways in which international domination creates the conditions for domestic domination remains outside the purview of the republican law of peoples. Without an account of the interrelated character of international and domestic domination, Pettit excludes nonrepresentative states from claiming the principle of nondomination. As a result, this model of the law of people does not extend far beyond Rawls's duty of assistance in the case of burdened societies.[88]

A postcolonial cosmopolitanism that takes seriously the idea that hierarchy and unequal integration are structural features of the international order entails a more expansive account of political responsibility rather than a limited duty of assistance.[89] In both its legal and its political and economic constitution, the contemporary international order facilitates international domination and contributes to practices of domestic domination associated with so-called burdened and outlaw states. The claim here is not that international structures are the only or primary factors at play in promoting authoritarianism or weakening state capacity. Instead, the perspective advanced here urges a reconsideration of a picture of the international order in which already constituted peoples freely and equally decide on international principles. Moreover, it highlights the ways that state formation and self-government occur against an international back-drop of hierarchy and domination and understands that rectifying these international conditions through a commitment to nondomination is a necessary component of ensuring self-government.

In looking forward to a postcolonial cosmopolitanism, we should look back toward the anti-imperial efforts to remake the international order. As we shall see, contemporary debates about what political forms are suit-able for supranational government and how to justify robust demands for redistribution across borders have historical analogues in anticolonial visions of self-determination. But for the worldmakers at the center of this study, the emphasis on the problem of international hierarchy gave these questions a distinctive orientation and led them to prioritize secur-ing nondomination. The central lessons of anticolonial worldmaking—that hierarchy rather than sovereign equality structures the international order, that nondomination must be a central principle of a postimperial international order, and that a commitment to nondomination enhances rather than detracts from internationalism—can inform our own projects of worldmaking. To set the stage for this vision of a world after empire, I turn in the next chapter to the imperial world order anticolonial national-ists sought to displace.

CHAPTER TWO

The Counterrevolutionary Moment

PRESERVING RACIAL HIERARCHY
IN THE LEAGUE OF NATIONS

ON APRIL 4, 1917, on returning to Petrograd from his exile in Switzerland, Vladimir Lenin delivered his famous April theses. Drawing from his *Imperialism: The Highest Stage of Capitalism*, published that same year, the first thesis denounced World War I as "an imperialist war" driven by capitalist interests and envisioned a peace that would bring an end to both empire and capitalism. These theses thus demanded that power pass to the proletariat and peasantry, that peace be concluded on the basis of no annexations, and that "a complete break be affected in actual fact with all capitalist interests."[1] Anticipating the global reverberations of the Bolshevik Revolution, thesis 10 called for the formation of a new revolutionary International. Six months later, the Bolshevik Decree on Peace restated and clarified the demand for a peace without annexation: occupied and subject nations must be "accorded the right to decide the forms of its state existence by a free vote, taken after the complete evacuation of the troops of the incorporating or, generally, of the stronger nation and without the least pressure being brought to bear."[2]

Though the decree left self-determination unmentioned, its account of nonannexation resonated with Lenin's earlier definition as the right to "exist as a separate state."[3] Lenin's 1915–16 writings contributed to a longstanding debate about the place of nationalist movements within socialism. For Lenin, democratic struggles for independent nationhood were an inextricable part of class struggle. First, the nation-state and bourgeois democracy, Lenin argued, were the "rule and the 'norm' of capitalism." Insofar as the road to socialism was through capitalism and the "complete development of commodity production," the formation of nation-states was to be supported.[4] Second, and from a more immediately strategic perspective, Lenin argued that Eastern Europe and Asia found themselves in the early twentieth century in the context of "a *whole series* of bourgeois-democratic national movements."[5] Within this context, socialists could not ignore the demand for self-determination and had to support the revolutionary elements of the nationalist movements.[6] In keeping with his later calls for a new International, Lenin argued that the socialist endorsement of self-determination must look "towards the East, towards Asia, Africa, and the colonies, where this movement is a thing of the present and the future."[7]

By the beginning of 1918, the Bolshevik government had placed self-determination into the debate on war aims. The principle was included in the armistice agreed to between the Bolshevik government and the Central powers at Brest-Litovsk.[8] And with this victory in hand, Lenin called for a "a democratic peace between the nations, without annexations and indemnities and on the basis of the free self-determination of nations."[9] For observers among the Allied powers and elsewhere, the Russian Revolution "seemed to have all the qualities of the opening act of a revolutionary drama shortly to be enacted all over Europe."[10] According to US secretary of state Robert Lansing, the revolution threatened the domestic stability of states and the prospects for a stable postwar world order. While Lansing agreed that some "principle of local self-government" might be justified, "the necessities of preserving an orderly world require that there should be a national authority with sovereign rights to defend and control the communities within the national boundaries."[11]

Between 1917 and 1919, this specter of revolution was not limited to Europe. Colonial subjects and critics of empire saw in World War I what Lenin called the "barbarous policy of bourgeois civilization."[12] In 1915, W.E.B. Du Bois penned "The African Roots of War," tracing the origins of the World War to the "desperate flames" that emerged from colonial aggrandizement after the Berlin Conference. Despite all claims to the contrary, Du Bois argued, "the ownership of materials and men in the darker world is the real prize that is setting the nations of Europe at each other's throats today."[13] While he would controversially call on African Americans to close ranks in the fight for democracy, Du Bois described imperialism as a form of democratic despotism in which the world's democracies addressed crises of national identity and the internal distribution of wealth through imperial exploitation. Critics of empire and pacifists in Europe and across the colonized world echoed Du Bois's analysis of democratic empires and challenged the claims of Europe's civilizational superiority.[14] During the spring of 1919, in Egypt, India, China, and Korea, anticolonial protests erupted and laid claim to the right to self-determination.[15]

In this context of upheaval, the Allied powers, led by Woodrow Wilson, hoped to contain the threat of revolution, in part through an effort to claim the moral high ground in the debate about war aims. In January 1918, Wilson gave his famous wartime declaration—the Fourteen Points. Almost simultaneously, Lloyd George updated British war aims to include the principle that territorial settlements must be based on "the right of self-determination or the consent of the governed."[16] The following month, in a February 11, 1918, address to a joint session of Congress, Wilson used *self-determination* for the first time, noting that "self-determination is not a mere phrase but an imperative principle of action," which entailed that "national aspiration must be respected; peoples may now be dominated and governed only by their own consent."[17]

Despite this late embrace of the term and because of the United States' dominant economic and military position after the war, Wilson's appropriation was successful, as Wilsonism and self-determination came to be viewed as synonymous.[18] Even historians who otherwise cast doubt on the centrality of self-determination to Wilson's thought continue to link him to the principle.[19] When self-determination is viewed as a constitutive piece of Wilson's postwar plans, the aftermath of the war and particularly the founding of the League of Nations appears as a tragic failure to realize political ideals in practice. The Wilsonian moment ended with Europe's overseas colonies still maintained and the league itself participating in colonial oversight through the new mandates system.[20] Article 10 protected "the territorial integrity and existing political independence" of member states, but self-determination appeared nowhere in the text of the covenant.[21]

In explaining the failure to realize principled commitments in practice, historians point to the ways that the process of realization is truncated by an external limit. On the one hand, Wilsonian ideals are limited by his equivocation between a commitment to universal ideals and an effort to ward off the revolutions they might unleash. On the other hand, ideals are sacrificed on the altar of diplomatic negotiations as European imperial powers rejected the inclusion of self-determination in the covenant.[22] This truncation view of Wilsonian ideals assumes that principles like self-determination have stable unequivocal meanings that need only be applied and realized in practice. Truncation does not destabilize or undermine the content of principles and, as a result, their future realization is still possible. What were truncated universals in the Wilsonian moment would be slowly achieved after the Second World War. This vision of the progressive extension of self-determination understands the content of the ideal as already anti-imperial and fixed from the Wilsonian moment to the age of decolonization.

This chapter takes an alternative position, arguing that Wilson and Jan Smuts, a fellow architect of the League of Nations, recast self-determination in the service of empire. These statesmen, engaged in what Stephen Skowronek terms the "reassociation of ideas," by laying claim to the revolutionary principle of self-determination and repurposing it in ways that supported unequal integration and preserved a structure of racial hierarchy within the league.[23] The shift from truncation to reassociation reframes the relationship between principles and practices. While truncation assumes that principles have a stable meaning, which only requires translation into practice, reassociation suggests it is practice itself that imbues principles like self-determination with their content and meaning. Thus the principle of self-determination must be excavated through careful attention to the contexts in which it emerges and the uses for which it is mobilized. Wilson and Smuts's reassociation effectively recast self-determination as a racially differentiated principle, which was fully compatible with imperial rule. Their shared project of appropriation and resignification was mobilized in service of counterrevolutionary ends and drew explicitly from Edmund Burke's critique of the French Revolution, as well as their rejection of nineteenth-century experiments in emancipation.

The Wilsonian moment is thus best characterized as a counterrevolutionary moment, and the hierarchical world order of the League of Nations carried the imprints of these origins. While the mandates system has received sustained attention as a site of the league's contradictions with regard to empire, this chapter turns to the only two African member states—Ethiopia and Liberia. These states were not subject to alien rule, but their membership illustrates the reach of unequal integration and the burdened and racialized membership it produced. Far from protecting Ethiopia's and Liberia's independence, their inclusion as member states produced the conditions for their domination. The drama of this racialized international hierarchy would reach its denouement when Italy cast its 1935 invasion and occupation of Ethiopia as a humanitarian intervention.

Making Self-Determination Safe for Empire

Noting the forty-two founding members of the League of Nations, commentators have argued that the new international organization marked a major rupture in international relations that was made possible in part by the partial realization of Wilsonian ideals. For the German jurist Carl Schmitt, the inclusive membership of the league was the endpoint of a transition from a spatially bound *jus Publicum Europaeum* to an unbound universal international law that had begun with the Berlin Conference and the formation of the Congo Free State.[24] As argued in Hedley Bull and Adam Watson's classic text on decolonization, the fact that states such as Haiti and Liberia were represented in the league constitutes an unprecedented expansion of international society that would culminate in decolonization after World War II.[25] Offered from radically different political perspectives, both of these assessments understand the league to be internally governed by the principle of equality and inspired by Wilsonian ideals.

Such accounts, however, miss the ways in which unequal membership was a key feature of the league. Article 1 of the covenant already indicated this hierarchy by noting that "any fully self-governing State, Dominion, or Colony may become a Member of the League."[26] This allowed for the membership of the self-governing British dominions and India (represented by the British raj), but their status as part of the British Empire—and thus not fully autonomous—was always marked in league documents.[27] Moreover, following the league's founding, the question of membership was raised again as small eastern European states sought inclusion. Before eventually granting membership to Latvia, Estonia, and Lithuania, the league recommended limited forms of membership for small states, including associated status without voting rights, restricted voting rights, or representation via a larger state.[28]

Beyond these qualifications of membership, the mandates system, which governed the former territories of the German and Ottoman Empires, represented the most explicitly hierarchical institution within the league. The mandates were not excluded from Wilsonian ideals. Instead, the new institution recognized mandated peoples' latent capacity for self-rule and deferred its realization because of their backwardness. The articulation of universal principles such as self-determination was concomitant with the elaboration of a set of deviations and deficiencies that would be overcome through the disciplining mechanisms of empire. Situated at the nexus of universalism and hierarchy, mandated territories experienced unequal political and economic integration. They occupied a distinctive legal standing as neither colonies nor states.[29] As we shall see, Ethiopia and Liberia—both independent and self-governing—occupied a similarly ambivalent position that facilitated their domination.

Rather than truncations of the principle of self-determination, these instances of inequality and domination are in fact reflections of a refashioned account of the principle that Woodrow Wilson and Jan Smuts made compatible with racial hierarchy and empire. Wilson and Smuts belatedly adopted the principle of self-determination but rejected the Leninist demands for separate national states and secession. Through their reassociation, self-determination would mean the consent of the governed and consultation with subject peoples. In his first mention of the term on February 11, 1918, Wilson had effectively made this transposition. Self-determination meant that "national aspirations must be respected" and "peoples may now be dominated and governed only by their own consent." Far from being a call for the dissolution of empire and the formation of national states, self-determination is equated here with Wilson's long-standing commitment to the "consent of the governed." And if consent suggested anything like democratic decision-making, Wilson and Smuts argued that racially backward people were not suited for democracy but could partake in minimal forms of consent and were owed some modicum of respect.

This reassociation of self-determination—the ease with which Wilson and Smuts could remake the principle to serve entirely different political ends while fashioning themselves as its defenders—illustrates both the malleability of the principle and its enduring connection to national liberation. Thus even as Wilson offered a radically circumscribed vision of self-determination that was not incompatible with empire, anticolonial nationalists and African American activists found in his appropriation support for their own struggles. Even his secretary of state worried that the president was offering a principle "loaded with dynamite" that was bound to "breed discontent, disorder, and rebellion" as the "Irish, Indian, Egyptians, nationalists among the Boers [and] Mohammadans" laid claim to self-determination.[30]

While Lansing saw Wilson's adoption of self-determination as continuous with the revolutionary project implied in Lenin's articulation, for both Wilson and Smuts, the appropriation and redefinition of self-determination was a counterrevolutionary project aimed at warding off its radical implications. Both statesmen drew on Edmund Burke's critique of the Jacobins to point to the dangerous and unstable nature of universal principles like self-determination. Moreover, they saw World

War I as a crisis of white civilization that they had already experienced in their domestic contexts with the US Civil War and the Boer Wars at the end of the nineteenth century. The dual task of warding off a world revolution fueled by the Bolsheviks and preserving "white supremacy on this planet" were thus the purposes for which Wilson and Smuts remade self-determination.[31]

Revolution and the fracturing of white civilization were already entangled in Wilson's early writings on the Civil War and Reconstruction. Evading the question of slavery, Wilson portrayed the Civil War as an unavoidable "fraternal strife" that was fought to overcome sectional conflicts and lay the groundwork for a new national union.[32] The emancipation of slaves was an unintended and regretful outcome of the war. It left the United States with the problem of assimilating African Americans, whom Wilson described as "dusky children untimely put out of school."[33] Reconstruction for Wilson was the wrong solution to this "Negro Question." Granting African Americans equal citizenship when they were unqualified for the rights and duties of full membership would prove to be a disastrous political experiment. African Americans' suffrage introduced an unstable class into the polity. The former slaves were a "laboring, landless, homeless class, once slaves, now free; unpracticed in liberty, unschooled in self-control, never sobered by the discipline of self-support, never established in any habit of prudence; excited by a freedom they did not understand."[34] By the time Reconstruction ended, "the Negroes were exalted; the states were misgoverned and looted in their name; and a few men, not of their number, not really of their interest, went away with the gains. They were left to carry the discredit and reap the consequences of ruin, when at last the whites who were real citizens got control again."[35] The tyranny and "mischief" of Reconstruction was undone only when southern states were allowed to exclude "illiterate negroes" from the vote and "the rest of the country withheld its hand from interference."[36]

For Wilson, Reconstruction was akin to Jacobinism as radical Republicans exhibited a dangerous and unyielding commitment to liberty and equality. Against this revolutionary spirit, Wilson endorsed a Burkean commitment to reform, preservation, and attention to the necessary habits and dispositions inculcated by existing institutions. Over the course of his academic career, Wilson wrote a biographical sketch of Burke, an introduction to the 1896 edition of *Conciliation with the Colonies*, and an essay, "Burke and the French Revolution." He saw Burke, the Irish parliamentarian, as the consummate Englishman, who rejected abstract thought and speculative politics in favor of practice and history. Burke, he argued, understood that "the history of England [and of the English-speaking peoples] is a continuous thesis against revolution."[37]

Wilson read the history of the American Revolution from this Burkean perspective, arguing that it was not in fact a revolution of the French variety, but a historical development that emerged from a long habituation to and training in self-government.[38] The United States "never had any business harkening to Rousseau or consorting with Europe in revolutionary sentiment."[39] For this reason, Wilson dismissed Thomas Jefferson's "speculative philosophy" and its articulation in the Declaration of Independence as "exotic," "false," and "artificial," as too tainted by revolutionary sentiment to have any place in America's founding.[40] Rather than a universal ideal to be adopted, self-government was built on the stable foundation of character that required "conscious effort" and "transmitted aptitudes."[41] These transmitted aptitudes were specific to the English-speaking peoples. While continental Europe was consumed by revolutionary fervor, "only in the United States, in a few other governments begotten of the English race, and in Switzerland, where old Teutonic habit has had the same persistency as in England, have examples yet been furnished of successful democracy of the modern type."[42]

It was this organic Anglo-Saxon historical development that the revolutionary project of Reconstruction threatened to undermine. In its aftermath, national reconciliation paved the way for America to take its "place of power in the field of international politics" by acquiring a "colonial empire."[43] Wilson often spoke of America's empire in passive voice, as if it accidently befell the nation, as if, to use J. R. Seeley's expression, it were acquired "in a fit of absence of mind."[44] For instance, he described the Philippines as "our almost accidental possession," which had "fallen to us by the willful fortune of war."[45] And prior to ordering the invasion of Haiti, Wilson insisted that the United States did not want "a foot of anybody's territory." Only "when obliged by circumstances" had the United States taken territory, "which we ourselves would have not thought of taking."[46] The passive construction elided the founding violence of imperial expansion and constructed imperial rule as a burden borne by the metropole.[47] Turning once again to Burke, Wilson understood this burden as a form of trusteeship. According to Wilson, it was "our to duty to administer the territory, not for ourselves, but for the people living in it . . . to regard ourselves as trustees of the great business for those to whom it does really belong." As "trustees," Americans should be "ready to hand over [the business of government] to the *cestui que trust* at any time when the business seems to make that possible and feasible."[48]

But crucially, trusteeship could not be handed over "at any time." Wilson urged against a universal right to independence, which assumed that all people were equal in their rights and capacities. As revolutionaries fought for independence in the Philippines, Wilson argued that self-government is not a given right, but "gained, earned, graduated into from the hard school of life."[49] Written the same year as his essay on Reconstruction, the metaphor of "school" returns in the imperial context. Like African Americans, Filipinos were also children in "matters of government and justice" and thus required tutelage.[50] Those who recalled American independence in support of the claims of Filipino revolutionaries relied on a distorted view of America's own history that linked it to the revolutionary spirit of the Jacobins. Echoing his account of American democracy as an organic development, Wilson argued that America was also schooled through a "long subjection to Kings and Parliaments" they did not elect.[51] By "serving under kings" and organizing themselves as commonwealths while still British colonies, Americans had developed the habits and discipline that self-government required well before they gained independence.[52] Given this historical experience, the United States should not hasten to extend independence to the Philippines.

Wilson recognized that the ideals of self-government and equality were dangerously abstract, but increasingly popular in an age of democracy and growing anti-imperialism. To counteract and circumvent their revolutionary implications, these ideals could not be rejected wholesale but would have to be remade and filled with a sense of the capacities, characteristics, and habits that constituted their necessary pretext. As Wilson reminded Americans, *self-government* was a compound term that required an assessment of "which word of the compound we shall emphasize in any given case."[53] In the case of African Americans and colonial subjects, the self of self-government required detailed specification.

In Wilson's thinking, the self was on the one hand qualified by reference to capacity and development and on the other hand limited to those of Anglo-Saxon inheritance. This was a productive equivocation. It acknowledged the value of self-government for all peoples while delaying its attainment for much of the world. However, if it allowed for the possibility that colonial subjects might embody the character and habits required for self-government, it also ruled out this possibility by naturalizing and racializing those capacities. For instance, Wilson wrote of the Filipinos' incapacity for self-government, "No people can form a community or be wisely subjected to common forms of government who are as diverse and as heterogeneous as the people of the Philippine Islands."[54] The problem of incapacity appears not as a temporary problem of education but as an insurmountable difference. Similarly, American self-government is presented as the result of English inheritance, which provided "the blood of freedom."[55] Here, the naturalization of an Anglo-American capacity for freedom displaces the earlier invocation of tutelage under unelected kings and parliaments. In light of this account, Wilson argued that "one kind of self-government is suitable for one sort of community, one stage of development, another for another." When it comes to government, "there is no universal form or method either of preparation or of practice."[56]

The upshot of Wilson's reassociation of self-determination was to transform it from a right to which all people were entitled to an achievement of historical development and a specific inheritance of the Anglo-Saxon race. In claiming both possibilities, Wilson included colonial subjects in the future realization of self-government and justified empire as a project of improvement while simultaneously suggesting that such a realization was impossible. This latter account implied that empire would be a perpetual feature of the international order. Jan Smuts's engagement with the meaning of self-government and self-determination complemented Wilson's reassociation by normalizing and defending perpetual empire. For Smuts, even if colonial subjects would never realize democratic self-government in the European sense, they were still participating in a form of self-determination. If Wilson focused on the "self" and offered a thick definition of the collective self that could achieve independence, Smuts focused on what "determination" could mean in the new phrase *self-determination*. His innovation was to offer a minimalist account of self-determination that could make it compatible with the racialized exclusion that Wilson had already indicated.

Like Wilson, Smuts developed his thinking on race, revolution, and self-government in the context of the domestic Negro Question. In 1895, he argued that the "theory of Democracy as currently understood and practiced in Europe and America is inapplicable to the colored races of South Africa."[57] His most immediate target was the voting laws of the British Cape Colony. After emancipation in 1834, the franchise was restricted by property ownership and gender rather than by race, allowing African men who either earned fifty pounds per year or owned land worth twenty-five pounds to vote. According to Smuts, this racially inclusive franchise treated democracy as a principle to be universally applied rather than the practical result of political habits and development. The African native, he argued, "cannot in a day cover the distance which it took the most highly endowed white races hundreds of years to travel."[58]

To insist otherwise and hold on to a "well-meaning attachment to racial equality" was for Smuts an abdication of political realities for the "utopian cloudland of abstract theory."[59] In terms similar to Wilson's Burkean orientation, Smuts associated this attachment to universals with Jacobinism, and in particular with "Rousseau's theory of equality [that] set Europe in a blaze of revolution."[60] Those who preached equality and assimilation sought to apply the French Revolution's principles of liberty, equality, and fraternity to colonial subjects.[61] South Africa's white settlers, especially the Afrikaners, who had left Europe long before the upheavals of the late eighteenth and nineteenth centuries, had not succumbed to the intoxicating pull of this revolutionary spirit. Moreover, unlike their metropolitan counterparts who naively preached equality and fraternity, settlers, living in outposts of European civilization, understood that racial difference could not be swept aside in the name of democracy. Instead, it required a politics that understood and reflected these differences. Smuts thus endorsed Cecil Rhodes's attempts to curtail the African franchise in the Cape Colony and compared them favorably to the rise of Jim Crow in the United States.[62] He insisted that these restrictions were necessary adjustments to racial realities rather than retrogression from the ideal of a democratic South Africa.[63]

While Smuts rejected racial equality as a form of Jacobinism, he argued that the enslavement of Africans, which had preceded calls for equal rights, was also a form of extremism. European thinking about the African, Smuts noted, had vacillated between a radical version of brotherhood and an equally untenable view of the African "as essentially inferior or sub-human, as having no soul, and as being only fit to be a slave."[64] This racial denigration led to tyranny and oppression against a population that, however different, was part of South Africa's "moral and social environment."[65] Against these extremes, Smuts urged a cautious, tentative approach that built on the lessons of past failures. The cautious road, however, was not one of deferring multiracial democracy for a future in which the African majority would have developed the necessary capacities. Deferral suggested a policy of assimilation where racial difference is eventually overcome. On Smuts's view, there would be no future point at which racial difference would be erased. Moreover, efforts aimed at achieving this goal by civilizing the native were detrimental to the colonized as Africans' contact with Europeans, and their assimilation to European ideals led to the deterioration of native forms of life.[66]

Against the civilizing mission's aims of assimilation, Smuts argued that colonial policy on the African continent should have the aim of preservation. The language of preservation echoed the imperial ideology of indirect rule that was developed in British India and could already be found in the General Act of the Berlin Conference.[67] With this emphasis on preservation, Smuts argued that the British Empire "does not stand for the assimilation of its peoples into a common type, it does not stand for standardization, but for the fullest, freest development of all its people along their own specific lines."[68] This required "creating parallel institutions—giving the natives their own separate institutions on parallel lines with institutions for whites."[69] Smuts euphemistically described this policy as "separate development."[70] This program acknowledged a belief that whites and blacks were "different not only in color but in minds and in political capacity."[71] For this reason, they required separate political institutions that are "always proceeding on the basis of self-government."[72] Separate development, or apartheid, would become South Africa's official policy when the Afrikaner-dominated National Party came to power in 1948.

The insistence on "separate development" recalls Wilson's view that there is "no universal form or method" when it comes to government. However, while Wilson's use of developmental language suggested at times that self-government was realizable for colonial subjects in the future, Smuts never equivocated between deferral and denial. Moreover, the denial of a European form of self-government did not mean that Africans were excluded from self-government altogether. Because Africans could govern themselves in their separate institutions, segregation did not violate the principle of self-determination. It was an application of the principle to peoples with different capacities, habits, and practices. Ultimately, this policy would result in "large areas cultivated by blacks and governed by blacks, where they will look after themselves in all their forms of living and development, while in the rest of the country you will have your white communities, which will govern themselves separately according to accepted European principles."[73] Rather than forestalling equal citizenship, Smuts argued that self-government was fully compatible with and equally realized in separate institutions demarcated by a racial hierarchy.

By the time discussions about a postwar international order began, Smuts had accomplished a reassociation of self-determination that made it compatible with empire in the arena of domestic policy. It was this vision of a racially adjusted form of self-rule that Smuts sought to project onto the international sphere. He began in that context by surprisingly claiming that World War I was the result of imperial aggrandizement. According to Smuts, if there were a return to the "old policy of grab and greed and partitions," the peace would be illusory.[74] In this claim, Smuts appears to echo the likes of Lenin and Du Bois, who also linked the war's origins to imperialism and argued that a peace that did not address empire would be a sham. But while these anti-imperialists formulated the connections between war and empire by drawing attention to the global scramble for colonies fueled by finance capital and led by the British, Smuts refashioned the argument to absolve the British Empire of the aggression and rapaciousness that led to war. In Smuts's account it was the Ottoman and German Empires, the "old Empires" constituted on the basis of "inequality and the bondage and oppression of the smaller national units" and grounded in theories of centralized sovereignty, that had contributed to the war.[75]

The British Empire, based on the "principles of national freedom and political decentralization," was exempt from this destructive imperialism and as a result could be the model for the new League of Nations. It was, Smuts argued, a "lesser league," a miniature form of what the international order could look like in the aftermath of war. Despite the hierarchies between the metropole, the dominions, and dependencies, Smuts argued that the British Empire realized the principles of freedom and equality. He defended this view by transposing equity for equality.[76] Equity moderated the absolute and universal claim of equality by indicating that the aim of political institutions was not to secure equal rights and full membership but instead to achieve an appropriate equilibrium attentive to differing capacities and levels of development.[77] Like the British Empire, the league would secure development for colonized peoples according to their specific capacities and cultures. This differentiation was the best means of realizing the principles of freedom and equality.

Smuts's mandates system embodied this differentiated application of self-determination. According to Smuts, the new institution would be guided by the general principles of "no annexation and the self-determination of nations."[78] And yet the "self-determination of nations" would have to be fitted for the capacities of different peoples. While nations like Poland could be immediately granted statehood, many of the nations under Ottoman rule were capable of autonomy but would need "the guiding hand of some external authority."[79] At the bottom of Smuts's hierarchy were the German colonies in the Pacific and Africa. Smuts viewed these colonial subjects similarly to black South Africans and argued, "It would be impracticable to apply any idea of political self-determination in the European sense" to the inhabitants of these territories.[80]

But even if they were excluded from self-determination in the European sense, the mandates were still governed by the principle of self-determination now fitted to their capacities. Self-determination in their case would mean consent and consultation. Smuts argued that the native populations must be consulted as to whether they wanted their former German masters back, but he noted that the results of such a consultation are already "a foregone conclusion," making consultation superfluous. In addition, he endorsed point 5 of Wilson's fourteen points, which stated that questions of sovereignty in colonial territories must take into consideration the "interests of the populations concerned" as well as "the equitable claims of the government whose title is to be determined."[81]

Through the minimalist requirement of consent and consultation, Smuts could effectively claim that the league was based on "universal human principles" while at the same time preserving hierarchy. In his re-association, self-determination was no longer independent statehood. For colonized people, consent was a sufficient realization of the principle. But as the history of colonial treaties suggests, consent operated as a mechanism of unequal integration. In the case of the mandates, consent was—in Timothy Mitchell's words—to be secured through "a process of recognizing (and in practice, of helping to constitute) forms of local despotism through which imperial control would continue to operate."[82] Central to this production of consent was the institution of treaties that recognized native sovereigns and their capacity to enter international agreements while effacing the historical conditions of inequality that were reproduced in the treaty. As Smuts's comment on the "foregone conclusion" of consultation suggests, the only thing natives could consent to would be British or French imperial rule. The only right such a process of consultation afforded was the "right [of natives] to dispose of themselves."[83]

Wilson's vision for the postwar settlement similarly combined the universal ideals of equality and self-determination with hierarchy. For instance, in his "Peace without Victory" speech, Wilson insisted that the equality of nations was a matter of equal rights, not "equipoises of power."[84] Although it would be challenged in the age of decolonization, the view that a commitment to formal equality in the international sphere can be fully compatible with material inequalities was not controversial. But Wilson was not simply disaggregating juridical equality from substantive political and economic differences. Instead, he argued that even equality of rights would be attenuated and qualified by reference to a state's level of development. International equality was not given in advance but "gained in the ordinary, peaceful and legitimate development of the peoples themselves."[85]

In Wilson's fourteen points, equal rights were limited to a subset of countries in Europe as only the national and territorial claims of Belgium,

France, Italy, and Poland were recognized.[86] On the other hand, the "relations of the several Balkan states to one another [were to be] determined by friendly counsel" rather than according to the principle of self-determination.[87] For the former colonies of the Ottoman and German Empires outside of Europe, which would not be guaranteed self-government and equality within the League of Nations, Wilson advocated "undoubted security of life and an absolutely unmolested opportunity of autonomous development."[88] Divorced entirely from any future realization of self-determination, these guarantees appeared to transform tutelage and trusteeship into a permanent state of affairs.

Racial hierarchy was thus constitutive of the League of Nations, which Smuts and Wilson founded. They created a distinctive set of institutional and discursive legacies in the league that preserved racial hierarchy by laying claim to the ideals of self-determination and equality of nations. On the one hand, the league was a more inclusive and universal project than prior iterations of international society. On the other hand, inclusion operated through a process of unequal integration in which self-determination could mean only consent, consultation, and "autonomous development" for much of the world. The reference to states, dominions, and colonies in article 1 of the covenant; the debate about limited forms of membership for eastern European states; the hierarchical mandates system that differentiated A, B, and C mandates; and the crisis over African membership in the league were not truncations of principles yet to be fully realized but effects of a counterrevolution that successfully preserved racial hierarchy.

As Smuts and Wilson worked to institute their version of the League of Nations at the Peace Conference, the Communist International held its founding meeting in March 1919 and called attention to the counterrevolutionary transformation of self-determination at hand. While almost every victor nation paid lip service to the principle of self-determination, it was denied in every instance. European territorial settlements like the French incorporation of Alsace-Lorraine occurred without plebiscite; "Ireland, Egypt, India have no national right of self-determination"; and the victors were in the process of distributing former German colonies among themselves.[89] European empires had drawn colonized subjects into the war on an unprecedented scale, but it appeared that "Indians, Negroes, Arabs and Madagascans [had] fought on the European continent . . . for their right to remain the slaves of England and France." According to the International, Wilson's project in the league "is meant only to change the commercial label of colonial slavery." The idealism and universalism with which Wilsonism had become associated only masked what was a preservation of racial hierarchy and colonial exploitation.[90] The League of Nations was a league of "imperialist counter-revolution" that could be defeated only through the combination of anti-imperialist and proletarian revolution.[91]

The language of "colonial slavery" would soon become the central metaphor of black anticolonial critique, but in February 1919, the Second Pan-African Congress, which Du Bois hastily organized in Paris to coincide with the treaty negotiations, made more moderate demands and did not break with the league. The fifty-seven delegates, with twelve representing the African continent, called for gradual self-government for Africans, giving the League of Nations authority to supervise native rights including in colonies outside of the mandate system, according equal rights and liberty of conscience to "educated" native subjects, safeguarding the rights of native labor, protecting land rights, and promoting mass education in the colonies.[92] Du Bois was able to meet with a few of the delegates at the Peace Conference, but on the whole the efforts of the Pan-African Congress were rebuffed.

Upon returning to the United States in the context of the Red Summer's racial violence, Du Bois wrote an article in the *Crisis* that set aside the moderate demands of the Congress and returned to the revolutionary possibilities opened in 1917. He argued that "the one new Idea of the World War—the one which may well stand in future years as the one thing that made the slaughter worthwhile—is an Idea which we are likely to fail to know because it is today hidden under the maledictions hurled at Bolshevism." This idea that "only those who work shall vote and rule" promised a new world order. For Du Bois, the next phase of this project was left to Negro laborers who "in Africa and the South Seas, in all the Americas and dimly in Asia" would lead the struggle against "white domination of black and brown and yellow serfs."[93]

The Impossibility of Black Sovereignty

Following the formation of the League of Nations, the International Labor Organization, league officials connected to the Permanent Mandates Commission, and nongovernmental organizations would also take an interest in the problem of Negro labor. But if for Du Bois the Negro laborer was figured as a possible revolutionary agent that would bring an end to the global color line, within the league, the question of Negro labor was primarily registered in terms of a humanitarian crisis of slavery—one that was located in the independent African states of Ethiopia and Liberia.

Indeed, well before Ethiopia became a member of the league, the East African country had entered the organization as the site of humanitarian crisis and object of international intervention.

In 1922, with the encouragement of the British Anti-slavery and Aborigines Protection Society, Sir Arthur Steel-Maitland, the New Zealand representative in the League of Nations Assembly, raised the pressing issue of the "recrudescence of slavery in Africa."[94] His concern was particularly targeted at practices of slavery and the ongoing slave trade in Ethiopia. Hoping to organize an international response to this crisis, he introduced two resolutions in the assembly—the first requested an inquiry into slave trading in Ethiopia, while the second focused more broadly on slavery in Africa. To avoid what could have appeared as undue attention directed at one country, the assembly passed the more general resolution, asking the league's council to collect information from all member states about slavery in Africa and to submit a report for the assembly's meeting the following year.[95]

While the 1922 resolution dropped any specific mention of Ethiopia, the humanitarian crisis of slavery shaped the league's relations with the East African country as well as Liberia a few years later. In locating their abolitionist efforts in Liberia and Ethiopia, league officials and member states deflected from the broader question of labor exploitation in colonized territories. Beginning with revelations about forced labor in the Belgian Congo, journalists, humanitarians, and anticolonial critics made the case that colonial governments were engaged in practices akin to slavery and sought imperial reform.[96] Within the league, however, European empires were largely absolved of past and present involvement with slavery, and slavery itself was disconnected from colonial labor and cast as an atavistic holdover in backward societies. By framing the slavery problem in this way, the league positioned itself as the agent of emancipation and Liberia and Ethiopia as either culprits of humanitarian harm or incapable of effectively addressing the crisis.

Significantly, the charge that slavery was practiced in Liberia and Ethiopia was mobilized not to exclude these African states from the league but instead to justify their unequal integration. Following the combination of self-determination with imperial hierarchy that Wilson and Smuts had articulated, Ethiopia and Liberia were subject to a qualified membership in the League of Nations that often appeared similar to the conditions imposed in the mandated territories. Indeed, at a number of moments, the league considered "mandation" of the two countries as a solution to the slavery problem. Even though the institution of a mandate was unsuccessful, Ethiopia and Liberia were subject to an international oversight that was legitimized through their own consent. In this context, the recognition of African sovereignty and the endowment of these states with international personality engendered their domination. Their unequal integration eroded and curtailed the significance of their legal standing.

Unequal integration produced a burdened and racialized membership for Ethiopia and Liberia. By "burdened membership," I mean a form of inclusion in international society where responsibilities and obligations were onerous and rights and entitlements limited and conditional. It is akin to what Saidiya Hartman has called "burdened individuality" in the context of emancipation in the United States, where the granting of freedom and equality to African Americans came laden with new forms of responsibility and indebtedness. For the formerly enslaved, Hartman argues, emancipation was a double bind that combined "the onerous responsibilities of freedom with few of its entitlements."[97] On the international stage, Liberia and Ethiopia would find themselves in a similar position as inclusion in the family of nations engendered distinctive burdens.

As described here, burdened membership stands in contrast to John Rawls's account of burdened societies in *The Law of Peoples*. In his definition, "burdened societies, while they are not expansive or aggressive, lack the political and cultural traditions, the human capital and know-how, and, often, the material and technological resources needed to be well-ordered."[98] They are owed "a duty of assistance" that aims to help burdened societies govern themselves rationally so that they may eventually enter the "Society of well-ordered Peoples."[99] Rawls understands burdens as domestic deficits that are disconnected from the international context. Moreover, like colonies in the alien rule framework, burdened societies stand outside of the economic and political relations of the international order as they are still awaiting entry and inclusion.

The case of Liberia and Ethiopia in the league reframes the problem of burdened societies in a number of ways. First, the crisis of slavery in these states not only was the result of inadequate political culture or internal disorder but was entangled with broader colonial labor conditions. This was especially true in Liberia, where slavery and forced labor could not be separated from the regional colonial economy. While perceived as an internal domestic deficit, the crisis of slavery was produced at the nexus of entanglements between the international and national. Moreover, framing slavery as an internal crisis served the strategic and ideological purposes of league officials and imperial powers insofar as it deflected and distracted from the larger question of colonial labor. Second, *burdened* here refers not to inadequate domestic endowments but to impositions that accompanied international assistance and oversight. Burdens are thus generated in the very process of the international community exercising a duty of assistance, as that assistance comes with particular kinds of obligations and responsibilities. Finally, these states experienced these internationally imposed burdens as a condition and consequence of inclusion within the bounds of international society. Ethiopia and Liberia were not excluded from, but instead unequally integrated into, international society.

Ethiopia and Liberia's burdened membership was also racialized as the league pointed to the absence of European rule to explain the persistence of slavery in the two African states. This insistence at times stood in tension with the league's project of reform. As with the mandates, the aim of international oversight in Ethiopia and Liberia was to transform states that could not yet implement international norms into ones that could. The oversight required the countries to make reports to the league, to meet special obligations, and to open their economies for integration into global markets. As the effort of international oversight appeared difficult to implement, was met with resistance, or did not yield the desired results, league officials returned to the lack of colonial rule as the primary reason for failure. In doing so, they emphasized and reproduced racial difference as an intransigent and insurmountable challenge to the aim of emancipation and conceived of white rule in Africa as a permanent feature of the international order. Black sovereignty appeared increasingly as a contradiction in terms, and the league's own efforts at oversight seemed destined for failure. As we shall see, when Italy finally invaded Ethiopia in 1935, Italian representatives at the league would present their country's actions to extend European rule as the logical conclusion of the league's abolitionist efforts.

Before this process of unequal integration could unfold, in the case of Ethiopia at least, the question of the league's jurisdiction would have to be resolved. Following the assembly's 1922 resolution, the league investigated why slavery continued to be practiced in Ethiopia and considered whether league supervision could be justified given the country's independence. The British Anti-slavery Society published a pamphlet arguing that the problem of slavery in Ethiopia resulted from the absence of European oversight, recommending that the league take up this role. According to the pamphlet, while slavery was abolished or severely curtailed in those African territories under European control, slavery, "open, cruel and fiendish, unfettered by European intervention and hardly discountenanced by the Foreign Offices of the European powers," was taking place in Ethiopia.

The absence of external oversight and a weak state had resulted in ownership of minority ethnic groups, slave raiding beyond Ethiopia's borders, and a flourishing slave trade with the Middle East.[100]

Although Ethiopia was not yet a league member, the society argued that the league had universal jurisdiction in humanitarian matters. Article 22 of the covenant had made the league responsible for the "prohibition of abuses such as the slave trade" in the mandated areas, and article 24 had placed all preexisting international organizations, including the Brussels-based Anti-slavery Bureau, under the league.[101] In addition, the league was responsible for investigating slavery in Ethiopia because it was the "policeman of the world."[102] Echoing Smuts's claim that the league was an extension of the British Empire, the society insisted that the international organization now shouldered the responsibility for Britain's centuries-long effort "to secure a higher standard of treatment for oppressed peoples." As the world's policeman, the league should place Ethiopia under a mandate so that slavery could be eradicated and the country could meet international humanitarian standards.[103]

Frederick Lugard, who served as the British representative to the league's Permanent Mandates Commission, took up the society's concerns and recommendations. He reiterated that ongoing practices of slavery in Ethiopia were the consequences of political instability and economic isolation and insisted that the league should intervene. However, because Ethiopia was not party to the Treaty of Versailles, he worried that the organization had "no *locus standi* whatsoever in regard to the affairs of the country."[104] Despite this apparent lack of jurisdiction, Lugard concluded that placing Ethiopia under mandate would be possible. The league would be "acting within its legitimate sphere" if it recommended that the signatories of the Treaty of Saint-Germain-en-Laye of 1919 and the Brussels Act of 1890 (both of which included abolitionist commitments) authorized the league to investigate slavery in Ethiopia and take "possible remedial action." This remedial action would take the form of "assistance, both moral and material," by instituting a "B mandate" over Ethiopia.[105]

Lugard and the Anti-slavery Society understood "mandation" as a mechanism for expanding the league's oversight and achieving the political and economic integration of Ethiopia. In their analysis, Ethiopia's backwardness and instability were the result of its isolation from international society and indicated an ineffective state that could not project authority over its entire territory. With its requirement of an open-door economic policy and administrative oversight by foreign advisors, a mandate was the solution to both problems. Economic integration would overcome the country's isolation and lead it toward a modern economy based on free labor, while the league's administrative assistance would bolster the state's capacity. According to Lugard, this program would lead to "a thorough reform of the government" that could "bring order out of chaos, liberate a people now held in slavery [and] bring commercial prosperity" to Ethiopia.[106] The mandate promised a tutelage that would eventually lead to the realization of international standards of statehood in the East African country.

In 1923, Ethiopia submitted a request for membership, which ended plans for mandation, but enabled the extension of the league's jurisdiction through its inclusion as a member state. This application for membership, led by the regent Haile Selassie, made the case for Ethiopia's inclusion by appealing to the country's Christianity and to its participation in other international institutions.[107] Through these appeals, Selassie hoped to secure equal membership, but his request initiated a process of unequal integration that resulted in a burdened membership where obligations became more pronounced than rights. Ethiopia's request reignited debates about the requirements of league membership and placed questions of political instability and slavery at the forefront. Members of the league questioned whether Ethiopia's inclusion would tarnish the league's image or be an opportunity to help the country meet international standards. According to the British representative, the league should consider "on the one hand, the desire to help Abyssinia to raise herself in the scale of civilization, which it was possible she might do more effectively if she became a Member of the League, and on the other hand, . . . whether Abyssinia was in a position to make a worthy contribution to the League."[108] While Ethiopia sought to ensure its independence and gain equality through league membership, league officials and member states believed that membership was an opportunity to extend its oversight over Ethiopia. Membership would now accomplish what the recommendations for a mandate a year earlier had failed to achieve.

International lawyers have largely overlooked the ways that membership functioned as a mechanism for extending international oversight and realizing the mandate proposal by other means. As a result, Ethiopia's entry into the league is often celebrated as an important turning point from an exclusionary international society based on the nineteenth-century standard of civilization to a more universal membership.[109] And in important ways, this is true. The subcommittee charged with reviewing Ethiopia's application for membership used a general questionnaire focused on whether Ethiopia was recognized by other states, possessed a stable government with well-defined frontiers, and was fully self-governing.

The committee found that it was a recognized state with a stable govern-ment and borders, but "was unable to determine the extent of the effec-tive control of the central authority over the provinces remote from the capital."[110]

Along with the uncertainty about the state's effective control over its territory, the last question the committee considered became an oppor-tunity to raise specific concerns about slavery and thereby extend league oversight. The question read: "What have been the acts and declarations of Abyssinia (a) as regards her international obligations, (b) as regards the stipulation of the League with reference to armaments?"[111] Despite its generality, international obligations regarding slavery became the most important concern. Ethiopia was not party to the 1890 Final Act of the Brussels Conference or the 1919 Treaty of Saint-Germain-en-Laye. As a condition of membership, Ethiopia was asked to retroactively accede to these legal instruments. In addition, the government was required to provide the league's council with information regarding its progress on the abolition of slavery and to take into consideration the league's rec-ommendations on the best means of fulfilling this aim.[112] The committee acknowledged that Ethiopia was being offered a conditional membership with special obligations but insisted that this was the appropriate measure given the country's backwardness. According to the Italian representative, the specific obligations required of the African nation should not "wound Abyssinia's susceptibilities, since other States, which had arrived at a higher degree of civilization, had already consented to undertake special engagements."[113]

Ethiopia's membership in 1923 thus provides a clear picture of what I have described as unequal integration. Rather than denying Ethiopia membership for having failed to meet the standards of statehood, inclu-sion within international society overcame the earlier problem of league jurisdiction and enlisted consent to inaugurate a program of international oversight. The system of oversight was designed to discipline and civilize Ethiopia so that it could raise itself to the ranks of other member states. Membership thus became mandation by other means. The result was an unequal and burdened form of membership. In this way, the expansion of international society and the entrenchment of international hierarchy went hand in hand.

This process of unequal integration became more explicitly racialized as the league expanded its concern with slavery to Liberia and reiterated that the chief cause for practices of slavery was the absence of European rule. Liberia was a signatory to the Treaty of Versailles and thus a member of the league since its founding. Liberia was not subject to special obligations when it first became a member, but concerns about slavery would revise and alter the terms of its inclusion. A 1925 memorandum from the International Labor Organization to the league's newly formed Temporary Slavery Commission noted that while slavery in Africa existed primarily within the borders of Ethiopia, it was also practiced in Liberia. According to the memo, Ethiopia and Liberia "are the only two African states, which are not under some sort of European control." "Where European powers exercise control of the administration of the territory, the slave trade and large scale raids have diminished and have become practically impossible."[114]

In the persistent claim that slavery was practiced in independent African states that did not have effective control over their territories, humanitarian crisis was tied to black sovereignty. This view implied that Africans could not rule themselves and their territories in ways that conformed to the standards of modern statehood. European oversight and intervention was constructed as the only mechanism that could secure humanitarian norms in Africa. That the charge of slavery became the idiom through which black self-government would be undermined should strike us as deeply perverse not only because of Europe's central role in the transatlantic slave trade and slavery in the Americas but also because of the labor practices that characterized colonial Africa in the twentieth century. Forced labor was a central practice in every colony, so much so that the largest imperial powers—Britain and France—successfully lobbied for its exemption from the 1926 Slavery Convention. While the signatories of the convention agreed to suppress the slave trade and abolish slavery as soon as possible, the convention allowed for forced and compulsory labor for public works.[115] Moreover, colonial powers represented forced labor as a traditional practice or native custom, recasting a modern system of labor extraction as an indication of African backwardness.[116] Thus, the 1930 Forced Labor Convention excluded "traditional practices" such as minor communal services, collective work, compulsory cultivation, and the right of chiefs to levy personal services from its prohibition on forced labor. These very exemptions would be deployed by colonial powers to extract the required labor for development projects.[117]

This widespread use of forced labor was quietly legitimized as the rhetoric of humanitarian crisis in Liberia and Ethiopia grew louder. In 1929, echoing the International Labor Organization and the Temporary Slavery Commission, the United States sent a "note of protest" alleging widespread practices of slavery in Liberia and requested an international investigation.[118] Composed of three members selected by the United States, Liberia, and the league, the International Commission of Enquiry in Liberia began its work in April 1930. Their report concluded that while slave markets and slave dealing were no longer practiced, inter- and intra-tribal domestic slavery as well as pawning existed. In addition, evidence suggested that forced labor for public and private purposes was used, that the migration of Liberians to other colonial territories was akin to slavery, and that government officials actively participated in and profited from these practices.[119]

To abolish slavery in Liberia, the commission recommended a thorough reorganization of the country's internal administration. The report argued that the district commissioners in charge of the interior counties should be removed for their corruption and participation in slavery and compulsory labor. According to the committee, the success of the administrative reorganization depended on choosing district commissioners who were "honest, fair-minded and free from graft." To meet these criteria, the selected commissioners would be either European or American.[120] League officials latched onto this recommendation as key to the successful abolition of slavery in Liberia. According to the secretary general of the league, "any reforms which were introduced would be of a paper character, unless and until the main reform was applied . . . [namely,] white administrators in the interior."[121] The report's recommendations on economic integration extended this association of black sovereignty with humanitarian crisis by separating its examination of Liberian labor practices from the region's colonial economy. According to the report, Liberia's closed door "impeded development by masking maladministration, discouraging research, delaying civilization and education, preventing competition and generally stifling commercial enterprise" and should be replaced with an open-door policy on the model of other "tropical African dependencies and colonies."[122]

This recommendation, however, diminished the extent to which Liberia already participated in the world economy. For instance, the International Commission had investigated the ways in which Liberian migrant workers were compelled to meet labor demands in other colonial territories, particularly the Spanish island of Fernando Po. Rather than situating the coerced migration of workers in this broader colonial economy, the report insisted that Liberia was entirely to blame for the "tragic effectiveness" of the trade.[123] League officials concluded, "Criticism must be directed against the Liberian Government" rather than the Spanish because "Liberian authorities received so much per head for each laborer who was shipped."[124] In addition to relieving the Spanish colonial government of any responsibility for the forced labor it employed, the report would also conclude that the Firestone Company, the largest private employer in the country, did not knowingly employ forced labor.[125] Only in those instances where the government was responsible for labor recruitment and the company had little control were laborers forcibly impressed.[126] In absolving the Firestone Company and the Spanish government from any responsibility, the commission's report once again focused international attention on the limits of black self-rule. This critique of Liberian sovereignty opened the door for reform proposals that ranged from administrators appointed by the league to military intervention on the model of the 1915 US intervention in Haiti.[127]

After the investigation in Liberia and hoping to avoid intervention in Ethiopia, the then emperor Haile Selassie agreed to an investigation led by the Anti-slavery Society. The society's 1932 report concluded that while the emperor possessed "the mentality which we associate with European political ethics, in a degree which is singular in an Eastern ruler, and still more singular in the ruler of an Eastern state whose traditions are those of violence, disunity and incompetence . . . government in the European sense does not exist."[128] Reiterating the debate about mandation during the early 1920s, the authors recommended assigning European administrative advisors to Ethiopia. But if Ethiopia's nonmembership raised questions of league jurisdiction in 1922, its membership now meant that it could not be forced to accept this recommendation. In a strategy that reproduced the very terms of Ethiopia's unequal integration, the report sought to mobilize consent to effect the goal of European oversight. Ethiopia would be offered international loans for public works and would be required to agree to European administrators as part of the loan's conditions.[129] The loans would thus serve a dual role—finally achieving the goal of European oversight in Ethiopia and facilitating Ethiopia's economic integration. For instance, the building of roads through a league loan would connect the country to "legitimate trade" and contribute to developing Ethiopia into an agricultural state like Palestine (a British mandate) and Syria (a French mandate).[130]

The loan program was not instituted, but it once again indicated the process of unequal integration. Like the proposed mandate of 1922, Ethiopia's conditional membership of 1923 and the 1930 recommendations of the International Commission in Liberia, the loan program indexed a strategy by which inclusion in international society served as a mechanism for the League of Nations to exercise a disciplining and regulatory function over these two African states. In each instance, unequal integration subjected Ethiopia and Liberia to special obligations designed to correct internal deviations and deficiencies. The effect of these processes was a distorted form of sovereignty. Instead of securing equality and nonintervention, their inclusion and membership engendered the conditions of their inequality and domination within international society.[131]

Scholars of the mandate system have often remarked on the sovereign inequality that the league produced by focusing on the division of political and economic power. According to Antony Anghie, "the acquisition of sovereignty, of political powers, was accompanied by the simultaneous withdrawal and transference of economic power to external forces," leading to a distinctive form of postcolonial sovereignty.[132] Examining Iraq, the only mandate to receive independence within the league, Susan Pedersen confirms this point. Iraq gained formal independence in 1933 but only as a condition of ceding economic and military privileges to Britain, its former mandatory power.[133] Iraq, like the mandates more generally, thus provided an early example of a postcolonial form of domination where formal independence and economic exploitation could be reconciled. As we shall see, anticolonial nationalists would be preoccupied with this postcolonial predicament in the age of decolonization.

However, there was more at stake in Ethiopia and Liberia than the disaggregation of political and economic sovereignty. Their sovereign inequality was produced in the distribution of legal rights and political obligations. In these two African states, the league posed a different question about political rule itself, asking whether the two African states were capable of exercising it according to international standards. In the persistent equation of black self-rule with practices of slavery, the league answered no to this question, and the consequences of this response were far reaching. The burdened and racialized membership the league produced rendered sovereignty conditional. If the two states were unable to meet the special requirements of their membership, the formal protections sovereignty and recognition afforded were also out of their grasp.

Imperial Expansion as Humanitarian Intervention

In April 1934, frustrated with the slow pace of reform in Liberia, Frederick Lugard circulated a searing critique of the Liberian government and urged the country's expulsion from the league should the government fail to accept the league's appointed administrators in the interior. Writing to the British House of Lords, he asked, "Suppose your Lordships, that the U.S. or any other State declined any longer to be flouted by Liberia and resorted to force is there any Member of the League which would be prepared to champion the cause of misrule?"[134] Lugard's question proved to be partly prescient. Not Liberia, but Ethiopia would be subject to force, and as Lugard suggested, no member of the league would support a country accused of misrule.

The infamous Italo-Ethiopian war, which started as a series of border disputes between Italian Somaliland and Ethiopia in late 1934, became a full-fledged invasion and occupation the following year. The standard narrative of the war understands the Italian invasion as an illegal act of aggression and focuses on the failure of the league's collective security system, which could not adequately respond to the crisis. This view returns to an account of truncated political principles and suggests that while collective security ultimately failed, the widespread international condemnation of the invasion demonstrated commitment to the principles of sovereign equality and nonaggression. For instance, according to Arnulf Becker Lorca, the invasion "occurred in a new international environment," and as a result, it was "mostly criticized, understood to be unlawful and met with economic sanctions by the League."[135] On this view, then, not the norms of international law but their application in practice led to the league's inaction. The architects of the United Nations would learn precisely these lessons from the league's failure and include more rigorous collective security institutions in the United Nations Charter.[136]

From Carl Schmitt's perspective, the invasion did not mark a breach between principle and practice. Instead, he argued that it indicated a crisis of the universal international norms that had underwritten the league. Italy's invasion and the league's unwillingness to intervene in support of Ethiopia was, he maintained, a subconscious return to the traditional division of European and non-European space.[137] It was a reversion to an older European international law that understood "war on non-European soil [to be] to outside its order" and positioned Africa as "colonial territory."[138] The invasion and the lack of response was for Schmitt further indication of the league's spatial chaos and demonstrated the destabilizing consequences of extending sovereign equality "beyond the line."[139] Schmitt's account, like the standard argument about the failure of implementation, understands the invasion and occupation as a departure from the league's universal principles.

However, the invasion and the lack of adequate response are neither a sign of unrealized principles nor a sudden collapse of universal international law and reversion to the spatially bound *jus Publicum Europaeum*.

When situated in the context of Ethiopia's burdened and racialized membership, the invasion appears continuous with the unequal integration and racial hierarchy that had structured the league since its founding. As Lugard had already indicated, who could fault a state for resorting to force in the face of intransigence, and what state would come to the rescue of another state embroiled in humanitarian crisis? Though Lugard himself opposed the Italian war along with many other league officials, Ethiopia's burdened membership, which Lugard had helped to produce, set the discursive and political stage on which Italy launched its attack.

Italy's justification for war was firmly situated within the conditions of Ethiopia's burdened membership. One month before its October 1935 invasion, the Italian government submitted a sixty-page memorandum to the league. The memo reminded the league of the deep uncertainty surrounding Ethiopia's 1923 request for membership. Almost all had agreed that Ethiopia had not achieved the required standards of statehood for league membership. However, the country was admitted "based on the belief that, through participation in the system of international cooperation represented by the League, Ethiopia could be led to make by herself the efforts necessary to approach, even though only gradually, the level of civilization of the other peoples belonging to the international community."[140] In returning to this justification of Ethiopia's membership, the Italian memo recalled the process of unequal integration that had left Ethiopia with more onerous responsibilities than rights and reminded the league that Ethiopian sovereignty was conditional on the fulfillment of those very responsibilities.

From the perspective of the Italian government, the two special obligations Ethiopia had accepted as conditions of its membership—the abolition of slavery and the regulation of its arms trade—had not been achieved. Slavery and the slave trade continued unabated and often with the tacit support of government officials. The Ethiopian government was furthermore violating the arms agreement covering East Africa by selling munitions to private persons.[141] Beyond violating the specific obligations of its membership, Ethiopia had also allegedly breached other international laws and bilateral treaties. For instance, Ethiopia flouted the open-door provisions of article 23 in the League of Nations Covenant and did not adhere to bilateral Italo-Ethiopian agreements that granted Italy "most favored nation" status.[142]

The memo declared explicitly what league officials had already implied. The twelve-year experiment to raise Ethiopia's level of civilization through membership had failed and illustrated that Ethiopia "does not possess the necessary qualifications . . . to raise herself by voluntary efforts to the level of other civilized nations."[143] The Italian government explained this failure in two ways. In the first case, Ethiopia was portrayed as a failed state that suffered from a "chronic state of disorder."[144] The absence of effective government denied Ethiopian subjects the protections and rights they ought to have been guaranteed, while the disorder in the country threatened to spill over into neighboring countries. On the question of slavery in particular, it had become clear that abolition would not be realized "unless there is a fundamental change in the conditions of the country which cannot come about so long as government is non-existent, inchoate and impotent."[145] The Italian government concluded that Ethiopia could not "carry out unaided the thorough reorganization without which it must remain a permanent danger."[146] Setting the stage for its intervention, the Italian memo noted that the League of Nations is "a system of obligations and rights, which are interdependent. No member of the League can invoke rights arising from the Covenant when it has not fulfilled its own obligations."[147] Because Ethiopia had not fulfilled the onerous obligations of its membership, it was not entitled the rights of membership.

Ethiopia's status as an outlaw state further justified intervention. The country not only lacked the capacity to fulfill its obligations to the league but also was actively violating international law. Ethiopia demonstrated "a cynical indifference for her international obligations and the undertakings assumed toward the League of Nations."[148] It was, according to the memorandum, a barbaric nation, one that practiced emasculation, torture, and cannibalism within its borders, and aggression and xenophobia toward its neighbors.[149] On this view, Ethiopia rather than Italy was the criminal state under international law. This characterization would have consequences for the war. While its status as a failed state robbed Ethiopia of its claims to rights of membership, its position as an outlaw canceled any obligations Italy or other members of the league might have had to Ethiopia. Through "barbarous custom and archaic laws," Ethiopia "openly placed herself outside the Covenant of the League and has rendered herself unworthy of the trust placed in her when she was admitted to membership."[150] As the closing paragraph of the memo noted, "it would be contrary to every principle of law and justice to claim that Members of the League are bound to observe the rules of the Covenant in their relations with a State Member which has placed itself outside the Covenant through a breach of its undertakings."[151]

The league's initial response to the Italian memo did not dispute the characterization of Ethiopia or the need for tutelage. Instead, less than two weeks after the Italian government submitted its memorandum, a special committee outlined a new program of international assistance. This plan called for a cohort of foreign specialists who would be charged with organizing a corps of police and gendarmerie, facilitating the opening up of the country to foreign corporations and reorganizing its fiscal policy.[152] With the invasion well under way, the Italian delegate to the assembly argued that his country's actions were more in line with the league's own practices than this plan. The delegate asked, "Why, instead of proposing a form of collective assistance, has [the league] not borne in mind that the covenant itself provides an effective method of aiding peoples who, owing to their present conditions, are not able to stand by themselves?"[153] According to the Italian representative, article 22 of the covenant was designed for states like Ethiopia, a point the league had already conceded a decade ago. Assigning Italy as a mandatory power in Ethiopia could solve the league's problem of providing assistance to the backward country. As if to confirm its reformist and humanitarian intentions, the Italian general in East Africa announced a declaration suppressing slavery ten days after the invasion began. In 1936, as Italy gradually extended its occupation, the Italian government reported to the league that Italy had freed all slaves in occupied territories.[154]

While justifying its invasion in the league's own abolitionist terms, Italy stripped Ethiopia of the protections afforded not only by league membership but also through the laws of war. If Ethiopia was barbaric, the impending invasion and occupation was not a war between equal members of the international community that would have to follow the guidelines outlined in The Hague and Geneva conventions. Instead, it was a "colonial" or "small war," which covered "expeditions against savages and semi-civilized races by disciplined soldiers."[155] These wars, unlike traditional interstate conflicts, could involve outlawed modes of warfare including indiscriminate killings, the destruction of villages, and the torture of captured combatants.[156] Thus, by invoking Ethiopia's barbarism a month before its invasion, Italy prepared for the use of overwhelming violence, illegal use of mustard gas, indiscriminate killings of noncombatants, the torture of captured soldiers, and other war crimes.[157]

These war crimes are often understood as the height of Italy's illegal act of aggression. However, rereading its justification of the invasion in light of Ethiopia's burdened and racialized membership suggests that Italy's actions should be understood as following from international society's processes and discourses of unequal integration. By invoking the special conditions of Ethiopia's membership and returning to the international community's frequent attempt to extend international oversight to Ethiopia, Italy was able to present Ethiopia as the outlaw state while presenting its own actions as a fulfillment of the league's aims of abolishing slavery and developing a backward state. If by portraying Ethiopia as a failed and outlaw state Italy hoped to recast its imperial ambitions as a humanitarian project, this account also made possible the international community's silence and tacit endorsement of the invasion. Ethiopian independence could be sacrificed for the greater cause of maintaining European peace in part because that independence was already in question through a burdened membership and a racialized discourse that equated black sovereignty with humanitarian crisis.

Toward a Critique of Colonial Slavery

The Italian invasion galvanized critics of empire throughout the African diaspora and marked a critical turning point in the politics of black anticolonialism. The worldmakers in this study fashioned a new Pan-Africanism in the context of their increasing disillusionment with the League of Nations and their efforts to come to terms with the limits of the Communist International. Exemplary of this shift, the works and political activities of W.E.B. Du Bois, C.L.R. James, and George Padmore during the 1930s index an effort to revise and restate the critique of imperialism. The upshot of this effort was the revival of Pan-Africanism as a distinctive internationalism—one that centered a critique of colonialism as a dual structure of slavery and racial hierarchy. This Pan-Africanism drew on and was deeply influenced by Lenin's account of self-determination but increasingly fashioned itself as an autonomous project of world revolution in which colonized subjects, rather than the metropolitan proletariat, were the key agents of global transformation.

These intellectual and political shifts were sharp and had lasting implications for anticolonial nationalism in the Black Atlantic. In 1919, even after being unable to secure the moderate demands of the Second Pan-African Congress, Du Bois insisted that the League of Nations was "absolutely necessary to the salvation of the Negro race." As a site of enlightened and "organized Public opinion," it could be mobilized to further the aims of people of African descent.[158] Hoping that the league would take up the congress's recommendations, which were ignored during the Paris Peace Conference, Du Bois forwarded the resolutions to the league's secretary general in 1921.[159] In this moment, he sought to reform rather than reject the tutelary model of the mandate system. For instance, as the Firestone Rubber Company made inroads in Liberia in the late 1920s, Du Bois supported its efforts and urged the corporation to employ "trained American Negros" who could lead the development of their race. According to Du Bois, he had "not then lost faith in the capitalistic system."[160] By 1933, armed with a more thoroughgoing Marxist critique, Du Bois rejected the collusion between Firestone, the State Department, and the league that had led to the 1930 investigation into slavery and almost resulted in a US military intervention. He argued that while Liberia was not faultless, "her chief crime is to be black and poor in a rich, white world; and in precisely that portion of the world where color is ruthlessly exploited as a foundation for American and European wealth." He concluded that Liberia's subordination was part of the transatlantic effort to preserve the "whole colonial slave labor system."[161]

Du Bois extended this critique in his discussion of Italy's invasion in Ethiopia, arguing that Italy's actions confirmed that "economic exploitation based on the excuse of race prejudice is the program of the white world."[162] That this exploitation was in part justified by reference to ongoing practices of slavery in Ethiopia only masked the colonial slavery that most of the world experienced. While the league investigated slavery in Ethiopia (and Liberia), colonialism had already enslaved much of the world. From Asia to Africa, European imperial policy sought to "dominate native labor, pay it low wages, give it little political control and small chance for education or even industrial training; in short, to seek to get the largest possible profit out of the laboring class."[163]

Writing from London, James experienced a similar conversion toward a more radical critique of imperialism during the Italian invasion and occupation. In a 1933 essay marking the centenary of emancipation in the West Indies, James urged the British Empire to once again take the lead in the international struggle against slavery. While he mentioned that forced labor and slavery were practiced throughout the colonized world including within the British Empire, he named China, Arabia, Ethiopia, and Liberia as places where slavery remained deeply entrenched.[164] Despite being in the midst of researching the Haitian Revolution, James argued that the path toward emancipation for the five million slaves lay in appealing to the conscience of the British public and government in order to force the League of Nations to act.[165]

By 1936, James, now embracing Trotskyism, abandoned his faith in the British Empire and the league. He argued that the invasion of Ethiopia taught a lesson to "Africans and people of African descent, especially those who have been poisoned by British imperialist education." The occupation and the league's failure to act illustrated "the real motives which move imperialism in its contact with Africa [and] show[ed] the incredible savagery and duplicity of European imperialism in its quest for markets and raw materials."[166] As chair of the newly formed International African Friends of Abyssinia, James successfully convinced fellow members of the organization that appeals to the League of Nations would not bring relief to Ethiopia. Rather than league sanctions he called for global "workers' sanctions" that would stop Mussolini. These sanctions from below, James argued, would create alliances between European and colonized workers in preparation for the coming world war and the political revolutions it would inevitably unleash.[167]

James's call for workers' sanctions was tied to his vision of an anti-imperial struggle situated within the Communist International and supported by the Soviet Union. However, by 1935, the International was weakened, and the Soviet Union, having recently joined the league, toed the line. James sought to make sense of the failures of the International in his 1937 *World Revolution*. He argued that the International's efforts to mobilize workers to fight for peace-loving democracies against war-making fascists marked the complete collapse of the anti-imperialist vision that had distinguished its early phase. Rather than a sudden volte-face, however, James traced the fall of the International to the failure of the German Revolution in 1923 and Joseph Stalin's announcement of socialism in one country the following year.

In this critique of the International, James made the Ethiopian crisis central, arguing that the International lost an opportunity to revive the world revolution. According to James, "the International from the first moment could have pointed out that nothing but working-class action could have saved Abyssinia, and as the whole dirty record of lies and greed and hypocrisy unfolds itself could have driven home nail after nail into the coffin of the League." By "com[ing] out clearly for a boycott against all war-materials to Italy or any other country which interfered in Abyssinian affairs," the Soviet Union and the International would have harnessed the emerging anti-imperial forces and positioned itself as the vanguard in the movement.[168] Not only that it failed to do so but also that the Soviet Union was selling supplies to Italy marked for James the end of the Third International. The coming struggle against imperialism required a new "Fourth International of Trotsky" that would organize the working-class movement in Europe and colonized subjects under the banners of "turn the imperialist war into civil war. Abolish capitalism. Build international Socialism."[169]

George Padmore, who had worked for the Comintern, was less optimistic about its revival and would lead the shift from the Communist

International to what Brent Hayes Edwards has called the "Black International." Unlike Du Bois and James, Padmore did not experience disillusionment with the league in the 1930s, as his own political development began squarely in the orbit of communist internationalism. Having joined the Communist Party while in the United States in the late 1920s, he was soon elevated in the Comintern as the key theoretician of the "Negro Question." Beginning in 1929, he chaired the Negro Bureau of the Red International of Labor Unions from Moscow. While living in Germany from 1930 to 1933, Padmore organized the International Trade Union Committee of Negro Workers, edited its publication the *Negro Worker*, and published a global study of black workers in a pamphlet titled *The Life and Struggle of Negro Toilers*. In 1933, he broke with the Communist International, citing its lack of investment in the colonial question, and was deported from Germany to the United Kingdom as the Nazis took power.[170] Padmore regrouped in Paris between 1933 and 1935, where in collaboration with another expelled black communist, Tiemoko Garan Kouyaté, he planned a Negro World Unity Congress.[171]

The congress was aborted, but the plans and manifesto Padmore and Kouyaté put together laid the foundations for a new iteration of Pan-Africanism. Padmore's version of the manifesto directed the new project of Negro World Unity to the condition of black enslavement and impending world war. He declared, "In Africa, in America, in the West Indies, in South and Central America—to be Black is to be a slave. Despised, humiliated, denied justice and human rights in every walk of life."[172] While imperial powers prepared "to use [blacks] once more as cannon fodder," the task of the Congress would be to "[establish] unity in our ranks and [adopt] a platform of struggle for the Africans and people of African descent the world over."[173]

The Black International imagined in the unrealized congress and subsequently enacted in Padmore and James's 1937 International African Service Bureau, and the 1945 Fifth Pan-African Congress in Manchester staked out an autonomous space for black radicalism. Emerging "out of and against the communist international," this iteration of Pan-Africanism fashioned itself as the site of a new project of world revolution directed against colonial slavery. The institutional contours of this project were as yet undecided at the dawn of World War II. But as we shall see, in its aftermath, the growing cohort of Pan-Africanists would pursue a project of national independence coupled with anticolonial worldmaking that sought to secure nondomination within the international order. Central to this was a return to and refashioning of the revolutionary possibilities that the right to self-determination had promised in 1917.

CHAPTER THREE

From Principle to Right

THE ANTICOLONIAL REINVENTION
OF SELF-DETERMINATION

FROM THE PERSPECTIVE of anticolonial critics and nationalists, 1945 was eerily reminiscent of 1919. The end of the Second World War heralded renewed commitments to internationalism. As with the Wilsonian moment, calls for a new international organization were couched in the language of universal ideals. The 1941 Atlantic Charter, which articulated Anglo-American war aims, looked forward to the restoration of sovereignty and self-government to all peoples. And in the United Nations Charter, human rights and equality of nations were invoked as founding principles of a new world order. Yet, once again, the avowal of these principles did not entail the end of colonial rule. Soon after signing the Atlantic Charter, Winston Churchill insisted that it did not apply to the territories of the British Empire.[1]

This was confirmed in the United Nations Charter, which extended the League of Nations' hierarchies. As great power states, members of the Security Council issued binding resolutions and had the power of the veto. The mandates were renamed trustees while colonies were euphemistically described as "non-self-governing territories." The inclusion of colonies within the purview of the UN Charter marked a shift from the league, which had limited its oversight to the mandates. However, self-determination was not referenced in relationship to either non-self-governing territories or the new trusteeship system. Self-determination appeared only twice, in articles 1 and 55 of the charter, and, in both instances, the "principle of equal rights and self-determination of peoples" was subordinated to the larger aim of securing "peaceful and friendly relations among nations."[2]

As the United Nations Organization Conference met in San Francisco in 1945 to finalize the plans for the new organization, the Nigerian nationalist Nnamdi Azikiwe watched from Lagos in dismay. In 1943, he had joined fellow African journalists in demanding that the provisions of the Atlantic Charter be extended to the colonies. Their memorandum on postwar reconstruction called for political and civil rights for colonized subjects and laid out extensive social and economic reforms that included a living wage, an end to forced labor, rights to collective bargaining, the nationalization of mines, and increased investments in education, housing, and health care. These reforms would be instituted alongside a gradual movement toward independence that required a period of "responsible self-government" before achieving sovereignty.[3] Azikiwe argued that the economic and social reforms required democratic self-government. Only "the crystallization of democracy in the social, economic and political life of the territories," which entailed "the full control of the essential means of production and distribution by the indigenous communities of the territories," would "effectively promote social equality and communal welfare."[4]

If Azikiwe hoped that postwar reconstruction offered an opportunity to overcome the "factors of capitalism and imperialism [that] have stultified the normal growth of these territories," the United Nations appeared to entrench the status quo.[5] According to Azikiwe, in San Francisco "there is no New Deal for the black man. . . . Colonialism and economic enslavement of the Negro are to be maintained."[6] The deep continuity between the imperial world order and the United Nations was embodied in the presence of Jan Smuts in San Francisco.[7] That the same man who had developed the mandates system and envisioned extending apartheid from South Africa to Kenya was now appealing for a preamble that affirmed human rights struck W.E.B. Du Bois as deeply ironic.[8] For Du Bois, Smuts's presence illustrated the hypocritical character of the new international body. He noted, "We have conquered Germany . . . but not their ideas. We still believe in white supremacy, keeping Negroes in their place and lying about democracy when we mean imperial control of 750 millions of human beings in colonies."[9]

Organized in part as a response and rejoinder to the San Francisco meeting, the Fifth Pan-African Congress met in Manchester, England, in October to outline its vision of the postwar world order. With George Padmore and Kwame Nkrumah at its helm, this meeting marked a departure from the reformist orientation of previous congresses and embodied the radical black internationalism that Padmore and others had articulated

beginning in the 1930s. The congress demanded "for Black Africa autonomy and independence, so far and no further than it is possible in this
'One World' for groups and people to rule themselves subject to inevitable
world unity and federation."[10] Echoing the Comintern's League against
Imperialism and revising the *Communist Manifesto*, the congress called
on "colonial and subject peoples of the world" to unite in what organizers
believed was the new phase of world revolution.[11]

Fifteen years later, in September 1960, Kwame Nkrumah addressed
the General Assembly as president of independent Ghana and used his
new platform to refashion the United Nations as the international forum
for decolonization. Declaring the dawn of a new era, Nkrumah argued
that the UN should lead the fight against imperialism by protecting all
peoples' right to self-determination and by excluding obstinate imperial
powers from membership in the international body.[12] As if in confirmation of Nkrumah's vision of the UN, the assembly passed the historic resolution 1514, Declaration on the Granting of Independence to Colonial
Countries and Peoples, three months later. Resolution 1514 conceived of
self-determination as a right of all peoples and declared: "The subjection of peoples to alien subjugation, domination and exploitation constitutes a denial of fundamental human rights."[13] The resolution marked
an important victory for the Pan-Africanism outlined in 1945. According
to Alex Quaison-Sackey, Ghana's representative at the United Nations,
the declaration corrected the limitations of the UN Charter. "If indeed
Africa was a forgotten continent at the time of the promulgation of the
Charter . . . the Declaration calling for an immediate end to colonialism
in all territories has redressed that balance."[14] His Guinean counterpart echoed this point and noted that the 1960 declaration was "a just
atonement for the serious omissions of San Francisco."[15] Outside the
halls of the United Nations, Amilcar Cabral, who was leading a guerrilla
war against Portuguese rule in Guinea-Bissau, argued, "The UN resolution on decolonization has created a new situation for our struggle," in
which "colonialism is now an international crime." In this context, he
argued, anticolonial struggle "has lost its strictly national character and
has moved onto an international level." The guerrilla warriors in Guinea-
Bissau and elsewhere were, in his words, "anonymous soldiers for the
United Nations."[16]

Within fifteen years, anticolonial nationalists had successfully captured the UN and transformed the General Assembly into a platform for
the international politics of decolonization. Central to this transformation was a novel account of self-determination as a human right. The UN

Charter had relegated self-determination to a secondary principle, and the authors of the 1948 UN Universal Declaration of Human Rights had also assiduously avoided mention of self-determination. In this context, anticolonial nationalists refashioned self-determination as a right, positioned it as a prerequisite to other human rights, and argued that it entailed an immediate end to colonial rule. Understood as a claim to independence and equality, the right to self-determination served as the foundation for a domination-free and postimperial international order. This refashioning of the UN and self-determination set the stage for anticolonial nationalists to challenge the remnants of colonial rule and to legitimize new postcolonial states on the international stage.

This chapter takes up the question of how self-determination emerged as a right and examines the political and theoretical implications of this transformation. I argue that anticolonial nationalists appropriated the principle of self-determination but reinvented its meaning through a novel critique of imperialism that centered on the problems of slavery and racial hierarchy. While decolonization is often understood as a realization of the principles underlying the United Nations and the culmination of a Westphalian regime of sovereignty, the emergence of a right to self-determination was not an inevitable outgrowth of the United Nations Charter but instead a contested and contingent reinvention, secured in the face of deep suspicion and opposition. The anticolonial right to self-determination functioned as the juridical component of international nondomination. It created the external legal context in which popular sovereignty within independent states could be instituted. This vision of an international order, premised on the independence and equality of states, which are to be free from domination, was not born in the Westphalian Treaty or the UN Charter. Instead, it should be understood as an anti-imperial project that went beyond the inclusion of new states to demand an expansive vision of an egalitarian world order.

But while the right to self-determination secured the legal foundations of an anti-imperial world, it was not without its limits. As I show, the formulation of empire as enslavement and the commitment to territorial integrity could not fully address settler colonial contexts or secession in new postcolonial states, while the anticolonial view that human rights were to be secured in self-government and statehood offered no adequate response to instances where the state itself violated the rights of citizens. The right to self-determination was thus both an important victory for anticolonial worldmakers and one that revealed the tensions and contradictions at the center of their project.

Rethinking Anticolonial Appropriation

Historians have tended to treat anticolonial politics at the UN, and in particular the right to self-determination, as an extension and expansion of the organization's founding documents. On this view, the Atlantic Charter, the UN Charter, and the Universal Declaration of Human Rights are remembered as bearers of the universal ideals that would reshape the postwar international order while figures such as Eleanor Roosevelt, René Cassin, and Raphael Lemkin are cast as crusaders of the cause.[17] From this perspective, the postwar international order marks a break from the League of Nations as new norms and institutions sought to limit state power and recognize the dignity of persons in international law. While these norms were not immediately realized, subaltern actors, especially anticolonial nationalists, are included in these narratives of progress as agents of expansion that propelled the universalization of self-determination and human rights.[18]

This account relies on an idealized account of the UN's founding that ignores the continuities between the League of Nations and the UN and dismisses the deep disappointment of anticolonial critics like Du Bois and Azikiwe in 1945.[19] By framing the UN as the embodiment of a "new deal for the world" that needed only to be expanded, anticolonial nationalism and decolonization are assimilated into a progressive history of postwar ideals and institutions. This reinforces standard histories of decolonization in which the end of empire is framed as a universalization of Western ideals and an expansion of the existing norms and frameworks of international society.[20] It recognizes anticolonial political action only in the register of application and extension of existing norms and, as a result, disregards anticolonial nationalism as a site of conceptual and political innovation.

In contrast to these more recent narratives, observers and commentators during the 1950s and 1960s had a more ambivalent and at times critical orientation to anticolonial nationalism. While the likes of Rupert Emerson and John Plamenatz at least initially celebrated decolonization as a universalization of Western ideals, others critiqued the demands of anticolonial nationalists as incompatible with liberal principles and a threat to the new international system. For instance, well before self-determination's transformation from principle to right had been completed, the American international lawyer Clyde Eagleton, who was part of the delegation at Dumbarton Oaks and San Francisco, argued that invocations of a right to self-determination in the UN were abusing the principle by unsustainably extending it to mean economic as well as political sovereignty and claiming that it should apply to all colonized peoples.[21] This anticolonial view had little to do with self-determination in the liberal tradition of Giuseppe Mazzini and Woodrow Wilson. It was Soviet in inspiration and exploited the inclusion of self-determination in article 1 of the UN Charter, which Eagleton believed was "crowded in . . . without relevance or explanation." For Eagleton, self-determination required responsibility. Echoing the charter's language on the trusteeship system and the non-self-governing territories, he argued that rather than producing "more and more infant states" the UN should generate adequate standards for bestowing self-government.[22]

Removed from the UN debates, Isaiah Berlin in his classic essay "Two Concepts of Liberty" located anticolonial struggles as aspirations for neither negative nor positive liberty. While anticolonial nationalists presented their project as a universal demand for liberty, in Berlin's view they occupied a third category of "pagan self-assertion" where the singular aim was asserting the "personality" of the group. As a result, the preoccupying questions were around ensuring native (as opposed to alien) rule regardless of whether the representatives of the group "govern well or badly, liberally or oppressively." Berlin called this a "hybrid form of freedom," which, in its embrace of Marxism and nationalism, shared features of positive liberty and similarly threatened to devolve into authoritarianism.[23] Far from viewing this hybrid freedom as an extension of liberal ideals, Berlin saw "pagan self-assertion" as a threat to the negative concept of liberty he endorsed.[24]

Anticolonial nationalists, for their part, resisted the move to subsume decolonization and self-determination under the auspices of the Soviet Union and reduce it to a claim of cultural or national recognition. In *Pan-Africanism or Communism*, Padmore argued that the effort to credit "political awakening in Africa to Communist inspiration" was hypocritical and part of Cold War propaganda designed to alienate African nationalists from their sympathizers in the West.[25] While this book is often seen to mark his transition from Marxist to nationalist, Padmore presented a complex view of Pan-Africanism's autonomy that did not reject communism altogether. In doing so, he traced its origins to the back-to-Africa movements of the nineteenth century. Echoing Marcus Garvey, whom he had once dismissed as "national reformist misleader," Padmore argued, "Pan-Africanism seeks the attainment of the government of Africans by Africans for Africans."[26] In this aim, Padmore argued that Pan-Africanists endorsed the Universal Declaration of Human Rights and sought to achieve the right to self-determination as a "prerequisite to the federation of self-governing states on a regional basis, leading ultimately to the creation of a United States of Africa."[27] While Pan-Africanism was independent of official Communism, it recognized "much that is true in the Marxist interpretation of history" and strove for "Democratic Socialism, with state control of the basic means of production and distribution."[28]

In staking out Pan-Africanism's autonomy in these terms, Padmore was not claiming authenticity or demanding the recognition of difference on the model of Berlin's "pagan self-assertion." As Padmore's references to human rights, self-determination, Marxism, and democratic socialism suggest, autonomy did not mean that Pan-Africanism was a self-contained tradition of thought that stood outside the idioms and terms of Western political thinking. Instead, it emerged from a creative and combative relationship with those terms as it responded to distinctive and evolving political dilemmas. In its central preoccupation with New World slavery and its legacies, Pan-Africanism reinvented and remade inherited ideals and principles.

In the context of twentieth-century decolonization, self-determination was the target of this kind of reinvention. Staking out the contours of anticolonial reinvention requires rethinking the politics of appropriation as a creative intervention that responded to specific political questions and conditions. Anticolonial nationalists appropriated self-determination in the context of what David Scott calls "a problem-space." Drawing on R. G. Collingwood's "logic of question and answer" and Quentin Skinner's reformulation, the problem-space is a conceptual tool for conceiving of the way in which political thought and practice are responses to specific, historically situated questions.[29] On this view, the right to self-determination was not continuous with prior versions of the principle. Instead, it was remade and reconstituted in response to a particular way of posing the problem of empire. As the following sections illustrate, between the 1930s and 1960s, anticolonial nationalists increasingly framed empire as enslavement and conceived of the right to self-determination as the response to this problem. In this pairing of question and answer, the anticolonial account of self-determination was invented.

However, the problem-space does not simply describe the ideational context in which question and answer are paired. It also includes the institutional and political backdrop that enables certain kinds of answers while disabling others. In other words, question and answer are linked, but those linkages are governed less by an inevitable logic and instead articulated on a historically contingent stage. The right to self-determination emerged as the answer not because it was the only logical or available response. Instead, specific historical conditions helped to elevate this particular response. On the one hand, metropolitan intransigence vis-à-vis alternative demands for equal political and economic rights as well as institutional integration put forward largely by African labor movements laid the groundwork for nationalist calls for self-determination.[30] While the vision of integration within a reconstituted federal structure persisted in French Africa and the Francophone Caribbean, by the 1940s self-determination and independence emerged as the dominant answer to the problem of empire within the British Empire.[31] On the other hand, the UN, the emerging language of human rights, and the Cold War created institutional and discursive openings for the pairing of empire as enslavement with the right to self-determination. While anticolonial nationalists had invoked human rights prior to the founding of the UN, the effort to write binding covenants provided opportunities for anticolonial nationalists to explicitly mobilize the nascent and still malleable discourse of international human rights in service of a critique of imperialism and racism.

The Cold War further enhanced these openings as new postcolonial states used their growing majority to bypass the stalemate in the Security Council and transform the General Assembly into the primary site of political action within the UN. The bifurcated international order also produced a set of constraints on the United States and European imperial powers, which were largely opposed to the right of self-determination, but were at least partly deferential to the anticolonial agenda in the hopes of not fully ceding the moral high ground on empire to the Soviet Union. Thus, while the United States and the European powers had resisted the right to self-determination throughout the 1950s, resolution 1514 passed with no votes in opposition. Nine states, including the United States, the United Kingdom, France, and the Union of South Africa, Portugal, and Spain, registered their disagreement through abstention rather than rejection.

If this set of contexts was enabling for the formulation of a right to self-determination, this answer also appeared unable to fully respond to the expansive critique of empire as enslavement. Anticolonial nationalists for their part always framed the right to self-determination as the first step in their project of worldmaking, which entailed world federation according to the 1945 Pan-African Congress and a United States of Africa according to Padmore in 1953. But within the context of the United Nations, the critique of colonial slavery largely registered as a denial of fundamental human rights. This narrowing of the anticolonial critique meant that the more radical demands around economic self-determination, for instance, would have to be set aside in the institutionalization of a right to self-determination. The right to self-determination thus emerged in a context of both "possibility and constraint," to use Frederick Cooper's felicitous phrase.[32]

Yet despite its limits the transformation of self-determination from principle to right constituted a reinvention of the ideal that departed from its mobilization at the end of World War I and established self-determination as the dominant principle of political legitimacy in the international order. In codifying a right to self-determination, anticolonial nationalists harkened back to the anti-imperial and universal aspirations of Lenin's formulation and repudiated Wilsonian reassociation. Yet they also rejected Lenin's emphasis on secession in favor of articulating the international conditions of nondomination for existing territorial units in which popular sovereignty would be constituted. This was a distinctively anticolonial account of self-determination. Anticolonial nationalists indicated their aspirations to political innovation and the refounding of international society by describing their 1960 resolution as a "Declaration on the Granting of Independence." Following David Armitage's work on declaration as genre and Ayten Gündoğdu's account of rights declarations as acts of political founding, the declaration can be read as an effort to break with a world order that was built on racial hierarchy and facilitated empire as enslavement.[33] In declaring a right to self-determination, resolution 1514 announced in its place an anti-imperial world order in which the rights to independence and equality constituted the legal basis of nondomination within international society.

Empire as Enslavement

Following the founding of the United Nations, W.E.B. Du Bois bitterly observed: "There will be at least 750 million colored and black folk inhabiting colonies owned by white nations, who will have no rights that the white people of the world are bound to respect."[34] In this characterization of colonialism, Du Bois implicitly cited the decision in the landmark 1857 *Dred Scott v. Sandford* Supreme Court case in which Chief Justice Roger B. Taney, writing for the majority, concluded that blacks "had no rights which the white man was bound to respect; and that the Negro might justly and lawfully be reduced to slavery for his benefit."[35] The decision permanently barred freed blacks from claims of citizenship and extended slavery to the western territories while securing the rights of slave owners from federal encroachment.[36] By alluding to Taney's opinion in 1945, Du Bois linked enslavement and colonization. This linkage complemented his long-standing view that the world was structured by a global color line.[37] International racial hierarchy facilitated the domination of black and colored colonial subjects through alien rule. And this system of domination, according to Du Bois, ought to be understood as a form of enslavement. The colonial subject could "justly and lawfully be reduced to slavery" for the benefit of the "white people of the world."

This dual critique of empire as a form of enslavement and international racial hierarchy emerged in the context of renewed interest in the history of the transatlantic slave trade and slavery among black intellectuals. While Wilson and Smuts had mobilized what they perceived as an unstable and dangerous Jacobinism in nineteenth-century emancipation to ward off and subvert demands for self-determination, Du Bois, C.L.R. James, Eric Williams, and others rewrote the history of African enslavement in service of the impending anticolonial revolutions in the black world. In their classic texts *Black Reconstruction* (1935), *The Black Jacobins* (1938), and *Capitalism and Slavery* (1944), Du Bois, James, and Williams first sought to establish the centrality of slavery to the modern world. The enslavement of Africans, they argued, contributed to the emergence of a bourgeoisie and to the rise of industrialization.[38] Second, they rejected a moralized narrative of abolition for an account that centered the role of the enslaved in achieving emancipation.[39] From Du Bois's account of the slaves' general strike during the US Civil War to James's narrative of Toussaint L'Ouverture, black revolutionaries rather than metropolitan abolitionists are the main protagonists in the demise of slavery in the Americas. Third, they linked the nineteenth-century struggles for emancipation to twentieth-century decolonization. For James, in particular, the Haitian Revolution, the first to overcome slavery and colonialism, prefigured the struggle for independence in Africa.[40]

Anticolonial nationalists mobilized these histories in their effort to frame the problem of empire as one of enslavement. By highlighting the ways in which slavery was a modern form of labor extraction and exploitation, anticolonial critics established continuities between New World slavery and colonialism in the nineteenth and twentieth centuries. Nkrumah linked the two regimes of domination through race. He begins his 1963 *Africa Must Unite* with a quote from Eric Williams's *Capitalism and Slavery*: "Slavery was not born of racism, rather racism was the consequence of slavery." Nkrumah argued that with this "racial twist" the "myth of color inferiority" was invented. The myth facilitated "the rape of the [African] continent" during the slave trade and subsequent "exploitation under the advanced forms of colonialism and imperialism."[41] For George

Padmore, economic exploitation of black labor linked slavery and colonialism. He argued that while emancipation in the Americas was thought to have ended "the slave status of the African," imperial expansion in Africa "forced the Natives into wage-slavery."[42]

The through-line linking New World slavery and the scramble for Africa was a racialized structure of domination and exploitation. This account of slavery transcended the limited definitions of slavery that dominated the League of Nations' abolitionist efforts. As the previous chapter illustrated, the 1926 Convention on Slavery reduced slavery to the ownership and sale of persons, ignoring broader practices of colonial forced labor. Moreover, the league's narrow definition of slavery was mobilized to call into question and curtail black sovereignty in Liberia and Ethiopia. In contrast, the anticolonial critique offered an expansive account of slavery that combined a republican emphasis on arbitrary power and domination with a Marxist critique of exploitation. The critique of domination and exploitation led anticolonial nationalists to endorse domestic self-government and international nondomination in the right to self-determination.

Anticolonial critics highlighted the problem of empire as enslavement by exposing the hypocritical nature of liberal and humanitarian justifications of colonial rule. The 1885 General Act of the Berlin Conference, the League of Nations Covenant, and the United Nations Charter all described colonial rule as a form of trusteeship where the colonial power functioned as a "trustee" who exercised political power for the benefit of the colonized subjects. Azikiwe pointed out the Burkean origins of this account of political rule as trusteeship.[43] In his early critique of British rule in India, Edmund Burke had argued that "all political power which is set over men . . . ought to be some way or other exercised ultimately for their benefit," and described the rights and privileges of rule as a trust.[44] While Burke invoked trusteeship to argue for limitations on imperial rule, by the late nineteenth century, this language was redeployed in service of expanding imperial power. As we saw in the previous chapter, Wilson and Smuts turned to Burke's model of trusteeship in service of their counter-revolutionary preservation of racial hierarchy.

For twentieth-century anticolonial critics, the paternalistic premises of trusteeship had no place in a democratic age.[45] Moreover, trusteeship had amounted to nothing more than an ideological gloss intended to mask the true aims of imperialism.[46] Imperial rule, they argued, could not be exercised in the interests of the ruled because its structure did not facilitate any way of ascertaining those interests and addressing instances of their

violation. Colonial subjects were denied civil liberties and political participation. Without the franchise and with limitations on freedom of speech
and press, the colonized had no means of expressing their interests.[47] The
colonial power both decided what those interests might be and adjudicated how best to realize them. This paternalistic exercise of power stood
in stark contrast to the exercise of political power in the metropole, which
was bound by the law and operated through democratic self-government.
Against this norm, imperial rule operated through an "ethics of force." [48]

By exposing the domination that masqueraded as trusteeship, they
sought to reveal that the economic interests of European powers, rather
than the well-being of colonial subjects, were the underlying motivations
for imperialism. According to Nkrumah, "imperialism knows no law beyond its own interests." And its primary interests were the exploitation of
labor, the extraction of raw materials, and the creation of new markets.[49]
This thesis of imperialism's economic logic drew on J. A. Hobson's and V. I.
Lenin's accounts of finance capital's role in the late nineteenth-century era
of imperial expansion.[50] However, where Hobson and Lenin highlighted
the unprecedented nature of the new imperialism, anticolonial nationalists offered a long history of economic exploitation that centered the exploitation of black labor. According to Du Bois, "Today instead of remov-
ing laborers from Africa to distant slavery, industry built on a new slavery
approaches Africa to deprive the natives of their land, to force them to toil,
and to reap all the profit for the white world."[51]

Expulsion from land and taxation were the primary means by which
colonial subjects in Africa were forced into production for export.[52] Having lost lands formerly used for subsistence farming and now required to
pay taxes, colonial subjects took employment in European-owned mines
and plantations. A largely independent and autonomous peasantry thus
became dependent on wage labor throughout much of the African continent.[53] According to Nkrumah, "they have either to accept the pitifully
low wages offered to them or suffer the consequences of being without
work, which in certain regimes, makes them liable to a variety of punish-
ments."[54] In addition to the indirect compulsion of landlessness and taxes,
forced labor for public works such as the building of roads and railroads
was also used in British and French territories. According to its advocates,
forced labor was not slavery because it did not entail ownership of laborers and it contributed to the development of the colonies as opposed to
enriching private interests.[55] But despite this distinction, the dependence
and exploitation characteristic of slavery were on full display in the practice of forced labor. As Nkrumah noted, "men are not treated as men, but

as chattel, to be pushed around from place to place at the whim of the district officer."[56]

Du Bois and Padmore joined Nkrumah in arguing that colonial labor practices were slavery by another name.[57] While the Marxist orientation that informed their use of wage slavery made them suspicious of the category of free labor altogether, they differentiated between metropolitan and colonial labor. Metropolitan laborers were also entangled in relations of wage slavery, but a powerful trade union movement had followed the rise of industrialization in Europe and shifted the balance of power. In the colonies, trade unions were often illegal, and if they existed, most African workers remained unorganized.[58] According to Du Bois, colonial laborers worked under conditions where "there will be no voice of law or custom to protect labor, no trade unions, no eight-hour laws, no factory legislation— nothing of the great body of legislation built up in modern days to protect mankind from sinking to the level of beasts of burden."[59]

In formulating empire as a problem of enslavement, anticolonial nationalists framed their revolution as a movement from slavery to freedom.[60] Historians of political thought have identified this narrative and the juxtaposition of slavery and freedom, in particular, with the republican tradition.[61] Like this tradition and its contemporary revival, anticolonial nationalists argued that arbitrary power and dependence were characteristic features of slavery. But in keeping with the radicalization of republicanism during the nineteenth century, recently reconstructed in the work of Alex Gourevitch and William Roberts, the anticolonial account of enslavement gave extensive attention to labor exploitation as a central site of servitude and enslavement.[62] It was in the realm of labor that the colonial condition most resembled the condition of African slavery in the New World. And for black anticolonial nationalists, this modern and racialized chattel slavery rather than the ancient Roman iteration was the primary referent of their account of empire as enslavement.

The critique of arbitrary and despotic power at the core of the empire-as-enslavement thesis did not issue in a negative account of nondomination. Nor did it entail an argument for native over alien rule regardless of whether the former ruled "well or badly, liberally or oppressively," as Berlin had concluded. First, anticolonial critics argued that liberal and benevolent alien rule was never an available option. Because of its paternalism, distance, and difference, it contained within itself the seeds of despotism. But replacing foreign rulers with native ones alone would not rectify the threat of arbitrary and despotic power. Anticolonial nationalists were largely opposed to the power of native authorities on these same grounds. For instance, Nkrumah opposed maintaining the power of chiefs in the Ghanaian constitution, arguing that because no democratic principles were applied, the chiefs represented an instance of arbitrary power.[63] The critique of empire as enslavement thus did not simply result in a demand for native rule as such but entailed a particular vision of the postcolonial state that included all inhabitants as citizens and was democratic, developmental, and redistributive. Native rule had to take the form of democratic self-government to adequately overcome domination and exploitation.

Democratic self-government, however, could be only part of the answer to the problem of empire. On its own, it left unaddressed the racial hierarchy that structured that international order and made empire as enslavement possible in the colony. The focus on international racial hierarchy and unequal integration gave the critique of empire as enslavement a global scope. As Du Bois's formulation of the global color line suggested, imperial enslavement was organized at an international level through a collaborative pan-European process by which European states collectively exercised a right of ownership and expropriation over the rest of the world.[64] More than any other event, the Berlin Conference of 1884–85 that divided the African continent between European states exemplified this collaborative spirit. Conceived as unequal members of international society, African territories could be parceled out between European powers in order to stem intra-European conflicts and competition. Central to this scramble for Africa was a growing sense of racial superiority. According to Du Bois, the distribution of the African continent among European states occurred because once "color became in the world's thought synonymous with inferiority, 'Negro' lost its capitalization and Africa was another name for bestiality and barbarism."[65]

International hierarchy not only constituted the terms of colonial slavery but also structured the nature of rivalry, competition, and conflict between states. Like Hobson and Lenin, Padmore traced the origins of world war to imperial aggrandizement. He argued that the "chain of events beginning with the partition of Africa" generated an expansive form of interstate rivalry that soon extended beyond the colonial frontier and emerged within Europe itself when World War I broke out.[66] While European states had collectively and collaboratively pursued their economic interests vis-à-vis the extra-European world, the colonial periphery was also a site of European conflict and competition. Imperial states were never fully capable of projecting their sovereignty onto their colonial holdings, which often resulted in competing claims and territorial disputes. Moreover, the dominance of the British Empire (and to a lesser extent the French Empire) sparked competition between what Padmore called imperial "haves" and "have nots."[67]

The peace agreed to at Versailles left unaddressed "the [primary] causes of war, especially those causes which lurk in rivalry for power and prestige, race dominance, and income arising from the ownership of men, land, and materials."[68] As a result, the League of Nations could not fulfill its mission of securing international peace, and this set the stage for a second world war. Still intact, international racial hierarchy divided the world vertically along racial lines and also created divisions between powers with significant colonial territory and those without. It was the competition between expanding imperial powers—the haves and have nots—that led to international war.[69] Germany stripped of her colonies and subject to reparations, Italy excluded from the promised territorial gains in the 1915 Treaty of London, and Japan, whose claim of racial equality had been denied, constituted the Axis powers and aimed to exercise the imperialist expansion denied to them in the interwar period. Thus, the failure to address imperial expansion and white supremacy in 1919 led to the crises of the late 1930s.[70] The result was violence on the vertical axis of international hierarchy as exemplified in Italy's 1935 invasion of Ethiopia and on the horizontal interimperial arena as Germany sought expansion within Europe.[71]

At the end of World War II, Du Bois worried that the world had not yet learned the lesson of two world wars. The international racial hierarchy and colonial domination it facilitated remained unchallenged even as the world once again prepared for a lasting peace. Without challenging this global color line, the postwar settlement, like the League of Nations before it, would leave open the possibility for new forms of international conflict.[72] International hierarchy thus threatened the anticolonial project in two ways. First, it maintained the background conditions of colonial enslavement. Even after the war, according to Du Bois, Europe continued to believe that racial difference marked "congenital inferiority," which justified the treatment of colonial subjects "as serfs to minister to his own comfort and luxury."[73] Second, even if this structure allowed some colonies to gain independence or let states like Ethiopia and Liberia retain their formal sovereignty, the possibility of conflict and competition threatened the prospects for self-government.

The empire-as-enslavement thesis thus offered an expansive critique of colonial rule. Starting with the district officer and colonized subject, this critique cascaded out to the international sphere and required a wholesale transformation of domestic and international politics. But for all its power and expansiveness, this anticolonial emphasis on slavery ignored the problem of dispossession so central to settler colonial formations.[74] In the empire-as-enslavement framing, dispossession entered the picture only as a form of primitive accumulation that constituted the necessary backdrop for labor exploitation in the colony. Absent from this account is what scholars of settler colonialism describe as a distinctive experience of empire, which operates as a "form of structured dispossession."[75] On this view, dispossession is a form of injustice on its own terms that does not depend on the later exploitation of the dispossessed, a sequence that was often not pursued in instances of settlement.[76]

With regard to the anticolonial nationalists surveyed here, the failure to recognize dispossession as a separate and autonomous form of imperial injustice stemmed from the focus on Africa, where the paradigmatic cases of colonialism were the protectorates, mandates, dependencies, and crown colonies in which European settlement was limited. Thus, even as they supplemented and expanded the critique of alien rule to include unequal integration and international racial hierarchy, alien rule was emblematic of their understanding of empire. As a result, the critique of empire and the right to self-determination they formulated in response left unaddressed the specificities of the settler colonial experience in the Americas, Australia, New Zealand, and southern Africa. While there were important resonances between the empire-as-enslavement thesis and the critique of settler colonialism, especially in contexts where African slavery and Native dispossession were coconstituted, the emphasis on domination and exploitation at the hands of imperial elites had significant implications for the articulation of a right to self-determination.

As it was codified in the 1950s and 1960s, the right to self-determination came to be limited to instances of alien rule. Sometimes referred to as "blue water" or "saltwater" imperialism, alien rule was differentiated from settler colonial experiences through the requirement of geographic distance. The United States initially championed this standard in the 1950s in an effort to ensure that the newly established international requirements for non-self-governing territories would not apply to indigenous communities and minorities within states.[77] As anticolonial nationalists pushed for a right to self-determination and secured passage of resolution 1514, they inadvertently reinforced the saltwater standard by insisting on territorial integrity. This commitment to territorial integrity, to which I will return, was largely aimed at warding off violent secessions in plural postcolonial societies, but it also had the effect of excluding indigenous claims to self-determination in the classic cases of settler colonialism. This delimitation also tempered the reach of self-determination in southern Africa, where colonial rule stubbornly persisted. South Africa and the Portuguese colonial states in Angola and Mozambique as well as settlers in Rhodesia laid claim to the saltwater thesis and insisted that the right to self-determination could not apply in their cases, as the territories they governed were internal to their own political units. However facetious these claims were, they exploited a contradiction at the heart of how anticolonial nationalists articulated the right to self-determination.

From Principle to Right

Despite these important limitations, the transformation of self-determination from principle to right was an important step in inaugurating an anti-imperial world order based on the universalization of independence and equality. The right to self-determination was a highly contested claim—one that great power states first rejected and later acquiesced to in the face of a growing majority of postcolonial states within the General Assembly. The emergence of a right to self-determination was thus less an inevitable development of postwar institutions and ideals and more an effort to break with the racial hierarchy and colonial slavery that continued to structure the international sphere. It was conceived as a new foundation for the United Nations and perceived as a threat by those who defended the status quo.

Anticolonial nationalists first articulated the right to self-determination outside the halls of the UN in contexts like the Fifth Pan-African Congress. Already in 1940, the West Indies National Emergency Committee put forward the Declaration of Rights of the Caribbean Peoples to Self-Determination and Self-Government, calling for the recognition of West Indian peoples' "inalienable human and democratic right of self-determination."[78] Presented to the Pan-American Foreign Ministers Conference, this document precedes the Atlantic Charter but already contains the anticolonial refashioning of self-determination as a human right. In 1945, the West Indies National Emergency Committee submitted its declaration for a right to self-government to the United Nations.[79] The Pan-African Congress in Manchester echoed this demand for a collective right to self-determination and connected it to individual rights. The congress demanded complete independence and autonomy for Africa and the West Indies and connected this demand to "the right to education, the right to earn a decent living; the right to express our thoughts and emotions, to adopt and create forms of beauty."[80] At the 1955 Afro-Asian conference in Bandung, anticolonial nationalists reinforced this view, declaring, "The rights of peoples and nations to self-determination is conceived as a prerequisite for the enjoyment of all fundamental human rights."[81] In this statement, self-determination was itself a right, and this collective right of "peoples and nations" was a necessary condition for individual human rights. It was this vision of self-determination that anticolonial nationalists introduced into the debates in the General Assembly and the Commission on Human Rights, where the binding human rights covenants were being drafted.

In response to a 1950 draft covenant on human rights that did not include self-determination, the growing coalition of postcolonial states passed General Assembly resolutions requesting that the Commission on Human Rights and the Economic and Social Council study "ways and means which would ensure the [right of self-determination] because the violation of this right has resulted in bloodshed and war in the past and is considered a continuous threat to peace."[82] These early resolutions also insisted that self-determination was a human right and a prerequisite for other human rights.[83] When the debate moved from the assembly to the Commission on Human Rights, imperial powers challenged the anticolonial position on three fronts. First, opponents of a right to self-determination argued that rights accrued to individuals and not collectivities. A people's right to self-determination was thus a contradiction in terms. Secondly, the right to self-determination conflated the political and legal realms. Rights were a legal concept with universal application, but ascertaining which groups constituted peoples and whether they were capable of self-government were political questions to be judged differently according to each case.[84] Finally, critics insisted that self-determination was a principle rather than a right. Citing the UN Charter, Great Britain's representative reminded the commission that self-determination was a secondary principle that would support the more central aim of maintaining international peace. To identify self-determination as a right that supersedes other claims singled out countries with colonial holdings and thereby undermined the principles of sovereign equality and nonintervention that were central to maintaining international peace.[85]

In returning to the UN Charter, critics acknowledged the anticolonial reinvention at hand and hoped to stem this new tide by invoking a prior instantiation of self-determination—one that entailed gradualism and left unaddressed broader questions of international hierarchy. Rather than offering a competing interpretation of the UN's founding document, anticolonial nationalists self-consciously embraced their intervention as a reinvention of international society. They returned to the problem of empire and insisted that the right to self-determination was the only available answer to questions of colonial domination and exploitation. In the General Assembly, proponents of the right to self-determination argued that from the perspective of "dependent peoples, a state of subjection to another power was little better than slavery."[86] The colonized, like the enslaved, experienced a violation of rights of citizenship and personhood that denied them individual human dignity.[87] This line of argument indicated that the separation of individual rights from the collective right of self-determination did not recognize the ways that subjection to foreign rule made subjects rightless.

Beyond linking self-determination to the achievement of individual rights domestically, anticolonial nationalists also argued that the right to self-determination was a better foundation for international peace. A universal right to self-determination would transcend international hierarchy, which enabled colonial domination and engendered imperial rivalry and war. As long as hierarchy remained a feature of international society, equality was limited to the existing states. This partial recognition of equality created conditions for the violent subjection of colonized peoples and for imperial competition between states.[88] On this view, if the UN recognized and protected a universal right to self-determination, the principle of sovereign equality and the aim of international peace would be better realized.

By 1956, the anticolonial position prevailed in the Commission on Human Rights. Drafts of the Covenant on Political and Civil Rights as well as the Covenant on Economic, Social and Cultural Rights included a right to self-determination. The drafts were then sent to the Third Committee of the General Assembly, where the right to self-determination elicited the most disagreement. Twenty-six meetings were dedicated to discussing the right.[89] To avoid an impasse that would derail passage of the covenants, the UN secretary general recommended that the Third Committee leave self-determination out of the covenants and create an ad hoc committee to prepare a separate declaration on self-determination. Postcolonial states rejected this recommendation. A separate declaration would sever the link between self-determination and human rights and relegate self-determination to a declaration, which, unlike the covenants, would not be legally binding.[90]

After revising the language of the article on self-determination and dropping a controversial clause that gave peoples permanent sovereignty over natural resources, the committee adopted it with thirty-three yes votes, twelve no votes, and thirteen abstentions.[91] Self-determination was prominently included as article 1, with the following language:

1. All peoples have the right of self-determination. By virtue of that right they freely determine their political status and freely pursue their economic, social and cultural development.

2. All peoples may, for their own ends, freely dispose of their natural wealth and resources without prejudice to any obligations arising out of international economic co-operation, based upon the principle of mutual benefit, and international law. In no case may a people be deprived of its own means of subsistence.

3. The States Parties to the present Covenant, including those having responsibility for the administration of Non-Self-Governing and Trust Territories, shall promote the realization of the right of self-determination, and shall respect that right, in conformity with the provisions of the Charter of the United Nations.[92]

With the growing number of African states in the UN General Assembly, postcolonial states expanded and enhanced the emerging right to self-determination with the 1960 passage of resolution 1514. Passed with an overwhelming majority, resolution 1514 reproduced the problem-and-answer pair through which the anticolonial right to self-determination was articulated. First, colonialism was conceived as a form of slavery in which the colonized were rightless subjects. In the debates that preceded passage of the resolution, subjection to foreign rule was declared a "colonial bondage" that denied its subjects human rights and dignity.[93] Only with the recognition of a right to self-determination, now restated as "an inalienable right to complete freedom, the exercise of their sovereignty and the integrity of their national territory," could the bondage of colonialism be overcome.[94] Secondly, foreign rule was identified as "an impediment to world peace." The international hierarchy on which colonial domination was instituted not only enabled violence against subject peoples but also incited imperial competition between states. To counter the problem of hierarchy, the resolution insisted on equality. According to the declaration, "inadequacy of political, economic, social or educational preparedness should never serve as a pretext for delaying independence." Incapacity for self-rule had been the central justification for denying or delaying self-government to colonized peoples, creating a hierarchical world order. The resolution called for the immediate transfer of power to peoples in trusteeships and colonies "without any conditions or reservations."[95]

The demand for an immediate end to all forms of foreign rule went beyond article 1 of the covenants. Article 1 called on states to "promote the realization of the right of self-determination . . . in conformity with the provisions of the Charter of the United Nations." In chapters 11 and 12, the charter called for a gradual rather than an immediate transfer of power to dependent peoples. States with colonies and trusteeships were asked to promote the development of self-government in ways that were appropriate to each territory. By requiring conformity to the charter, article 1 of the covenants reproduced this gradualist approach. Resolution 1514, on the other hand, rejected gradualism. Political independence and sovereign equality were not achieved through development under colonial rule but were foundations for a postimperial world order in which people "freely develop their own political, economic, social and cultural institutions."[96]

In positioning self-determination as an "inviolable right to complete freedom" and by rejecting the gradualism implicit in article 1 of the covenants, resolution 1514 marked the culmination of self-determination's reinvention. Self-determination was no longer an end state reached after developing the capacities for self-government. Moreover, it could no longer be satisfied with minimalist definitions of consent and consultation. Instead, the right to self-determination now entailed freedom from foreign rule and intervention secured through equal membership within international society. For the African representatives who worked to pass the declaration, the distance between 1945 and 1960 was profound.[97]

However, it was also a limited victory. For instance, when the empire-as-enslavement critique moved into the space of the United Nations, it primarily registered in terms of violations of human rights. Rightlessness had been part of the anticolonial critique of enslavement and was already present in Du Bois's citation of Chief Justice Taney as well as in the Bandung communiqué. But rightlessness was only one piece of a broader experience of domination. Within the United Nations, however, this became the primary term for understanding the wrong of colonialism. Thus in resolution 1514, "the subjection of peoples to alien subjugation, domination and exploitation" was equated with and said to constitute "a denial of fundamental human rights."[98] This delimitation of enslavement to rightlessness meant that the new right to self-determination had only a tangential connection to the economic critique central to the empire-as-enslavement framework. For instance, to get self-determination included in the human rights covenants the representatives of postcolonial states were forced to abandon the more radical demand of permanent sovereignty over natural resources. What appeared instead was a weaker claim that peoples had a right to subsistence along with a clause delimiting a people's right to dispose of their resources by reference to the state's obligations under international law. The arguments for a more egalitarian global economy, which would soon be taken up in the United Nations Conference on Trade and Development and would form the basis for the New International Economic Order (NIEO), were thus largely left out of this formulation of the right to self-determination.

Founding an Anti-imperial World Order

For anticolonial nationalists, the right to self-determination was never conceived as the culmination of their worldmaking aspirations. It was always a first step in political and economic transformations, both domestically and internationally. For instance, even as they struggled to have the right to self-determination recognized in the United Nations, they were already in the midst of constituting regional federations and would soon follow the victory of a right to self-determination with the more demanding project of the NIEO. In relation to these projects, the right to self-determination was meant to constitute the formal foundations of a new postimperial world order. Through guarantees of independence and equality, the right to self-determination secured the legal component of international nondomination necessary for the exercise of popular sovereignty and self-rule within the former colony.

To understand the significance of the right to self-determination, we must consider its relationship to human rights more generally. Over the last few years, there has been an important debate among historians about the relationship between anticolonial nationalism and human rights. According to Samuel Moyn, anticolonial demands for national self-determination privileged collective rights over the enumeration of individual rights in the Universal Declaration of Human Rights (UDHR). Moyn argues that anticolonial nationalism was not a human rights movement and that human rights as claims made beyond the state gained prominence only after the height of decolonization and in response to failures of the postcolonial state.[99] Historians such as Roland Burke and Steven Jensen, however, have argued that human rights were central to the early phase of anticolonial nationalism and that anticolonial nationalists in turn helped to shape the nature of the postwar human rights instruments.[100] On this view, postcolonial states used their majorities to overcome the paralysis that blocked codification of human rights law at the United Nations and mobilized the debates to publicize and prioritize racial discrimination and religious persecution.[101]

The position taken here is that human rights were an important part of anticolonial nationalism but were not the central or primary mode of critique. Before the end of World War II and the writing of the UDHR, "rights talk" was already a crucial site of political contestation in colonial Africa that facilitated the critique of imperialism. Colonial subjects laid claim to the rights and liberties offered in treaties and official discourse to challenge the lawless imposition of colonial rule and demand remedy for the excesses of colonial power.[102] As anticolonial critics turned toward independence, this existing language informed their critique of colonial rule and was supplemented by the emerging international discourse of human rights. For instance, in 1943, Azikiwe enumerated political and civil rights along with the right to self-determination in his *Political Blueprint for Nigeria*, and Nkrumah situated the African struggle for independence within a broader "quest for human rights."[103]

Rather than being unprecedented or novel, these references to human rights "marked a new chapter in an evolving tradition of rights talk."[104] Moreover, this mobilization of human rights discourse was always situated in a broader account of empire as enslavement. This form of enslavement included the denial of "elementary human rights" as well as "political servitude . . . and economic serfdom."[105] As I have noted above, within the context of the United Nations, the violation of human rights came to stand in for this larger critique of empire as enslavement. Using the institutional and discursive opening made possible by the language of human rights, representatives of postcolonial states elevated the violation of human rights in the colony and, in response to colonial rightlessness, formulated the right to self-determination, conceived as a prerequisite for other human rights.

The relationship between self-determination and human rights thus depends on how we understand the language of prerequisite. Anticolonial nationalists deployed prerequisite to signal the political and strategic priority of independence and self-government. Captured in Nkrumah's famous dictum that fellow nationalists should "seek ye first the political kingdom" and Azikiwe's vision of political autonomy as "the *summum bonum* of political existence," they ranked the right to self-determination as lexically prior to individual human rights, as well as other projects like economic development, which were part of the broader vision of postcolonial transformation.[106] Nkrumah argued that a "complete and absolute independence from the control of any foreign government" enables the "establishment of a democracy in which sovereignty is vested in the broad masses of the people," so that they "might be able to find better means of achieving livelihood and asserting their right to human life and happiness."[107] Against the elision of self-determination in the UDHR, Julius Nyerere argued that the rights enumerated in the declaration required the formation of new postcolonial societies. The declaration, he noted, was the "basis for both our external and our internal policies." It "represented [the] goals [of postcolonial states] rather than something that [was] already achieved."[108] On this view, postcolonial independence set the foundation for the gradual implementation of human rights as the rights of citizenship within new states.

This lexical ordering of self-determination and human rights emerged from the view that rights could be secured only in the framework of self-rule. Parliamentary democracy, Nkrumah argued, "offers the most opportunities to every individual in the state to express his personality to the fullest and to enjoy all the basic human rights."[109] Only when citizens had the right to decide in full freedom could their human rights be protected and their needs fulfilled. In the absence of democratic self-government, "no matter how benevolent that government may be," the rights of persons would not be protected. In conceiving of self-determination as the necessary framework in which rights might be protected and realized, Nkrumah rejected the paternalism of imperial rule.[110] Without self-government, rights were not rights, but privileges granted at the whims of an unaccountable political authority.

This critique of imperial paternalism called into question the UDHR's universalism. Article 2 declared that "the political, jurisdictional or international status of the country or territory to which a person belongs, whether it be independent, trust, non-self-governing or under any other limitation of sovereignty" should have no bearing on individuals' entitlement to rights.[111] The force of the anticolonial critique was to question the separation of rights from the "political, jurisdictional or international status of [one's] country or territory." In framing colonialism itself as a violation of human rights, nationalists argued that the colonial subject's rightlessness was precisely the result of the colonial status of the country or territory. Securing the rights of the colonized would require the institutionalization of democratic self-government on the one hand and "complete and independent sovereignty over its territory" on the other.[112]

Viewed from this perspective, anticolonial nationalists' relationship to human rights was more than an instrumental and strategic invocation of rights but did not reflect a commitment to human rights as internationally guaranteed individual entitlements that were aimed at curtailing the power of states. Human rights—the rights of man—were in the anticolonial account realizable only as the rights of citizens. Though postcolonial states had endorsed the international covenants on human rights and secured their passage, nationalists largely viewed rights as principles that "states should embody, not superordinate rules to which they must defer."[113] For liberal advocates of human rights, this effort to subsume human rights within the state and self-government was a sign that anticolonial invocations of human rights were politically opportunistic. According to Eagleton, the right to self-determination was not articulated "with regard to some consistent principle" and was "in accord with the political opportunism of the moment."[114] The international lawyer Louis Henkin concurred, arguing, "The struggle to end colonialism . . . swallowed up the original purpose of cooperation for the promotion of human rights."[115] In the anticolonial fusion of self-determination and human rights, Henkin worried that "human rights was being used as a political weapon against colonialism or economic imperialism, not to enhance the rights of all persons against all government."[116] For Henkin, collective self-government did not entail the protection of individual rights, and even democratic self-government with its majoritarian tendencies could violate the rights of citizens, particularly those that constituted political, religious, or ethnic minorities.

These questions would soon dominate discussions of postcolonial states, but the view that rights were to be secured through self-government was not simply an opportunistic mobilization of human rights in service of the collective right to self-determination. For Henkin and others, who were concerned with totalitarianism and curbing the excesses of state sovereignty, individuals required protections from the state. In contrast, anticolonial nationalists argued that it was the absence of statehood and democratic government that had rendered colonial subjects vulnerable to rights violations. This argument had been a central element of black nationalist thought in the nineteenth and early twentieth centuries. For instance, Marcus Garvey, whom Padmore identified as the progenitor of Pan-Africanism and Nkrumah credited as the most influential person on his political thinking, conceived of the solution to rightlessness as black self-government. He argued that across the Atlantic world, blacks are "denied the common rights due to human beings."[117] They are cast as slaves and are perceived as "outcast[s] and leper[s] among the races of men."[118]

It was this designation as slave, outcast, and leper that made possible the worst forms of violence against black people. The practices of "lynching by burning, hanging, or by any other means" and "whipping, flogging and overworking" became possible because black people were without a place in the world and a government that could protect their rights. According to Garvey, Englishmen, Germans, Frenchmen, and the Japanese are not lynched "because these people are represented by great governments, mighty nations and empires, highly organized. If the Negro did not reach "this point of national independence," he had no hope of securing his human rights, and his future, particularly in the Western Hemisphere, was bound to "spell ruin and disaster."[119] Like the movement for a "free Ireland" and the "determination of the Jews to recover Palestine, the Negro peoples of the world should be so determined to reclaim Africa and found a government there, so that if any black man in any part of the world is abused we can call the mighty power of Africa to come to our aid."[120]

Garvey's Negro government did not offer a fully developed institutional account of how black self-government might govern and protect a far-flung diaspora. However, at its center was the view that the injustices and rights violations that blacks faced could not be disconnected from their collective position as stateless people. While anticolonial nationalists gave up on Garvey's transnational vision in favor of territorially grounded political institutions in the form of the nation-state and regional federations, they shared in this tradition of thinking that recognized the interconnection between individual liberty and the collective conditions of possibility for its realization. According to Nyerere, anticolonial struggle was fought "on the ground of individual liberty and equality and on the grounds that every peoples must have the right to determine for themselves the conditions under which they would be governed." The task for nationalists was to work out "the constitutional and other arrangements which [were] appropriate to the most essential functions of a state—that is the safeguarding of life and liberty for its inhabitants."[121] For Nyerere, as with Nkrumah, citizenship within the postcolonial state was to provide the institutional context and conditions for safeguarding individual rights and liberties.

Though largely silent about, and at times critical of, the anticolonial revolutions during her time, Hannah Arendt's critique of the rights of man bears similarities with this anticolonial account of human rights as rights made possible through political membership. For Arendt, the UDHR, like previous efforts to enumerate the rights of man, were beset by a "lack of reality."[122] While the UDHR offers a "welter of rights of the most heterogeneous nature and origin," she worried it would result in the neglect of the "one right without which no other can materialize—the right to belong to a political community."[123] The insight that rights require what Arendt called "the right to have rights," a right "to belong to some kind of organized community," drew on her analysis of statelessness in Europe. Arendt analogized the experience of European statelessness to the condition of colonial Africa, arguing that "a growing number of people and peoples suddenly appeared whose elementary rights were as little safeguarded by the ordinary functioning of the nation-state in the middle of Europe as they had been in the heart of Africa."[124]

Rightlessness, for Arendt, illustrated that "the moment human beings lacked their own government and had to fall back upon their minimum rights, no authority was left to protect them and no institution was willing to guarantee them."[125] In light of the simultaneity of statelessness and rightlessness, Arendt argued that it was only when individuals had a "place in the world," a right "to belong to some kind of organized community," that human rights could be guaranteed.[126] Rights, in her account, "are conventions, forms of recognition produced by human agreement, fragile artifacts of human living together."[127] According to Arendt, "rights materialize only within a given political community. . . . They depend on our fellow-man and on a tacit guarantee that the members of a community give to each other."[128]

The anticolonial right to self-determination shared in Arendt's view that individual rights should be situated within political communities, but the right to membership could be only one part of the response to the problem of colonial rightlessness. In addition to grounding human rights in the right of political membership, the relationship between the political communities in which individuals had a right to membership and international society would have to be addressed. If the individual liberty and equality of former colonial subjects depended on the constitutional and other arrangements of the postcolonial state, the state would have to be embedded in an international society that preserved its existence.

In its external and international orientation, the right to self-determination went beyond the right to have rights. It aimed at transcending alien rule and hierarchy through international guarantees of independence and equality. By rejecting "the subjection of peoples to alien subjugation, domination and exploitation," and insisting that "all people have the right to self-determination," resolution 1514 sought to delegitimize imperial rule and establish self-determination as a new principle of political legitimacy within international society.[129] The new account of international legitimacy guaranteed all states freedom from alien rule and secured their independence. External independence was central to securing the boundaries of the political space in which colonial subjects turned citizens could exercise popular sovereignty and self-government.

However, on its own, independence from alien rule could not sufficiently guard against international hierarchy. While it might have overcome foreign rule and intervention, it did not fully address the problems
of hierarchy and unequal membership in international society. Independence thus required the institution of equality between these communities. Anticolonial nationalists accomplished this by rejecting hierarchies of
development and capacity and extending the principle of sovereign equality to all political communities.[130] Despite vast inequalities in the political, military, and economic endowments of each state, sovereign equality
ensured all political communities equal legal status within international
society. Equality in the international order preserved the independence
of each political community. It ensured that the powerful states of the
world would not dominate weaker and smaller members of international
society, denying the latter the external freedom required for internal self-
government. By delimiting political communities from each other and
ensuring all equal status within international society, sovereign equality
would protect and preserve the plurality of political communities within
the international sphere.

Though I earlier argued that the empire-as-enslavement critique
pointed to the positive liberty of self-rule within the colony, in its external
face, self-determination's guarantees of independence and equality might
be profitably read as efforts to secure nondomination in international society. In this context, the right to self-determination mitigated the effects
of the substantive hierarchies that structured international society, by limiting the exercise of power between states. Self-determination thus created
the external conditions for "political and legal relationships within a polity
by establishing domestic jurisdiction and differentiating among distinct
legal and political systems."[131] In this sense, the right to self-determination
set juridical limits on domination in the international sphere and aimed
for a "domination-free" international society.[132] Without international
institutions that preserved this right, the efforts at self-rule domestically
were always subject to possible foreign intervention and encroachment at
the hands of more powerful states and nonstate actors. In universalizing
the right to self-determination, nationalists sought to guard against this
domination.

The anticolonial commitments to independence, equality, and nonintervention are often viewed as indications of the ways decolonization universalized a Westphalian regime of sovereignty and extended the United
Nations Charter.[133] But this mischaracterizes both Westphalia and the UN
Charter while minimizing the significance of the anticolonial reinvention

of self-determination. As I noted in chapter 1, the characterization of Westphalia as inaugurating an international society of sovereign and equal states ignores the imperial history of sovereign inequality and hierarchy. Moreover, the ideal of a world of sovereign and equal states was a belated attribution to the Treaty of Westphalia—one that can actually be traced to the twentieth-century moment of decolonization. And while the UN Charter did include guarantees of sovereign equality, like the League of Nations Covenant before it, it combined this with sovereign inequality and contained within it gradations of legal standing. These marks of hierarchy could be found in the charter's inclusion of trust and non-self-governing territories and in the outsized power of the Security Council.

If, as I have argued, the history of modern international society was structured by unequal integration rather than merely the exclusion of non-European peoples, then we should understand the ideal of a universal international society to be of anti-imperial rather than European provenance. Resolution 1514 and, more broadly, the anticolonial politics of reinventing self-determination were efforts to constitute the foundations of an anti-imperial world order—one in which colonial domination was illegitimate for the first time in modern international society, racial hierarchy was abolished, and sovereign equality extended to all member states. Far from the realization and unfolding of Westphalia, the universalization of independence and equality became possible only with European decline and was predicated on the revision and remaking of a Eurocentric international society.[134]

Especially in their vision of sovereign equality, anticolonial nationalists reached far beyond the terms of existing international society.[135] Armed with the right to self-determination, nationalists argued that an anti-imperial world order required not only equal legal standing but also equal decision-making power. Thus, they rejected the veto power of the Security Council's five permanent members and the outsized decision-making and enforcing power of the council relative to the assembly as vestiges of a hierarchical world order. On the one hand, Nkrumah and Ghana's UN representative Quaison-Sackey called for a more representative council in which each region of the world (the Americas, Europe, Africa, Asia, and the Middle East) would hold a permanent seat in the Security Council.[136] This effort to address the "inequitable and unbalanced" composition of the Security Council did not yield to shifts in the permanent members but did lead in 1963 to an expansion of the council's nonpermanent seats.[137] On the other hand, nationalists sought to redirect decision-making powers toward the representative and egalitarian General Assembly, which they envisioned as the parliament of a new anti-imperial world order. This expansive vision of sovereign equality would reach its height in the New International Economic Order as postcolonial states deployed what they understood to be the legislative power of the General Assembly to create an egalitarian global economy.

But for all its novelty and significance as the formal condition of anticolonial worldmaking, it should be noted that the reinvention of self-determination described here turned to the international sphere to secure the conditions of postcolonial statehood. Worldmaking here was largely envisioned as an effort to preserve the state by guaranteeing a set of legal rights that delimited the exercise of power in the international sphere. While worldmaking took this defensive and negative posture in the universalization of the right to self-determination, in the formation of regional federations and the creation of the NIEO, anticolonial nationalists envisioned political and economic institutions that promised to displace, transcend, or at least constrain the state. In these projects, international society was not only a site for protecting independent statehood but also an arena in which regional and international institutions were required to address the limits of the nation-state in the face of persistent dependence and domination.

The Limits of Anticolonial Self-Determination

While resolution 1514 set the formal foundations for these more expansive projects and marked the peak of the anticolonial reinvention of self-determination, 1960, the year of its passage, also indicated its limits. Just weeks after the Republic of Congo's achievement of independence in June, the southern province of Katanga declared its independence, plunging the new state into political crisis. The arrival of the United Nations peacekeeping forces just days later—the first such operation in postcolonial Africa and the largest until the 1990s—inaugurated the five-year Congo crisis, which was a flashpoint in the Cold War and dominated discussions about the limits of decolonization among both anticolonial nationalists and their critics. By the time the crisis ended, the leader of the Congo, Patrice Lumumba, had been assassinated, the UN's first secretary general, Dag Hammarskjöld, had been killed when his plane suspiciously crashed, and with the blessing of the United States for his anticommunist stance, Joseph Mobutu had cemented his political power.

During his September 1960 address to the UN General Assembly, in which he celebrated the victories of decolonization thus far, Nkrumah

also sounded the alarms about the Congo crisis. He argued that the secession was an example of the consequences of "clientele-sovereignty, or
fake independence, namely the practice of granting a sort of independence
by the metropolitan power, with the concealed intention of making the
liberated country a client-state and controlling it effectively by means
other than political ones."[138] Nkrumah would describe this phenomenon
in other contexts as neocolonialism, "the last stage of imperialism."[139]
For Nkrumah, the United Nations had to protect the hard-won right of
self-determination against this illusory independence. Thus, while he
supported the peacekeeping mission, he rejected the secretary general's
insistence that UN forces remain neutral in the conflict between the se-
cessionists and the central government. "It is impossible," he argued, "for
the United Nations at one and the same time to preserve law and order
and to be neutral between the legal authorities and the lawbreakers." He
urged the General Assembly to impress on the secretary general and the
peacekeeping forces that preserving law and order required "supporting,
safeguarding and maintaining the legal and existing parliamentary framework of the State."[140]

A central part of Nkrumah's analysis of the Congo crisis as laid out
in his book-length *Challenge of the Congo* emphasized the ways in which
the weakness of new postcolonial states combined with persistent international hierarchies to once again constitute Africa as a site of imperial
rivalry, competition, and war. Returning to the anticolonial critique of international hierarchy's causal role in the two world wars, he saw in the international talk of the "strategic importance of the Congo" a new scramble
for Africa that threatened to cascade into a broader conflict. Moreover, as
journalists and other commentators began to portray the Congo as confirmation of the African state's artificiality and invoked African incapacity
for self-rule to return once again to models of trusteeship, Nkrumah saw
evidence of the "unchanging attitudes of western thought" with respect to
Africa—"racial contempt," "economic greed," and "the complete absence of
any thought for the well-being of the [people]."[141]

The persistence of racial hierarchy and the threats it posed to self-
determination informed the efforts of postcolonial states to re-entrench
the principle of nonintervention. Though resolution 1514 had already indicated fidelity to nonintervention and territorial integrity, the 1965 General
Assembly resolution 2131 would expand these principles to include pro-
hibitions not only against armed intervention (as in the UN Charter) but
also against informal intervention and any "measures to coerce a state to
either subordinate . . . its sovereignty rights or to secure from it advantages

of any kind."[142] In line with Nkrumah's account of the Congo crisis, resolution 2131 connected the protection of states' independence and sovereignty with the preservation of international peace, arguing that in the absence of higher barriers to intervention, the international rivalry and competition of the Cold War would once again lead to interstate conflict.[143] This expansive account of nonintervention extended resolution 1514's defensive vision of worldmaking where international institutions reinforce the state.

Nkrumah endorsed a conception of the United Nations as an institution for securing and expanding the rights that would guarantee international nondomination. But his efforts to ward off the threats of a new imperialism were not limited to a defensive mobilization of the principle of nonintervention on the international stage. Instead, as we shall see in the following chapter, he argued that the fake independence to which the Congo and other African states had fallen victim required the formation of a United States of Africa. Continental union was a central element of Nkrumah's Pan-African vision since the 1940s, but the call for federation became more urgent in the context of the Congo crisis. In this account, neocolonialism was not only the result of inadequate defenses against intervention but also attributable to the economic, and by extension, political weakness of postcolonial states. Directly addressing the vulnerabilities of the postcolonial state required thinking beyond it.

Yet, for all of Nkrumah's insights into the persistence of racial hierarchy, the instability of new states, and the need for concerted collective action against the forces of empire, he did not fully capture the challenge of the Congo. The Congo crisis not only was the result of foreign intervention and Cold War proxy wars; it also raised questions about the internal instability of the anticolonial right to self-determination. As Ryan Irwin has recently argued, at the highpoint of decolonization, the Katanga secession brought to the forefront "a quintessentially postcolonial problem: the relationship of borders to people."[144] While claiming that all peoples had a right to self-determination, anticolonial nationalists had limited its extension to peoples subjected to alien rule, accepted inherited colonial boundaries, and insisted on territorial integrity. Anticolonial nationalists were well aware that the colonial-era borders cut across ethnic and national groups but hoped to thwart a process of increasing fragmentation by extending citizenship to all and mitigating potential conflicts that would arise from ethnic, national, and religious diversity.[145] But as the Katanga secession illustrated, whether self-determination required smaller units that more closely mapped onto ties of kinship, language, and region remained an open question.[146] And even when ethnic conflicts did not escalate into calls for secession, the politics of citizenship appeared unable to transcend the deep divisions that characterized postcolonial societies.[147]

If the Katanga secession appeared too mired in the politics of the Cold War, the Biafran bid for independence and ensuing war in Nigeria between 1967 and 1970 would magnify the urgency of these questions. Stemming from conflicts about the distribution of political power and resources within Nigeria's federal structure and initiated by a series of coups and countercoups in 1966 that resulted in massacres of the Igbo, the secession sought to create a new state in the eastern province, an area considered the historic homeland of the Igbo people. Deeply committed to preserving postcolonial sovereignty, the Organization of African Unity (OAU), which as we shall see emerged as a very limited version of Nkrumah's continental union, approached the conflict as an internal matter. Though it offered mediation between the federal state and the Biafran leaders, the OAU did not take up the Biafran cause as a quest for self-determination of the kind that it was promoting in southern Africa where alien rule persisted.

Breaking with this consensus, Nyerere's government in Tanzania extended recognition to the Biafran state in 1968, and Nyerere reflected on the ways that the Biafran war indicated the limits of the anticolonial account of self-determination. He argued that anticolonial nationalists' acceptance of the boundaries inherited from colonialism was predicated on the premise that they could transform the former colonies into political communities that protected the life and liberty of all citizens. While the 1960 Nigerian federal constitution embodied this commitment, the 1966 coups and pogroms had broken its promise as well as "all hope of its resuscitation." According to Nyerere, there was nothing sacrosanct about Nigeria's border, and the federal government's claims that it was "defending the integrity of the country" could not be accepted when the state "had failed to guarantee the most elementary safety of the twelve million peoples of Eastern Nigeria."[148]

In defending the cause of independence, Nyerere called for a revision and not a repudiation of the terms of anticolonial self-determination. In doing so he mobilized the language of "slavery and domination" so central to the anticolonial critique of empire, analogizing the Biafran experience to colonial subjection and returning to the right to self-determination as the adequate response. Alongside this older anticolonial argument, however, Nyerere also adopted the charge of genocide. Drawing on the Igbos' self-representation as "the Jews of Africa," Nyerere likened the Biafran state to Israel. In this analogy, the Igbos faced an existential threat, which entitled them to a separate state that secured their existence as a people and preserved individual liberty and equality.[149] Though grounded in different genealogies and experiences, Nyerere's return to the slavery metaphor and his invocation of genocide mutually reinforced the claim of self-determination and separate statehood.

Biafran officials similarly presented their demand as an extension and expansion of African decolonization. Echoing the UN debates leading up to the formulation of the right to self-determination, they and their allies argued that extending the right to self-determination to Biafra would rectify the Nigerian state's violation of human rights.[150] Understood in these terms, what Biafra required was an adjustment of the postcolonial settlement such that the relationship between borders and peoples ensured that "states are made to serve people [and] governments are established to protect the citizens."[151] While decolonization had stopped short of challenging colonial borders, Biafrans argued, "self-defined linguistic and 'tribal' groups, were the logical unit of organization and governance in Africa."[152]

However, in a sign of the waning moral purchase of the right to self-determination, this argument, which kept the basic terms of the anticolonial reinvention intact, failed to win allies on the international stage. Coupled with the Nigerian government's intensification of the war through a blockade that resulted in widespread famine, the Biafran quest for independence raised more fundamental questions about the relationship between human rights and postcolonial sovereignty. As the Biafran war inaugurated the "age of televised disaster," the language of genocide dominated the depictions of the crisis, and the anticolonial appeal to slavery appeared out of place.[153] By the end of the war in 1970, Biafra had become a symbol "of the exhaustion of postcolonial optimisms, of the horrors of civil wars, [and] of the starving African child."[154] Represented in the 1971 formation of Médecins Sans Frontières (Doctors Without Borders) by doctors who had worked in Biafra, the crisis unleashed a new era of humanitarian politics that emphasized the experiences of individual suffering and framed nongovernmental organizations as apolitical advocates for the rights of victims of state violence.[155]

This new humanitarianism reiterated the early critiques of self-determination that Clyde Eagleton, Louis Henkin, and others had voiced during the process of anticolonial reinvention. Human rights were best conceived as individual entitlements that required supranational and nongovernmental guarantees. The state, especially the postcolonial state, was not the institutional guarantor of citizens' rights and liberties as Nyerere, Nkrumah, and others had argued, but the primary agent of their violation.

The critical attention new NGOs like Amnesty International directed toward human rights violations in the Third World joined a broader disillusionment with postcolonial sovereignty and anticolonial nationalism.[156] By 1975, Rupert Emerson, who had optimistically celebrated decolonization in 1960 as the extension of Western traditions of self-government, worried that "the wholly legitimate drive against colonialism and apartheid was in some measure called into question when the new countries habitually shrugged off any concern with massive violations of human rights and dignity in their own domain."[157] For Emerson, the problem was not only that independence offered no guarantees of human rights but also that self-determination "may serve to bar more tightly the sovereign-gates which exclude intervention of any kind, including intervention aimed at the protection and promotion of rights of individuals."[158]

Though Emerson himself did not take this argument to its logical conclusion, the view that state sovereignty shielded states from criticism and intervention would lead later critics to suggest that nonintervention and sovereign equality may be abridged in instances of gross human rights violations. On this view, decolonization had too rapidly extended self-determination to states that were now endowed with the formal rights of sovereignty but failed to correspond to the necessary empirical conditions of statehood. In response to the discrepancy between formal sovereignty and state failure or misrule, forms of international trusteeship and arrangements for limited sovereignty would be proposed as alternatives to self-determination and often combined with humanitarian intervention.[159]

The conflation of human rights and humanitarianism in what Didier Fassin calls "humanitarian government" and its combination with military intervention depended on the crisis and collapse of anticolonial nationalism, the emergence of a liberalism dissociated from its connection to empire, and the end of the Cold War.[160] But before this new politics could become ascendant, anticolonial worldmaking still offered an alternative and competing vision. Anticolonial nationalists recognized the right to self-determination as an important but limited victory on the road to national and international transformation. While critics argued that postcolonial crisis and state failure were the result of too hasty a process of decolonization, anticolonial nationalists returned to the limits of formal sovereignty, to what Nkrumah had called "fake independence," and sought to create new political and economic institutions that would address this problem.

In terms similar to contemporary critiques of international law, they perceived the problem of postcolonial statehood not as excessive sovereignty but as a distorted sovereignty where political, economic, and even legal impediments circumscribed their independence.[161] At issue was less that formal sovereignty did not map onto state capacity and more that it took a handicapped form in which former colonial powers and international institutions still played a dominant role in the newly independent states. This international context of hierarchy and domination could not be neatly separated from the domestic questions of authoritarianism, violence, and weak state institutions that were the site of humanitarian politics and grounded the critique of postcolonial states. Based on this account of postcolonial crisis as emerging from the nexus of the domestic and the international, anticolonial nationalists pursued combined projects of nation-building and worldmaking. While the right to self-determination had secured the legal conditions for domestic projects of political and economic reconstruction, the substantive dimensions of international hierarchy—economic dependence and the resulting forms of political domination—required more demanding forms of worldmaking. The following chapters trace two such efforts—the constitution of regional federations and the founding of a New International Economic Order.

CHAPTER FOUR

Revisiting the Federalists
in the Black Atlantic

THE 1960 DECLARATION on the Granting of Independence to Colonial Peoples and Countries was a watershed moment in the history of decolonization, marking the rise of an anticolonial account of self-determination. In rejecting the unequal membership and hierarchy that characterized international society in its imperial iteration, and by reconstructing self-determination as a universal right that accrued to all peoples, anticolonial nationalists secured the formal guarantees of international nondomination. The right to self-determination made foreign rule legally and morally objectionable, established independence and equality as the foundations of an anti-imperial world order, and extended full membership in international society to all states. Having universalized the right to self-determination, anticolonial nationalists deployed this new basis of international legitimacy to demand equal decision-making power in the United Nations.

While this anticolonial achievement is largely associated with the universalization of the nation-state form, the emergence of a right to self-determination coincided with projects of regional federation in Africa and the West Indies. When Ghana became a republic in 1960, Nkrumah successfully advocated for a clause in the new constitution that conferred on the parliament "the power to provide for the surrender of the whole or any part of the sovereignty of Ghana" once a Union of African States was formed.[1] The early constitutions of independent Guinea and Mali included similar provisions. That same year, ten Anglophone Caribbean islands—Antigua, Barbados, Dominica, Grenada, Jamaica, St. Kitts, Nevis and Anguilla, St. Lucia, St. Vincent, and Trinidad and Tobago—celebrated a second year as members of the West Indian Federation and looked forward to achieving independence in this new regional formation.

Anticolonial nationalists on both sides of the Black Atlantic framed regional federation as a central strategy for securing international nondomination. As the Congo crisis already revealed, political and economic hierarchies limited the right to self-determination and ensured that postcolonial sovereignty remained elusive. Understood only as freedom from alien rule, Nkrumah lamented that decolonization had become "a word much and unctuously used . . . to describe the transfer of political control from colonialist to African sovereignty."[2] Demonstrating its institutional flexibility, imperialism had "quickly adopted its outlook to [this] loss of direct political control [and] retained and extended its economic grip."[3] In the neocolonial phase of imperialism, imperial powers exploited their economic grip to indirectly realize political compulsion. The result was a distorted form of postcolonial sovereignty. While newly independent states sought to institutionalize the domestic dimension of the right to self-determination through popular sovereignty and representative governments, "the rulers of neocolonial states derive their authority to govern, not from the will of the people, but from the support which they obtain from their neocolonial masters."[4]

In his description of neocolonialism as the last stage of imperialism and his analysis of the dilemma it posed for anticolonial nationalists, Nkrumah drew on Lenin's analysis of the imbrication of imperialism and capitalism. Already in his 1915–16 writings on self-determination, Lenin had argued, "Finance capital, in its drive to expand, can 'freely' buy or bribe the freest democratic or republican government and the elective officials of any, even an 'independent', country."[5] Central to both Lenin and Nkrumah were the ways that freedom from direct interference and control did not necessarily entail national independence. States would be nominally free, and yet their economic dependence on particular states or their vulnerability to international trade and finance created the conditions in which political domination could be exercised by other means. In the context of this "postcolonial predicament"—the disjuncture between formal independence and de facto dependence—the nation-state appeared to bind former colonies in new relations of informal domination rather than securing the institutional conditions of self-determination.[6]

Black Atlantic federalists like Nkrumah and Eric Williams envisioned federation as a spatial and institutional fix for the postcolonial predicament. In their account of this predicament, they both focused on the ways that size and scale were at the center of the postcolonial state's limitations. As small economies tethered to metropolitan and global markets, postcolonial states were unable to achieve self-reliant economies. Governing a larger political space and operating at a regional rather than national scale, a federation would create a larger, more diverse regional economy that would slowly begin to undercut relations of dependence and could pool resources for regional economic development. Instead of serving as peripheral economies tethered to former imperial powers, the newly emerging European Economic Community, and the United States, regionally organized postcolonial states would develop linkages of trade, economic planning, and redistribution among themselves. Having broken the chains of economic dependence, a West Indian Federation and a Union of African States would also be able to guard against possible political and military interventions and demand greater representation in contexts like the United Nations Security Council.

This model of postcolonial federation was a central element of anticolonial worldmaking. While it was formulated at the regional scale, Nkrumah and Williams had not lost sight of the broader international field. They viewed the creation of regional federations as a mechanism for achieving nondomination within the international sphere. If the efforts to institutionalize a right to self-determination and to create a New International Economic Order took on international hierarchy directly, the federations addressed this problem indirectly. By restructuring the relationship of postcolonial states to each other through new institutional arrangements, Nkrumah and Williams hoped to gradually erode the relations of dependence and domination that subordinated postcolonial states in the international sphere. As a result, the Union of African States and West Indian Federation would be better positioned to secure self-determination. Thus even though the field of anticolonial worldmaking was limited in this case to the regional context, it still remained an effort to create an international sphere that was free from domination.

This chapter examines the political thought of Nkrumah and Williams as well as their two short-lived federal projects—the Union of African States and the West Indian Federation. The West Indian Federation, instituted through collaboration between the colonial office and Caribbean nationalists before independence, lasted for four years, between 1958 and 1962. During this time, a federal parliament and executive governed ten Anglophone Caribbean islands. A 1961 referendum in Jamaica, where the antifederalist position prevailed, led to the collapse of the federation. The following year, the federation's two largest members, Jamaica and Trinidad and Tobago, emerged as independent states.[7] Across the Atlantic, Nkrumah and Sékou Touré of Guinea launched the Ghana-Guinea union in 1958, which Mali joined two years later.[8] This union was to serve as the nucleus for a larger continental federation. However, between 1963 and 1965, most African states rejected federation in favor of the more loosely structured Organization of African Unity.[9]

I reconstruct the political conundrums and arguments that led Nkrumah and Williams to propose federation as a project of worldmaking, survey the contours of the regional debates in the two contexts, and reconsider the failure of these postcolonial federations. Drawing on new archival resources, I highlight a surprising origin story of the federal idea in the Black Atlantic by illustrating how Nkrumah and Williams recast the United States as an exemplary model of postcolonial federation. This provides occasion to reconsider the question of anticolonial appropriation. The example of the United States enabled Nkrumah's and Williams's accounts of the postcolonial predicament as a recurring dilemma and offered a critique of US hegemony while also papering over important differences between the aims and context of American federalism and their own projects. The failure of Black Atlantic federations, however, does not stem directly from the limits of the United States as example. Their collapse was also not the result of "narrow and competing nationalisms," an argument that pits nationalism against internationalism.[10]

Instead, I locate the demise of the West Indian Federation and the Union of African States in deep disagreements about the precise balance between federal union and independence of member states. Nkrumah's and Williams's attempts to create a federation capable of directing economic development and redistribution led both statesmen to endorse institutions that resembled a federal state rather than a federation. Their critics, represented here by Nnamdi Azikiwe and Norman Manley, also supported the idea of federal union but remained concerned that the centralized federations Nkrumah and Williams recommended appeared to inhibit rather than enhance postcolonial autonomy. I argue that the culmination of the federal project in functional integration illustrates the growing shift in anticolonial worldmaking, from a project of dispersing and delegating sovereignty through international institutions to one in which regional organizations bolstered the nation-state.

Recasting the Spirit of 1776

Before formal decolonization was at its height and while anticolonial nationalists were still articulating their early demands for a right to self-determination, Eric Williams reflected on the possible limits of a future transfer of political power. Having finished his doctoral work at Oxford University, Williams joined the Howard University faculty of political science in 1939. Along with colleagues such as Ralph Bunche and Rayford Logan, he was immersed in debates about the political and economic legacies of colonialism. In 1943, Williams organized a conference, "Economic Future of the Caribbean," where he presented a paper that explored the consequences of colonialism for political independence and economic development. He argued that the small islands of the West Indies had functioned as appendages to the British economy. As a result, their trade was entirely dominated by the metropole; their economies were centered on cash crops; and resources for export and basic necessities, particularly food, had to be imported. This economic dependence threatened to derail any future attainment of independence. Though not yet articulating it in terms of neocolonialism, Williams argued that a transfer of power to nationalists that left these economic structures intact would allow metropolitan powers to manipulate the policies of the island states.[11]

For Williams, the economic future of the Caribbean was not unlike other decolonizing countries in the past and present, and he argued that lessons could be learned from earlier moments of decolonization. In an unpublished essay written the same year as the conference, Williams turned in particular to the dilemmas of American independence. He argued that colonialism then and now was predicated on a form of economic exploitation that operated through political domination. "The colonies were condemned to an agricultural specialization, as they still are today in so many parts of the world, except where the necessities of modern production require the refining of oil and the mining of gold." Williams recast what he called "the spirit of 1776" through this emphasis on colonialism's economic dimensions. While Thomas Jefferson had emphasized the need "to dissolve the political bonds that connect [one nation] with another" in the Declaration of Independence, Williams insisted on the primacy of the economic bonds. For Williams, "political freedom predicates economic security and the removal of those economic fetters which restrict [the colonies'] full development and stunt their stature, in 1943 as they did in 1776."[12] Anticolonial struggles thus had to remain equally vigilant about both the political and economic conditions of self-determination.

Nkrumah similarly analogized the twentieth-century conditions of colonized territories to the eighteenth-century experience of the United States. Like Williams, he stressed the economic dimension of colonial rule in each case, noting in his 1963 *Africa Must Unite*,

I cannot understand why so many people in the United Kingdom still refuse to admit that local industry was deliberately discouraged in many of the colonies. After all, they learn in their school history books that the Americans complained of the same sort of thing in the eighteenth century. They too were not allowed to manufacture any commodity which might compete with industries in the metropolitan country.[13]

For Nkrumah, colonialism was primarily a strategy of economic exploitation where colonies produced raw materials for the metropole and consumed its manufactured goods. This economic exploitation had required political subordination, and as a result independence and autonomy were central to overcoming colonial exploitation. However, while Nkrumah urged his fellow nationalists to "seek ye first the political kingdom," he remained concerned that political independence alone would not transform economic dependence.[14] An end to colonialism entailed the creation of a political kingdom that could secure both political independence and a transformation of colonial economic relations.[15]

Through their invocation of American independence, Nkrumah and Williams cast themselves and fellow anticolonial nationalists across the world as "heirs to the tradition of 1776."[16] In recent accounts, the example and legacy of 1776 is often understood as one that privileges national sovereignty. The expansion and universalization of a Westphalian state system in twentieth-century decolonization is viewed as the final stage of this spirit of 1776. For instance, David Armitage argues that American independence marks the beginning of a "contagion of sovereignty" that infected the Americas in the nineteenth century and reached its height in the years after World War II. As a mark of this contagion, anti-imperialists and nationalists followed the American example by "claiming statehood as an escape from empire [and] declaring independence as the mark of sovereignty."[17] Williams and Nkrumah, however, drew a different lesson from 1776. American independence, they argued, did not foretell the triumph of postcolonial sovereignty. Instead, it illustrated its precariousness under conditions of international hierarchy.

In an age of decolonization so deeply associated with the universalization of the nation-state, the purported agents of this universalization—anticolonial nationalists—were thus also some of the most prescient critics of state sovereignty. But it is important to note the specificity of this anticolonial critique. While contemporaneous projects of founding a United States of Europe also turned to federation and invoked the example of the United States, these efforts were concerned with curtailing the excesses of nationalism and sovereignty in the aftermath of World War II's destruction.[18] Similarly, recent debates about the post-Westphalian world order often begin from the view that the formal rights of statehood give states impunity in their domestic context.[19] The excesses of Westphalian sovereignty, along with the recent challenges of economic globalization to the state's capacity for economic regulation, have inspired a renewed interest in regional federation. On this view, regional integration is a means for moderating interstate conflict, setting institutional limits on the internal exercise of sovereignty, and supplementing the steering functions of the state.[20]

Alternatively, Nkrumah and Williams's critique of state sovereignty begins not from an account of the excesses of sovereignty, but rather from its distortion and diminution. The problem with the rights states enjoyed in the international system was not that they enabled too much sovereignty but rather that they were meaningless in the context of international hierarchy and economic dependence. The protections that guarantees of sovereign equality and nonintervention afforded were unevenly distributed, making new and weak postcolonial states vulnerable to arbitrary interventions and encroachments at the hands of larger, more powerful states as well as private actors. Similarly, they viewed the economic dilemmas of the postcolonial state as vestiges of an imperial global economy. On this view, economic globalization was not a novel phenomenon of the twentieth century. Rather, it had its origins in empire's unequal integration, which both linked the globe and engendered relations of dependence. Reduced to the production and export of primary goods through this process of unequal integration, postcolonial states were not endowed with a capacity to steer and control a national economy that was subsequently limited.[21] Indeed, no such national economy existed.[22] Thus, the consequences of economic globalization in both its imperial and postcolonial forms were unevenly and distinctively experienced.

With this critique of postcolonial sovereignty on hand and the example of American federation in mind, Nkrumah and Williams formulated federation as the institutional solution to the postcolonial predicament. They argued that even after 1776, economic fetters characteristic of the colonial relations and political dominance of European empires undermined the independence of the American confederate states. The United States only really overcame the postcolonial predicament with a federal constitution in 1787. Having learned the power of acting in concert during the war against Britain, "the American states saw that they could not survive by living separately and managing their own affairs independently. [They knew that] America Must Unite."[23] The federal government, which emerged from this impulse, provided the necessary conditions for securing political and economic independence, enabling the United States to become "perhaps the richest and strongest nation in the world."[24] The implications of this argument were clear: if union through a federal arrangement had secured the economic and political independence of the thirteen American states, a federation of states in Africa and the Caribbean would be necessary to realize self-determination.

In this argument, Nkrumah and Williams associated "the spirit of 1776" not with the Declaration of Independence, but with its culmination in federation. This construction of the United States as a postcolonial federation involved an appropriation of *The Federalist Papers* that emphasized John Jay and Alexander Hamilton. Jay's and Hamilton's contributions to the federalist cause highlighted the external reasons for federation.[25] In Federalist No. 2–5, Jay reflected on how disunion among the American states could be exploited by foreign powers, while Hamilton, in Federalist No. 11–13, located this general concern with foreign intervention and domination in the nature of economic relations between America and Europe. From his reading of these papers and the political scientist Kenneth Wheare's 1946 *Federal Government*, Williams concluded that the American federalists had been motivated by "a desire to be independent of foreign powers, a realization that only through union could independence be secured; [and] a hope of economic advantage." He argued that a similar set of motivations were at the center of plans for a West Indian Federation.[26]

Readings of Jay and Hamilton also played a central role in demands for a Union of African States. As the Organization of African Unity met in Accra in 1965 and Nkrumah made the case for federation once again, the *Ghanaian Times* urged representatives of African states to "give us political union." Citing Jay's Federalist No. 4 and Hamilton's Federalist No. 11, the editorial argued that the American example illustrated the dangers of failing to form a postcolonial federation. According to this account, the central lesson Jay and Hamilton offered was that in the absence of union, the United States would fall victim to new imperial designs at the hands of Europe. Newly independent African states were in a similar position. While "36 states have attained independence, our degree of dependence upon Europe and now America, has not diminished and with that the degree of foreign domination and arrogance towards us." Only what Hamilton had called a "strict and indissoluble union" of African states could reverse the trends of dependence and domination to achieve postcolonial self-determination.[27]

This analogy to the American federalists required reading *The Federalist Papers* against the grain. For instance, when discussing the prerequisites of federation, Williams argued that Jay's claim in Federalist No. 2 that "Providence has been pleased to give this one connected country to one united people" has to be taken with "a grain of salt."[28] In the late eighteenth century, the United States of America did not constitute a "united people," as it was composed of descendants of different people. Moreover, "distance and detachment in the United States in 1787, before the railroads of the nineteenth century, the automobile of the early twentieth, and the aeroplane of today, were far more important than John Jay admitted."[29] In rejecting the need for a united people, Williams sought to put to rest arguments against West Indian federation that emphasized the diversities of the islands and the distance between them. If Americans had successfully created a federation without the benefits of modern communication and transportation, West Indians, he suggested, were better equipped to form a union of states.

Against the prerequisite of a "united people," Williams emphasized the international dimensions of the American constitution. The federation was not a national union based on ancestry and religion but rather constituted a composite body organized as sovereign states that were united in their aim of attaining independence. Like the United States, the West Indies were composed of many peoples, but if they were to cease being "anachronisms of eighteenth-century colonialism" and emerge as members of the international community, their hope lay in securing their independence through union in a federation.[30] On this view, a federation was not an expanded nation-state, but rather an interstate and international political structure. It promised a combination of union and autonomy that allowed each of the constituent states to retain arenas of jurisdiction while creating a new political body to respond to collective problems. According to Williams, this distinctive political structure was ideal for diverse political communities organized under separate governments, such as the United States and a future West Indian Federation.[31] Federation allowed for the preservation of political plurality within a new federal body while also creating a union government capable of securing the states' independence.

Nkrumah was similarly drawn to federation's capacity to combine union and independence. The American experience illustrated both that independence required union and that federal union was not based on national unity. In 1959, when Ghana and Guinea formed a union, which was to serve as a nucleus for a future federation of African states, their joint communiqué announced that they took "inspiration from the thirteen American colonies."[32] At his speech during the Organization of African Unity Summit Conference in 1963, Nkrumah likened the meeting of independent African states to the Philadelphia Congress. The delegates in 1787, he argued, did not yet see themselves as Americans. This identity "was a new and strange experience," but they still managed to act collectively. In calling attention to the novel nature of the term "Americans," Nkrumah, like Williams, emphasized the differences that separated the American states in 1787. Just as Americans had understood themselves as Pennsylvanians and Virginians, in 1963 delegates represented sovereign African states. Through union, African states could act collectively to secure their independence without the prerequisite that they understand themselves as a nation.[33]

Nkrumah juxtaposed the positive example of the United States, in which federation was successfully instituted to overcome the postcolonial predicament, to the cases of Latin America and Eastern Europe. In Latin America, the failure to form unions after independence was won in the nineteenth century made the continent "the unwilling and distressed prey of imperialism after one-and-a-half centuries of political independence." As small, disunited states, Latin America, unlike its northern neighbor, could not overcome its economic dependence and remained politically insecure.[34] Similarly, in Eastern Europe, the small states that emerged at the end of World War I were too weak and unstable to fend off external intervention. The failure to form unions in both cases had resulted in "balkanization," which exacerbated domination and dependence. Through this comparative perspective, the United States was positioned as the first and only successful instance of overcoming the postcolonial predicament. If African states failed to form a federal union on this model, Nkrumah argued that they would find themselves the victims of neocolonialism like postcolonial states in Latin America and Eastern Europe.[35]

In this conception of postcolonial federation as an institutional structure for uniting recently independent states, Nkrumah and Williams departed from their Francophone counterparts who envisioned federations that would include France and its former colonies. Anticolonial nationalists like Aimé Césaire of Martinique and Léopold Senghor of Senegal also argued that postcolonial sovereignty would not secure a meaningful independence from domination. They called for the formation of a federal French Union both as an effort to ward off the limits of independent statehood and as a demand for an equal share in the wealth that the colonies had produced.[36] In contrast to the project of a transnational French federation, the postcolonial federations Nkrumah and Williams modeled on the United States were to be organized among equally positioned states that all experienced the postcolonial predicament. Nkrumah explicitly positioned his project against models of Francafrique and Eurafrica, arguing that integration with European states would preserve and deepen economic dependence.[37] He remained skeptical that relations of hierarchy and dependence could be remade as egalitarian interdependence. As we shall see, this skepticism also made him wary of the welfare world, which the New International Economic Order proposed. He argued that the best path for postcolonial states was a horizontal integration that would indirectly and gradually restructure those relations of dependence.

Anticolonial Appropriation Redux

It is unsettling that anti-imperialists, who had critiqued empire as enslavement and international racial hierarchy, would model their vision of an egalitarian postcolonial federation on the United States. This requires a return to the question of anticolonial appropriation. I argued in chapter 3 that we should understand acts of appropriation as responses to political questions situated in a historically specific problem-space. Casting the United States as an exemplary model depended on framing the postcolonial predicament as a recurring political problem and the federal idea as a replicable answer. In their refashioning of self-determination as a human right, anticolonial critics emphasized a distinctive account of imperialism that centered slavery and racial hierarchy. But, in situating themselves as heirs to a habitual postcolonial predicament, Williams and Nkrumah suggested that federation in the American form could be reproduced in the twentieth century.

Williams and Nkrumah's appropriation of the American example as a response to the postcolonial predicament emerged in specific historical and intellectual contexts that made this example seem more appropriate than others. Two contexts appear particularly important for understanding their use of the American example. First, despite their internationalism and global orientation, their political thinking emerged from within the Anglo-American sphere. Their sojourns in the United States and United Kingdom shaped and informed what they took to be exemplary political institutions and foreclosed alternative models. For instance, it is significant that the United States as an imperial power became the model of regionalism, rather than anti-imperial formulations of the Americas put forward by Latin American thinkers that shared the postcolonial predicament.[38] In failing to engage alternative models outside of their Anglo-American inheritance, Nkrumah and Williams demonstrate the ways in which the appropriation of political ideas occurs in circumscribed contexts and is shaped by existing and inherited imperial spaces.[39]

In addition to their position within an Anglo-American field of political thought, their appeal to American federation occurred at a moment when the United States promoted itself as an anti-imperial power and actively exported its model of constitutional government. In its own self-representation, the Pax Americana was a force against oppression anchored in liberal democracy and UN-based internationalism. Central to this account was the US constitution, which simultaneously established American exceptionalism and was to be emulated by newly independent states.[40] Moreover, American observers of decolonization appealed to the spirit of 1776 either to approvingly cast anticolonial nationalists as an extension and universalization of this distinctive American project or in opprobrium of the ways that the revolutionary fervor of anticolonial nationalists threatened to destabilize the international order.[41] While their appropriation of the American example took a different direction, Nkrumah and Williams appeared conscripted to the terms of a newly emergent American hegemony in the international sphere.

The American example was thus not without its limits or contradictions. Nkrumah's and Williams's fidelity to the American example blinded them to the important disanalogies between the eighteenth-century United States and their own projects. Fashioning the United States as a postcolonial federation obscured the distinctively imperial ambitions and consequences that were part and parcel of the American federalist project. In seeking to ensure the United States' station "among the powers of the earth," American founders imagined the fledgling federation as an empire. The federal government created in 1787 would secure the United States as free and independent by providing the institutional structures and resources required for the pacification of its colonial periphery.[42] The aims of postcolonial independence and imperial expansion were intertwined and culminated in the Monroe Doctrine, which prevented European encroachment in the Western Hemisphere while sanctioning American hegemony and expansion.[43] The imperial character of the US federal government was directed not only outward with the aim of expansion but also inward in an effort to expropriate Native Americans, dominate enslaved Africans, and curtail populist politics.[44]

While Nkrumah and Williams recognized the United States as an imperial power, they did not understand its imperialism to be embedded within the structure of American federalism. In failing to consider the historical coconstitution of empire and federation in the case of the United States, Nkrumah and Williams minimized the divergences between the federal experiment of the late eighteenth century and their own. For instance, ignoring the imperial impulse of the American federalists led Nkrumah and Williams to misidentify the reasons for the United States' success in constituting a federation and overcoming the postcolonial predicament. First, imperial expansion contributed to a unifying ideology and project that made possible the realization of a federated United States.[45] While Williams rejected the claim that the former American colonies constituted a united people, Jay's insistence that Americans were "a people descended from the same ancestors, speaking the same language, professing the same religion, attached to the same principles of government" was a reference to the Anglo-Saxon settlers who would be the citizens of the postcolonial/imperial federation.[46] Second, if the imperial project gave settlers common cause in the formation of the federation, it also contributed to the political and economic success that Nkrumah and Williams admired. That is, the United States was the only former colony to have triumphed over the postcolonial predicament not because it had federated, but because it was an imperial federation.

If American federation could become a model for anticolonial nationalists after its imperial dimensions were elided, framing the postcolonial predicament as an external problem of reconciling de jure and de facto independence overshadowed the internal conditions of ethnic, racial, and religious pluralism that characterized twentieth-century postcolonial states. Nkrumah and Williams recognized federation as an institution ideally suited to the question of interstate legal pluralism, but they did not dwell on the question of intrastate diversity and thus did not consider institutional remedies for the conflicts it engendered. For instance, Nkrumah explicitly rejected a federal constitution for an independent Ghana at the consternation of subnational groups such as the Asante kingdom, which hoped to retain some autonomy from the new postcolonial state.[47] He argued that retaining the authority of native rulers was tantamount to substituting African tyranny for its British precursor.[48] While African states might pursue supranational federation, domestically he insisted on a unitary state. In the case of the West Indies, minority groups, particularly East Indian descendants who constituted 12 percent of the federal population but were 40 percent of the Trinidadian population and half of the Guyanese population, were anxious about a federation dominated by Afro-West Indians. Guyana would reject the West Indian Federation in part because it did not appear to have sufficient protections for ethnic minorities.[49] Although Williams recognized the racial and religious plurality of the West Indies, his plans for federation did not elaborate on antimajoritarian institutions. These concerns remained at the forefront for Indo-Trinidadians within his own party.[50]

Despite these important limitations, Nkrumah and Williams were not fully conscripted by their choice of example—theirs was a selective and strategic appropriation. It skipped over the Articles of Confederation to highlight the strong federal form agreed to in 1787 and read back the problem of economic dependence while giving short shrift to the military insecurities that were a core concern of the American federalists. In this selective rereading, these Black Atlantic federalists also invoked the United States as an example to critique its imperial ambitions. Neither Nkrumah nor Williams was naive about America's aspirations to global dominance. Nkrumah described the United States as the paradigmatic neocolonial power, which had already practiced the art of neocolonial domination in Latin America during the nineteenth and early twentieth centuries and was exporting those techniques to Vietnam and the Congo.[51] Williams was in the midst of a political struggle with the United States and the British Colonial Office to renegotiate the terms of the Chaguaramas base given to the United States during the Lend-Lease program. His appeals to the United States as a model were sometimes made at this very site of American dominance and hegemony, and he wrote extensively on US intervention in Latin America and the Caribbean.[52] By invoking a history of American anti-imperialism, both Williams and Nkrumah highlighted American hypocrisy in order to win the superpower to their cause. If, as Joshua Simon has recently argued, the American federalists embodied a distinct creole ideology of anti-imperial imperialism, they hoped that America might be persuaded to remember its anti-imperial past against its imperial aspirations.[53]

In framing themselves as heirs of 1776, Nkrumah and Williams also destabilized the claims of American exceptionalism. By portraying the limits of decolonization as recurring political problems that the United States had also faced, they offered an important rejoinder to observers who located postcolonial state weakness in cultural and sociological deficits. The experience of postcolonial states did not constitute deviations from Western models of the nation-state but were instead framed in a broader and recurring story of the limits of postcolonial independence in the context of hierarchy. The United States was simultaneously relativized such that its political and economic success was not the result of a people especially endowed for liberty. American success had little to do with what Wood-row Wilson had described as an Anglo-American capacity for freedom. Instead, its postcolonial success emerged from pursuing an institutional form that successfully overcame the postcolonial predicament. It was fed-eral union rather than racial endowment that distinguished the United States from Latin America. Nkrumah and Williams hoped that in pur-suing federation they too would follow this path of postcolonial success.

The appropriation of the American example thus enabled the argu-ment that independence required union and offered critical rhetorical resources against American exceptionalism and hegemony. At the same time, the analogy to the eighteenth century was possible only by disre-garding the coconstitution of settler colonialism and American federation and eliding the distinctive dynamics of twentieth-century postcolonial so-cieties. I raise these limitations and blind spots of the turn to the United States not so much because they reveal a fatal error that resulted in the demise of Nkrumah's and Williams's federalist projects. Rather, they make visible the particular inflections of their federal vision and highlight what would become the main sources of concern for their critics. In their pre-occupation with the external postcolonial predicament, their scant atten-tion to internal pluralism, and their turn to the United States as a model, Nkrumah and Williams fashioned postcolonial federation as a structure of augmenting and centralizing political authority. As we shall see in the fol-lowing section, their impulses toward centralization would become more pronounced as Nkrumah and Williams adapted the eighteenth-century federal model for the prevailing political and economic conditions of the twentieth century.

A Federalism Fit for the Twentieth Century

While Nkrumah and Williams elided questions of domestic ethnic, racial, and religious pluralism, they viewed federalism as a legally plural political form that combined the autonomy of member states and union. Diversity and difference between the states were at the forefront for both statesmen, and they favored federalism because it was best suited to preserve these distinctions. According to Williams, "differences of race, religion, language or nationality, far from encouraging hostility to federation, strengthen the sentiment for it, as the only means of securing the advantages of union whilst retaining separate allegiances."[54] Federation was able to achieve this combination of autonomy and union, Nkrumah argued, because each political unit enjoyed "legal equality under a constitution to which all

have laid their hand." Equality among members of the federation prevented the development of hierarchy and subordination within the new
political body.[55]

Williams drew on the work of political scientist Kenneth Wheare to
make this case for federation. A professor of government at Oxford University, Wheare was an expert on the history of commonwealth constitutions,
an advisor to constitutional assemblies in former British colonies, and an
active member of the Federal Union, a British organization that advocated
European integration in the 1930s and 1940s. His 1946 *Federal Government* justified the need for a theoretical and historical account of federation by noting that after being overshadowed in the nineteenth century
with the rise of the nation-state, "federalism [has become] fashionable . . .
as a means of solving or softening the problems of government of countries attaining or about to attain their independence."[56] Wheare defined
federation as a form of government with a "coordinate division of power"
in which the two branches of government (federal and regional) exercise
power in separate fields. Regional governments are not subordinated to
the federal government, and the federal government must exercise power
independent of the regional governments.[57] In order to define and delimit
the spheres of power, federalism requires a supreme constitution. Under
the constitution both the regional and federal governments are equal and
neither can arbitrarily override the terms set out in the constitution.[58]
Along with a constitution that specifies the powers of the regional and
federal governments, each branch of government must have independent
control of the financial resources necessary to execute its powers.[59]

Contemporary political scientists have similarly cast federation as a
distinctive form of government that eschews hierarchy in favor of heter-
archy and achieves union while preserving autonomy through a constitutional division of powers.[60] Federation is conceived as a political structure
that contains elements of a treaty alliance and aspects of a state while
remaining distinct from these forms.[61] Like an interstate treaty alliance, it
involves the recognition of the equality of constituent states, but, unlike an
alliance, it requires the formation of a permanent, collective political institution, which has independent authority and power. While the formation
of an independent authority resembles a state, federations do not subsume
and assimilate its constituent members. The resulting body allows for "the
collective existence of the federation and the individual existence of the
federation members."[62]

At stake in Wheare's account, however, was not an effort to isolate
federation as a distinctive form of government but rather one of tracing

the historical processes that had transformed the practice of federation. According to Wheare, the federal test required asking, "Does a system of government embody predominantly a division of powers between general and regional authorities, each of which, in its own sphere, is coordinate with the others and independent of them?" In the modern era, Wheare argued, only four federations fit this mold—the United States, Australia, Canada, and Switzerland. Yet during the twentieth century even these federations had undergone rapid transformations that shifted the practice of federation. Beginning at the turn of the century, the revolution in transport and industry, economic crises, the rise of welfarism, and the two world wars had resulted in the expansion of powers granted to federal governments. Federal income taxes were introduced for the first time, and the federal governments took greater responsibility for the provision of social services.[63] This growth of the federal government challenged the coordinate division of power central to the federal form. In Australia and Canada, for example, as the federal government claimed the right to levy direct taxes, it blocked the states from taxation. The states were thus denied an independent source of revenue and became financially dependent on the federal government.[64] In the United States, the states did not lose the right to levy taxes but grew increasingly dependent on grants-in-aid from the federal government.[65]

The growing power of federal governments vis-à-vis member states was debated and discussed by a range of scholars and commentators from the 1930s to the 1970s. For some, like the theorist of pluralism Harold Laski, with whom a number of anticolonial nationalists studied at the London School of Economics, a more energetic federal government was necessary to challenge monopolies and realize economic equality.[66] For others, the theory of federalism needed updating as a result of the transformations. According to Anthony Birch, a student of Laski's and a comparative political scientist, in former colonies where the need for economic development was central, federalists could no longer follow federalism's "guiding principle of the eighteenth and nineteenth century [and have] the watertight compartments in which state and federal government exercise power." The twentieth century required that power in a federal system be exercised cooperatively and concurrently rather than independently.[67]

Nkrumah and Williams framed their visions of postcolonial federation within this growing debate about the need for strong central governments. Their arguments in favor of federation thus tended to conflate a call for union and a demand for greater powers lodged in the federal government. In a 1955 speech, Williams made reference to Wheare's definition of federalism and asked whether "the theory of coordinate governments has been able to live up to its theoretical promise given the pressures of the modern era [which included] global wars, the economic depression and the struggle between classes and vested interests in the twentieth century."[68] Williams argued that these pressures had enlarged the federal governments' powers, particularly in the realm of taxation. While this had resulted in federal encroachment in spheres formerly reserved for state governments, Williams did not bemoan this development, arguing that an expansive and energetic federal government had made economic redistribution in the United States and elsewhere possible. With the Constitutional Conference of the West Indies scheduled for the following year, Williams ended the lecture with a call for a West Indian federal government empowered to create an integrated development plan for the region and authorized to levy income taxes.[69]

During an address to the Ghanaian Parliament six years later, Nkrumah echoed Williams's concerns. Thinking about African politics, Nkrumah argued, was dominated by two competing tendencies. On the one hand, scholars and statesmen called for strong central governments that could secure stability for foreign investment, direct development projects, and provide social services. On the other hand, those who argued for a decentralized federalism in African states were still operating from "the political and historical idea of the eighteenth century." Historical context rather than the logic of federalism had required the United States to limit the federal government's powers. In the eighteenth century, Nkrumah argued, the state was not expected to take on the task of economic planning, and only such a limited union could garner the consent of the people. In light of the political and economic challenges of the twentieth century, however, this model of federalism had become a liability: "[It] introduces an element of paralysis into the machinery of the state, and slows down the process of governmental action." The United States had to adapt its model of government to these new realities. Hoping to avoid this paralysis altogether, Ghana decided against a federal structure in 1957. Similarly, if an African union government was to be capable of exercising the necessary authority to realize the economic and political advantages of integration, there had to be greater centralization.[70]

In these calls for centralization, Williams and Nkrumah increasingly advocated for models of integration that appeared closer to a federal state than to a federation. In their framing of the postcolonial predicament and their turn to the eighteenth-century United States as an example, Nkrumah and Williams conceived of federation as an interstate structure suited

to autonomous and sovereign bodies who desired union in order to preserve their autonomy. Federation, on this view, would create a union government that had limited powers vis-à-vis the states. However, as they
argued for centralization and invoked the United States' own transformations in the late nineteenth and early twentieth centuries, they moved
closer to a federal state. Rather than organizing interstate relations, a federal state is often conceived as a mechanism for intrastate governance. It
allows for the devolution of some powers, but the federal government is
paramount over the states.

In their account, *federation* and *federal state* were synonymous, as the
only federal form that could achieve economic development and overcome
the postcolonial predicament would be one that had a strong central government. Nkrumah and Williams rarely considered what the consequences of
such centralization would be for the independence of member states within
the regional federation. What mattered, in their view, was creating an institutional form that secured international nondomination. And a strong
central government was the only structure capable of achieving this aim. In
contrast, their critics pointed to the ways that centralization threatened to
subject member states to new regional hierarchies. Azikiwe of Nigeria and
Manley of Jamaica supported the goal of union but advocated confederations. In their alternative formulation, a looser confederation was the best
institutional mechanism for attending to both independence and union.

Federal debates were waged on both sides of the Atlantic over the precise combination of union and autonomy captured in the distinction between federation and federal state. The debates over these two alternative
institutional forms took distinctive forms on either side of the Atlantic.
In the West Indies, the debate assumed an economic dimension, with
Williams arguing for centralization of development and industrialization
and Manley taking an increasingly protectionist stance where integration
would at least initially be limited to international relations. In the African
context, political anxieties about the emergence of a new kind of continental hegemony motivated Nkrumah's opponents, who argued for a union
that resembled a concert of states.

Between Federation and Federal State: The West Indian Debates

When Williams entered national and regional politics in 1955, West Indian
politicians and colonial officials were already in the process of working out
the details of the West Indian Federation. The constitution was completed

in 1956, and the federation was inaugurated two years later, with limited powers lodged in the federal government. Unlike the financial independence Wheare's theory of federation recommended, the West Indian federal government had no independent sources of revenue. Instead, it was financed through a mandatory levy from each island, the total of which could not exceed 9.1 million US dollars. Moreover, the colonial office and national representatives did not reach agreements on a customs union, free trade, and freedom of movement. As a result, they decided that while the constitution would affirm these goals in principle, the federal parliament could legislate on these matters only after a period of five years.

Despite a moratorium on constitutional amendments until 1962, almost immediately after the federal parliament was seated in 1958, discussions on the powers of the federal government reemerged with proponents for a stronger federal government as well as antifederalists calling for a review of the constitution. Like the federalists of 1787 who hoped to overcome the limitations of the initial Articles of Confederation, Williams saw the renewed constitutional debate as an opportunity to make the case for a stronger federal center, an argument he had also made leading up to the 1956 constitution. Speaking before the Inter-governmental Conference (IGC) where the constitution would be reviewed, Williams argued that the 1956 agreement was entirely out of sync with twentieth-century political and economic developments. While older federations were centralizing and European efforts at regional integration sought to rationalize regional economic policy, the West Indies appeared to be adopting a federal structure that could not meet the challenges of securing postcolonial independence in the twentieth century. He confessed his astonishment at the fact that "we [West Indians], weak and small as we are, we who have our way to make in the world should be behaving today as if we contemplate reversing the whole trend of world economy and politics."[71]

In his proposals, Williams outlined a number of reforms designed to enhance the power of the federal government and bring the West Indian Federation in sync with his view of global economic and political trends. These reforms ranged from enhancing the federal bill of rights by incorporating the human rights enshrined in the Universal Declaration of Human Rights to limiting the powers of the governor-general. However, many of his recommendations homed in on the economic powers of the federal government. Williams pushed for immediate implementation of free trade, freedom of movement, a customs union, and a common external tariff. Williams argued that these steps would create "a Federal Market" available to all member states and capable of attracting the capital necessary for development. In addition, taxation in the form of tariffs and income tax would be a federal power with member states receiving their revenues largely in the form of grants-in-aid. According to Williams, the total revenues of the federation would amount to $372 million with $242 million turned over to states and leaving $129 million to the federal government.[72] This amounted to more than a tenfold increase in the federal budget.

With the help of economists in the region, including the St. Lucian W. Arthur Lewis, who served as Nkrumah's first economic advisor and won the 1979 Nobel Prize in Economics, Williams's government in Trinidad released the *Economics of Nationhood* report to make his case to the region. Echoing Wheare's theory of coordinate powers, the report argued that federations required that "each layer of government have financial resources adequate to the purpose of its constitutionally allotted function." However, the report continued, the "division of functions between the Centre and the States is constantly shifting," and questions of industrialization, economic development, and social services had become the purview of federal governments. This justified lodging the power to levy income taxes in the federal government and, more broadly, required that the federal center have a monopoly on fiscal, monetary, and trade policy. According to the report, while member states lost independent sources of revenue, grants could ensure that both the states and the federal government had sufficient resources.[73]

The *Economics of Nationhood* report highlights the conflation of federation and federal state. In appropriating the American example of 1787, Williams had suggested (contra Jay) that a united people was not a necessary precondition for federation and that federal arrangements could achieve union while preserving autonomy. Yet the report transposed "nationhood" for federation, and its vision of the allocation of powers was closer to a federal state than to a federation. The member states appeared not as independent political communities engaged in self-rule as well as shared rule but were entirely dependent on the federal center. However, this move closer to a federal state was not prompted by an attachment to centralization as an end in itself. Instead, Williams argued that a confederation would be not able to direct economic development or effectively distribute the gains of regional trade. For instance, if economic integration allowed for free trade, but was not accompanied by federal taxation and redistribution, regional trade would only reproduce inequalities between member states and favor stronger economies. In the absence of redistributive mechanisms, the smaller islands would be reduced to protected consumer markets for the industries of Trinidad and Jamaica.[74]

Jamaican politicians voiced the strongest criticism of a centralized federal government. While regional federation had been a mainstay of anti-colonial politics in the eastern Caribbean for decades, it was a more recent idea in Jamaican circles. Moreover, as the most populous state and with a more industrialized economy, Jamaican critics worried that the economic burdens of a federation would fall largely on their island. For instance, once the West Indian Federation became independent, the British government would no longer supply grants that constituted a major portion of the budgets in the smaller islands. Colonial officials refused to agree to an economic aid package that would make up for budget shortfalls and support the federation in its early years.[75]

In 1956, Norman Manley backed free trade. However, under pressure from his domestic opposition, he would later insist on the need for at least initial protections that could safeguard Jamaican industry. Indicative of the ways that economic dependence made postcolonial economies competitive rather than complementary, Manley was particularly concerned about protecting a new oil refinery from Trinidad's better-established oil industry.[76] Moreover, during the renewed constitutional debate, he questioned Williams's insistence on centralization while sharing the general commitment to a West Indian Federation. In a 1960 radio broadcast, Manley noted, "Each of us alone is small in the world today as size goes in this world of ours. Because we are small it is the simple truth that for us unity is strength and the only hope of independence." Standing "in the doorway . . . that leads to the great hall of independence," unity would be essential in determining whether the West Indian islands would enter the world of independent states.[77] On the eve of the 1961 Jamaican referendum that ended the West Indian Federation, Manley reiterated this point, arguing that the right road to freedom and independence was to be found in a federation of the West Indies and predicted (wrongly) that Jamaicans would vote in favor of federation during the referendum scheduled for later that year.[78]

According to Manley, the key to a federal constitution was determining the relations between the federal and unit governments. The economic and financial powers Williams hoped to delegate to the federal government were too expansive and threatened "a serious and far-reaching disruption of Jamaica's attempt at developing and modernizing her own economy."[79] He argued that at this stage, the federal government needed to secure only "the minimum powers and capabilities . . . in order to satisfy the requirements of effective sovereignty and achieve membership of the [British] Commonwealth." This federation would be charged with defense and diplomatic representation and would oversee functional coordination.[80]

Starting with minimal powers did not preclude the federal government from exercising more expansive powers in the future, if it was desirable to the constituent states. Manley recommended that a customs union and freedom of movement be slowly introduced. But from his perspective, the reforms advocated in the *Economics of Nationhood* report resulted from a "confusion of thinking" that blurred the distinction between federation and federal state. For example, it was not clear why primary and secondary education should be the "exclusive prerogative" of the federal center in order to secure independence. Contrary to the automatic transfer of powers to the federal government that Williams advocated, Jamaica's position, as represented by Manley, was that the transfer of powers to the federal government should occur only when it was beneficial to the federation as a whole and to each of the units.[81]

To ensure this, Manley's recommendations focused on representation and the economic powers of the federation. First, representation in the House, the lower chamber of the federal legislature, would be based entirely on population. In the 1956 constitution, House seats were apportioned based on a complex calculation of population and monetary contributions to the federation so as to avoid a situation where Jamaica and Trinidad, the most populous states, would dominate the smaller states. Each state would have equal representation in the Senate. Manley's proposal left equal representation in the Senate intact but gave a majority of House seats to Jamaica. Second, Manley recommended that the power to levy income tax and engage in planning for economic development would require approval in the House, where Jamaica would hold a majority. Finally, a customs union would be phased in over a period of nine years.

Given the impasse between Manley's recommendation and the *Economics of Nationhood* report, the intergovernmental conference tasked with the constitutional review called in external experts to assess the two proposals. One of the experts, Taslim Olawale Elias, a Nigerian jurist and key figure in the writing of Nigeria's federal constitution, noted that the "constitutional argument would appear to have centered largely on the age-old distinction between a Federation and Confederation." Elias argued that federation entailed "a strong central government with a full international personality," while a confederation was an association of states designed "for the securing of certain limited objectives for each of the constituent units while leaving their individual legal personalities otherwise intact."[82] Drawing on the experience of Nigeria and pointing to international trends, Elias endorsed Williams's proposals for a strong federal government. According to Elias's report, "the [nineteenth-]century idea of economic laissez faire has given way to some measure of state control and planning in both the public and private sectors of the national economy. The effect of this new conception of the state has been to enhance the power of the central government in the organization and distribution of the national wealth as fairly as possible among the different sections of the people."[83] Reiterating the *Economics of Nationhood*, Elias thus concluded that the twentieth-century demands on the state required the federal government to exercise a "constitutional monopoly" in fiscal and financial matters.[84]

Fearing Jamaican exit, and despite Elias's report as well as the support of most members of the IGC, Williams agreed to all of Manley's demands at the 1961 Inter-governmental Conference. The federal structure that emerged from the 1961 compromise was thus even weaker than the structure put in place in 1956. It left the federal government power in the fields of defense and international relations, but none in the arenas of tax collection and economic planning. Moreover, the new arrangement made the future expansion of federal powers more difficult, as it gave Jamaica veto power over any future changes. That same year, Jamaicans voted against the federation in a referendum Manley had agreed to at the behest of his domestic opposition—the antifederalist Jamaican Labor Party. Manley had agreed, expecting a victory at the polls, and was shocked at the vote for exit, which prompted the demise of the West Indian Federation and paved the way for the island's independence in 1962.[85]

For Williams, the 1961 agreement and not the referendum marked the end of the West Indian Federation. He argued that the anemic federal structure agreed to in 1961 "violated every concept of federation" and "would have made the West Indies Federation the laughing stock of the entire world."[86] He insisted that even if Jamaica had voted yes in the referendum, he did not intend to support any changes to the federal structure inaugurated in 1958 "unless it was change in the direction of a strong Federal centre, making due concessions as far as timing was concerned, to any territory which faced difficulties or which was apprehensive about a strong Federal government."[87] But if the 1961 compromise was, according to Williams, "a bastardization" of the principles of federation, his own vision betrayed a conflation of federation and federal state.

This conflation was even more apparent once Jamaica had exited and proposals for a Federation of the Eastern Caribbean, which would include the remaining nine island states, emerged. While he initially resisted efforts at reconstituting the federal project, declaring infamously, "One from ten leaves naught," Williams then suggested that the smaller island states could join Trinidad in a unitary state. Williams was not the only one to move from a federal to a statist orientation. W. Arthur Lewis, one of the key proponents of a federation in the eastern Caribbean, suggested that the difference between federation and unitary state was a difference only in degree, not in kind. According to Lewis, each institutional arrangement "has central organs and peripheral organs" and involves different "division[s] of powers between the center and the periphery." However, while the differences were minimal, Lewis argued that "a constitution which all may accept if it is called federal, may equally be rejected by all if it is called unitary."[88]

The Federation of the Eastern Caribbean never got off the ground, but this episode helps to illuminate the broader dilemmas Black Atlantic federalists faced. While they embraced federation as a mechanism for securing a union of diverse and distinct political entities, their search for political institutions that could address economic underdevelopment and redistribution prompted their embrace of centralization. Their economic argument in favor of a strong federal center took two forms. First, both Williams and Nkrumah argued that free trade and a customs union would not address economic dependence and underdevelopment. Postcolonial states were better connected to metropolitan states than each other. Moreover, they tended to produce similar kinds of products.[89] The creation of a regional domestic market thus required an interventionist federal state that would gradually transform these conditions by creating the needed infrastructural connections and diversifying the economy. Second, even once a diverse and integrated regional economy had been created, federal taxation was necessary to ensure that gains were evenly and fairly distributed.[90]

The African Debates

While Nkrumah and other Pan-Africanists made this case for union as early as the 1940s, the question of what form an all-African union should take became a central issue for anticolonial nationalists only in the late 1950s and early 1960s as more African states gained independence. In 1962, after the collapse of the West Indian Federation and with over thirty independent African states, the work of constituting a Union of African States began in earnest with a preparatory conference of foreign ministers. At this meeting, two different visions of integration were articulated and shaped the contours of the debate in the years to come. The first draft proposal, presented by Ethiopia, eschewed the question of a political union altogether and called for the establishment of an organization of African states with a charter and permanent secretariat. The new organization would serve as a conduit for the creation of a collective defense system, the formation of regional and continental institutions dealing with economic development, and coordination in the international struggle against apartheid, colonialism, and racism.[91] The Ghanaian delegation countered with a proposal for a political union in the form of a federation. It recommended that a constitutional committee be appointed the following year to propose an appropriate structure for the new body.

Led by the foreign affairs minister Kojo Botsio, the Ghanaian delegation argued that only a continental government could ensure Africa's place in world affairs. First, a political union was required to realize the aims of economic integration. The creation of a free trade area and customs union, as well as industrialization and development, depended on a collective body that could direct planning at a regional level. Secondly, a federation allowed African states to represent a "consistent expression of a common foreign policy." This collective expression would be more influential than the aggregation of small independent states. Finally, defense of the continent against external aggression and interference would be better accomplished through an all-African defense force with a central command structure.[92] Unlike the debates in the West Indian context, where the disagreement centered on the extent to which a federal government should play an extensive role in economic planning and development, the African debate revolved around the question of whether the common goals of African states required political union or could be accomplished through a less demanding form of integration. On the questions of free trade and a customs union, which had been sticking points for Jamaica, there was consensus that functional and economic integration of this kind would be necessary in overcoming the continent's economic dependence.

However, critics of the Ghana plan insisted that economic integration, collective defense, and common foreign policy could be accomplished without a political union.[93] When a majority of states voted in favor of the Ethiopian proposal over Ghana's call for political union at the 1963 Summit Conference of the Heads of State and Government, Emperor Haile Selassie attempted to smooth over the differences between the two proposals.[94] He insisted that "while we agree that the ultimate destiny of this continent lies in political union, we must at the same time recognize that the obstacles to be overcome in its achievement are at once numerous and formidable." The creation of a Union of African States would begin with cooperation through the newly formed Organization of African Unity, and through collaboration at the United Nations, which would "slowly, but inexorably" lead to a political union.[95]

The idea that political union would develop out of more functional forms of coordination and integration papered over significant differences between the Ethiopian and Ghanaian proposals by drawing attention to their common concerns and aims while minimizing the distinction between a treaty organization and a regional federation of states. Selassie shared Nkrumah's diagnosis of the postcolonial predicament and also believed that union was necessary to realize independence. He argued that in the context of continued international hierarchy and economic dependence, "the emergence from colonialism is but illusory and the use of the word 'independence' would constitute not only a distortion, but also a disservice to the cause of African freedom."[96] In light of Africa's precarious independence, Selassie noted that "unity is the accepted goal" with divergences and disagreement only at the level of means and tactics.[97]

However, tactics were not the only question at stake. Instead, the two proposals offered starkly different visions of what African union might mean. Nkrumah's proposal for a Union of African States sought to institute a federal government empowered to act independently of the member states. As his commitments in the 1960 Ghanaian constitution suggested, the formation of a federal body required the delegation and dispersal of sovereignty. The OAU, for which Ethiopia and Nigeria advocated, had a secretariat and secretary general that did not have any independent political power, limited representation to state governments, and did not contain incremental plans for strengthening the union in the future.[98] The OAU was thus a treaty organization of independent and sovereign states that preserved state sovereignty through regional guarantees of sovereign equality and nonintervention. The failure to allocate any political power to the new organization would mean that the states retained a permanent veto over the OAU's actions.

This question of whether integration required independent political authority lodged in a federal government was the focal point of disagreement. According to the Ghanaian proposal, even the forms of integration and collaboration agreed to by all states, such as economic integration and collective defense, would falter without a political union. In a report circulated to delegates at the OAU, Nkrumah's government argued that without political coordination, the creation of an African common market would have limited and unevenly distributed benefits. Citing the example of the Latin American Free Trade Area, the report concluded that in the case of common markets among underdeveloped countries, "there is a real danger of existing urban and proto-industrial sectors capturing all the gains, operating 'like inter-connected soap bubbles—the largest absorbing the rest.'" Federation would create a political structure and administrative apparatus to distribute the benefits of free trade and compensate for losses when necessary.[99] This argument about the necessary relationship between political and economic integration reiterated Trinidad's *Economics of Nationhood* report. The central problem was that in the absence of a regional political body and redistributive taxation, the liberalization of regional trade would only reproduce and exacerbate inequalities between states in the free trade area. Semi-industrialized states would benefit from a larger protected market for their goods, which would be costlier to states that were largely agricultural. A program of postcolonial economic integration designed to overcome international dependence would thus inadvertently reproduce a similar structure of dependence and inequality within the region.

But while Nkrumah was concerned with achieving a federal structure that was egalitarian regionally and independent internationally, Nnamdi Azikiwe, who was now serving as governor-general of Nigeria, worried about the ramifications of a strong, possibly hegemonic, federal state on internally plural African states. Azikiwe argued that the Ghanaian plan intensified "deep-seated fears in the minds of certain African leaders" that a Pan-African organization would undermine the independence anticolonial nationalists had sought to secure.[100] The problem was not only the loss of sovereignty but also the legal, national, and cultural pluralism of independent African states. As Selassie noted during the first meeting of the OAU, "Africa's people did not emerge into liberty in uniform conditions. Africans maintain different political systems; our economies are diverse; our social orders are rooted in differing cultures and traditions."[101] As a result of this pluralism, Azikiwe argued that "the right of African states to equality of sovereignty irrespective of size and population; the right of each African state to self-determination and existence . . . and the principle of non-intervention" would have to be guaranteed within an African union.[102]

Azikiwe's critique of the Ghanaian plan drew on an alternative framing of the postcolonial predicament in which African states faced not only an external problem of economic dependence and political domination but also an internal question of ethnic and religious heterogeneity that posed equally pressing challenges. For large and diverse states like Nigeria and Ethiopia, the effort to constitute state institutions that accommodated ethnic and religious pluralism was an unstable balance that threatened to collapse at any moment. In this context, internal political conflicts also threatened the achievement of postcolonial independence. Thus, the instability of postcolonial sovereignty also motivated Azikiwe, but he understood the central contours of this instability differently, focusing on its internal dimensions rather than its external manifestations.

Preoccupied as he was with the external context of domination, Nkrumah's vision offered little in the way of institutional resources that could mitigate the internal challenges. As I argued in the previous chapter, Nkrumah was committed to the view that a politics of postcolonial citizenship would be sufficient to transcend internal religious and ethnic divisions. Thus, his reading of internal conflicts like the Katanga secession tended to emphasize the international condition of neocolonialism over debates about subnational autonomy. When pressed in the regional context to address anxieties about state fragmentation, Nkrumah at times suggested that freedom of movement within a Union of African States would diminish border conflicts, by transforming "our present boundaries" into "links instead of barriers."[103] Overall, however, his federal vision remained squarely concerned with the international problem of hierarchy rather than the internal question of pluralism and diversity.

For Azikiwe, a regional organization that defended the state's claims to autonomy, equality, and nonintervention was better suited to the internal postcolonial predicament. Invoking the arguments anticolonial nationalists had made in the demand for the right to self-determination at the United Nations, he framed his vision of African union as a "miniature United Nations" that "seeks to adapt to Africa the tried and tested principles which guide the conduct of the member states of that international organization."[104] On this view, union required an assembly with one vote for each member state and the formation of a secretariat, as well as the creation of an African court of justice, a convention on economic cooperation, a human rights convention, and a continental security apparatus. According to Azikiwe, such a structure would accomplish the collective goals of African states and adjudicate possible conflicts while still maintaining the independence and equality of states.[105]

The shift from Nkrumah's federal state, which required the delegation of state sovereignty, to Azikiwe's miniature United Nations, which would reinforce state sovereignty, highlighted the two different approaches to the relationship between nationalism and internationalism anticolonial worldmakers pursued. In the first, internationalism restructured sovereignty and created political authority that transcended the state. In the second, international institutions reinforced the state. Azikiwe acknowledged that his vision was a minimal project of union that amounted only to the creation of an African "concert of states." However, he argued that by creating the conditions for collaboration and coordination on economic issues, foreign policy, and defense, this international body would foster closer political ties between African states. Over time, these links would enable the delegation of independent authority to the union. Azikiwe identified this incremental process, in which economic and functional integration would initiate a process of political integration, with the newly created European Economic Community. According to Azikiwe, "although the Treaty of Rome [was] concerned with economic matters, it had an important political objective—namely, to promote unity and stability in Europe." Taking a lesson from Europe, Azikiwe argued that proponents of federation in Africa should also start with the economy and defense where there was already an established consensus among African states. In both Europe and Africa, a gradual process of functional integration would eventually lead to political union.[106]

Countering this gradualist position, Nkrumah maintained that economic and functional integration would not be successful without a federal structure in which the central government could direct these policies. Without "effective political machinery," the resolutions and conventions of the OAU were "no more than words on paper."[107] Moreover, the weak OAU, which was entirely subordinated to the states, could not fully address the postcolonial predicament federation was meant to overcome. The persistence of economic dependence and political insecurity ensured that "everywhere in Africa, our economies are crumbling, our treasuries are empty [and] we are becoming client states." Securing the independence and security of African states would require a federation on the model of the 1787 American constitution and not a weak concert of states.[108]

Nkrumah recognized the fears about the loss of autonomy but argued that the federation he proposed could preserve independence within the union. While the constitutions of Ghana, Guinea, and Mali allowed for the surrender of sovereignty in whole or in part to a future Union of African States, Nkrumah insisted that the total surrender of sovereignty was not necessary to create a strong and effective union, and that equality could be maintained within the union.[109] The creation of a federation protected the "legal equality" of all member states regardless of size or population under "a constitution to which all have laid their hand." Although some political authority would have to be ceded to the union government so that it could effectively carry out its mandate in specified areas, Nkrumah argued that because this government represented all the states, it should not be understood as a continental hegemon.[110]

Ghana's draft constitution for a Union of African States, submitted to the OAU in 1964, guaranteed equality and delimited the central government's role to those arenas of jurisdiction explicitly detailed in the constitution. Echoing Azikiwe's recommendations, the explanatory note prefacing the constitution declared: "The equality of the rights of each Member State is assumed under the Constitution irrespective of the extent of its territory, the size of its population, the economic or cultural development of its people."[111] The legislative body of the union preserved sovereign equality by ensuring that all member states were equally represented in both chambers. Moreover, article 116 noted, "All questions, which according to the UAS constitution, do not come under the jurisdiction of the Union shall remain under the authority of the member states."[112] Despite these guarantees of equality, the constitution closely resembled the energetic federal government Williams had argued for in the West Indies. The draft constitution included an extensive list of powers for the federal government, with exclusive powers in matters of defense, international relations, and international trade, as well as concurrent powers in a wide array of economic and social policy such as taxation, economic planning, social security, health services, and education.[113] It also enumerated a series of human rights (civil and political as well as economic and social) that would be guaranteed by the federal government.[114]

Azikiwe's vision of the African union in the form of a miniature United Nations was explicitly opposed to possible intervention. While union was necessary to successfully address the international insecurity of postcolonial states, union, according to Azikiwe, had to preserve the sovereignty of African states.[115] The UN model allowed for a union in which "African states can be as separate as the fingers in their domestic matters but as united as the fist in matters of external and general concern."[116] This unacknowledged allusion to Booker T. Washington's famous compromise on segregation, where he had insisted that "in all things social we can be as separate as the fingers, yet one as the hand in all things essential to mutual progress," indicated the importance of maintaining the political, legal, and cultural distinctions between African states. In Azikiwe's usage, the phrase sought to maintain the independence and territorial integrity of African states while allowing for a union that would make possible effective coordination on common aims. The combination of autonomy and union was precisely what had attracted a wide array of twentieth-century political actors to the federal idea. Yet to Azikiwe and many others, the proposed federation failed to strike the appropriate balance. Nkrumah's vision of a Union of African States with a centralized federal government appeared to impose a "uniform rigidity" on its constituent states.[117]

Against what was perceived as a hegemonic federation, Azikiwe turned to the United Nations as an alternative to Nkrumah's appropriation of the American example. The rights to independence and equality anti-colonial nationalists championed at the UN were thus revived in the regional context to forestall a political union of African states. As the previous chapter described, the anticolonial reinvention of self-determination had established the legal conditions of international nondomination as initial and partial answers to the problem of empire as enslavement. In the debates about a Union of African States, these same principles were directed against the creation of what was perceived to be a hegemonic union government. The possible loss of independence to a Union of African States and the ways that it might exacerbate internal instability and fragmentation produced as much concern as the external threats that the postcolonial predicament posed. The result was the formation of a treaty organization rather than federation. In Africa, the Caribbean, and elsewhere, the federal imaginaries of the mid-twentieth century gave way to functional integration.[118]

The Promise and Failure of Postcolonial Federalism

However, before the collapse of the "federal moment," federalists in the Black Atlantic gave voice to a distinctive vision of the postcolonial world.[119] Through a critique of neocolonial domination, they reimagined relations between postcolonial states and strove to transcend the limits of the nation-state through new regional formations. Their federal imaginaries blended their political and economic concerns and presented federation as a strategy for exiting international dependence while creating egalitarian regional institutions. If the right to self-determination prioritized the political and legal over the economic and the New International Economic Order privileged the economic realm over the political, this federal phase of anticolonial worldmaking marked the most sustained effort to design international political institutions that were directly linked to the remaking of the economic relations at the heart of neocolonial dependence.

Recovering this vision of postcolonial federation in the context of renewed interest in federation among historians and political theorists challenges and expands contemporary discussions. Historians of the French

Empire have recently pointed to the model of decolonization without independence advocated in the French Antilles and in French Africa as an exemplary instance of postcolonial federation. According to Gary Wilder, Senghor's and Césaire's visions of a federated French union "warrant the attention of those on the left now attempting to rethink democracy, solidarity, and pluralism beyond the limitations of methodological nationalism."[120] In contrast, the federations examined in this chapter emerged in a moment where decolonization without independence was neither available nor sought—a position that for better or worse Williams and Nkrumah shared with most anticolonial nationalists of the twentieth century. Their federal projects were as a result concerned with a different problematic— that of an independence made illusive in the face of new forms of international domination. In their hands, federation offered an institutional structure through which postcolonial states could secure nondomination in the international sphere while realizing self-government domestically.

The West Indian Federation and Union of African States also took a distinctive form in relation to the historically contemporaneous project of European integration. Though the fallout of the Great Recession, and more recently Brexit, has tempered optimism about European integration, the European Union functions as an exemplary case through which theorists grapple with the promises and perils of supranational government. However, portraying the EU as paradigmatic not only elides the concurrent projects of postcolonial integration but also casts the particular conundrums of European integration as generalizable. Attending to the specificity of postcolonial federation highlights how the anticolonial preoccupation with economic dependence gave postcolonial federation a distinctive orientation. Rather than mitigating interstate conflict, the social question was at the forefront of Nkrumah's and Williams's federal visions. Because of this orientation, they presciently pointed to the limits of economic integration without political union. In the efforts to dissociate regional free trade from the political question of federation, they saw the ways that regionalism could engender new forms of inequality and dependence. Their fears are borne out not only in the forms of regional integration that succeeded their federations in Africa and the Caribbean but also in the European Union, where functional integration has outpaced political union and continues to raise questions about the inequalities that regionalism preserves and exacerbates.

Yet for all the promise of postcolonial federation, the federal moment in the Black Atlantic was short-lived. The demise of the West Indian Federation and Union of African States cannot be understood either as an example of the necessary incompatibility of nationalism and internationalism or as an instance of a utopian project bound for failure. Instead, it reveals the ways in which federalists like Nkrumah and Williams misjudged the attachments sovereignty generated because they were convinced that postcolonial sovereignty was limited and precarious. As a result, they offered few responses to their critics. For instance, while Williams paid lip service to the need to accommodate states in the process of integration, he offered very little in the way of concrete proposals. Moreover, his endorsement of a unitary state for the eastern Caribbean suggested that he had little faith in the prospect of finding a federal structure that preserved the independence of member states while overcoming the postcolonial predicament.

Similarly, rather than seeking ways to accommodate and address his critics' concerns, Nkrumah expressed surprise that while centuries-old European states could set aside "national exclusivism" and yield some sovereign prerogatives to gain the advantages of integration, African states with their "new found" and unstable sovereignty were unwilling to entertain political union.[121] More attentive to the kinds of attachments sovereignty generated, Julius Nyerere argued that once independence had been achieved, African nationalists would be "flattered and filled with false nationalistic pride," and come to enjoy the "prestige and symbols" of sovereignty.[122] For Azikiwe and other critics of Nkrumah, however, the stakes were higher than these affective attachments to sovereignty. Faced with internal challenges to postcolonial statehood, the formal guarantees of sovereignty functioned as important safeguards against the fragmentation of the postcolonial state. While formal sovereignty was meaningless in the broader context of international hierarchy, the rights it nominally afforded—such as nonintervention and territorial integrity—could be effectively mobilized against the state's internal critics who demanded a revision of its settled boundaries. The Organization of African Unity, which emerged as a response to Nkrumah's calls for federation, reinforced these rights against both external encroachment and internal discord. The OAU's charter required member states to adhere to the principles of sovereign equality, "non-interference in the internal affairs of states, [and] respect for the sovereignty and territorial integrity of each state and for its inalienable right to existence."[123] While the charter insisted on the "inalienable right of all people to control their own destiny," it prioritized and privileged the preservation of African states.[124]

Thus, the preoccupation with the postcolonial state's instability cut both ways. It inspired Nkrumah's vision of delegating sovereignty to a regional authority, and it grounded Azikiwe's call for a miniature United Nations. The historically contingent resolution of the federal debates in a regionalism that preserved and reinforced state sovereignty would have immediate ramifications. Four years after the OAU's founding in 1963, the Biafran declaration of independence and the war that followed would be one of the first tests of this new regional institution. Committed to preserving the sovereignty of Nigeria, the OAU insisted, "Any solution to the Nigerian crisis must be in the context of preserving the territorial integrity of Nigeria."[125] Moreover, the charge of neocolonialism, mobilized in Nkrumah's account to motivate the aim of federation, was deployed in the General Assembly of the OAU and elsewhere, to undermine the legitimacy of the Biafran demand for independence.[126] In these usages, neocolonialism not only prioritized the precarious nature of external sovereignty over its internal instability but also equated internal dissent with external intervention, foreclosing the possibility of contesting the terms of postcolonial statehood.

What began as a postcolonial critique of the limits of sovereignty that prompted federal imaginaries thus ended in an institutional apparatus that zealously protected this limited sovereignty. Recovering the foreclosed political horizon of postcolonial federation and the debates that it engendered illustrates that the culmination of empire in nation-states continued to be challenged even at the highpoint of decolonization. During this brief federal moment, federation offered an institutional form that could achieve redistribution and address both the political and economic aspects of neocolonial domination. In new regional economies, nationalists found a way of out their entrapment as primary goods exporters and could approximate self-sufficiency within these larger markets. After the collapse of the federations, the question of economic dependence and its political consequences were back on the table. Faced once more with the postcolonial predicament, anticolonial nationalists returned to the global stage and articulated a new strategy of achieving international nondomination—the New International Economic Order.

CHAPTER FIVE

The Welfare World
of the New International
Economic Order

IN 1964, two years after the collapse of the West Indian Federation and his inauguration as prime minister of the independent Trinidad and Tobago, Eric Williams took a tour of African states. On his journey across the Atlantic, he jotted down some notes under the title "A Small Country in a Big World," and, following the subtitle, "The International Position of Trinidad and Tobago since August 31st, 1962," he listed the economic and political challenges the new country faced: "attacks on preferences—difficulties of citrus, textiles, coffee, and cocoa; search for new markets; Geneva Conference on Trade and Development; economic aid; cost of diplomatic representation."[1] In his speech to students in Dakar, Senegal, Williams noted that Senegal and many other African states were also small countries in a big world, facing similar economic and political challenges. According to Williams, African and Caribbean states "face today the problems faced by all developing countries—both the internal problem of satisfying the aspirations of our peoples and correcting the deficiencies left behind by the colonial regime [and] the external problem of protecting our developing economies from the more powerful economies of the developed countries, and achieving terms and relations of trade which will not jeopardize our political independence or perpetuate our economic dependence."[2]

Williams's account of the interrelated character of the political and economic, as well as the domestic and international, restaged the dilemmas of the postcolonial predicament that had preoccupied him for two decades. As he spoke in Dakar, this predicament was taking a new and heightened form. With the possibilities for overcoming dependence that regional federation promised no longer on the table, Caribbean and African states found themselves vulnerable to an increasingly unfavorable global economy. Beginning in the mid-1960s and accelerating in the 1970s, prices for products like cocoa, coffee, sisal, tea, and cotton experienced a precipitous decline. Postcolonial states, where the export of primary goods constituted large percentages of their overall exports, suddenly found themselves in the midst of steep foreign exchange shortages that limited their purchasing power. Pithily capturing the implications of this drop in commodity prices, Julius Nyerere noted that a tractor Tanzania imported for the price of 5.3 tons of sisal in 1965 required 17.3 tons in 1972.[3]

The declining terms of trade brought into sharp relief the extent to which postcolonial states were dependent on the global economy and raised questions about the vision of political economy that was concomitant with the project of anticolonial self-determination in the first two decades of decolonization. In what historian Frederick Cooper has called "the development era," both late colonial regimes and their postcolonial successors envisioned using state power to enhance productivity as well as modernize and industrialize what were largely agricultural economies.[4] The anticolonial right to self-determination was thus predicated on the view that the national state could orchestrate "a rational, state-centered plan of development."[5] It would be able to do so in part because the national state, unlike its colonial predecessor, was based on democratic representation.[6] According to Kwame Nkrumah, "The major advantage which our independence has bestowed upon us is the liberty to arrange our national life according to the interests of our people, and along with it, the freedom, in conjunction with other countries, to interfere with the play of forces in the world commodity markets."[7] This vision of development underwrote not only the postcolonial state but also the regional federations described in the previous chapter. For both Nkrumah and Williams, federation was a scaling up of the nationalist model of development. Larger regional markets, coupled with an assertive federal state, created the spatial and scalar context as well as institutional conditions that would better position postcolonial states to modernize colonial economies. While this developmental model was not realized in the form of regional federations, it generated important economic gains for postcolonial states during the first decade of independence. In the African context, economic growth remained positive while investment in social services like health and education paid off in declining mortality rates, increased life expectancies, and higher literacy rates.[8]

The irony of these successes, however, was that they came at the price of further entrenched economic dependence. While the development model aimed to gradually overcome the reliance on the export of primary goods and create more autonomous postcolonial economies, postcolonial states inadvertently "reinforced the externally dependent economy of the colonial era."⁹ Faced with declining terms of trade, the consequences of which would only be exacerbated in the 1973 oil crisis, the goal of economic independence appeared entirely out of reach for postcolonial states. To shore up budgetary gaps, postcolonial states increasingly relied on aid and debt. Aid, however, was very limited and came with conditions that dictated how money could be used while the servicing of debts would soon take significant portions of national budgets and be tied to harsh conditionality. To be a small postcolonial country in a big world of uneven trade relations would soon entail being caught in cycles of indebtedness. This iteration of the postcolonial predicament exacerbated dependence on powerful states and international institutions, illustrating that neocolonialism was embedded in the very structure of the global economy.

With the partial exit federation afforded no longer possible, anticolonial nationalists returned to the international stage with a new project of securing nondomination. Beginning in 1964 and formulated through a charter and declaration a decade later, the New International Economic Order (NIEO) marked the most ambitious project of anticolonial worldmaking. The NIEO sought to address a wide array of global economic questions, including the ownership of natural resources on land and in the seas, the relationship of multinational corporations to state authority, and the transportation and distribution of traded goods. But at its core, this project sought to address the unequal relations of trade between developing and developed nations.

This chapter argues that the NIEO envisioned international nondomination as a radical form of economic and political equality between states that would finally overcome the economic dependencies that threatened to undermine postcolonial self-government. From the perspective of the NIEO's proponents, the problem of dependence extended beyond external actors exploiting unequal economic relations to indirectly compel postcolonial states. Instead, postcolonial states were subject to the vagaries of the international market in ways that persistently limited postcolonial nation-building. In response to this structural dependence, nationalists envisioned an egalitarian global economy that required the internationalization of welfarism. Drawing on the work of Gunnar Myrdal, I thus characterize the NIEO as a welfare world that would enhance the bargaining

power of postcolonial states, institute international planning and coordination to generate equitable redistribution, and ensure democratic
decision-making.

Through the political thought of Michael Manley and Julius Nyerere,
I illustrate how this new political economy of self-determination engaged
in a distinctive politicization of the economy that located economic inequality in an international and imperial division of labor. On this view,
the global economy of the twentieth century was a product of centuries
of imperial domination that integrated the world on hierarchical and unequal terms. With this vision of the global economy in mind, anticolonial
nationalists represented the postcolonial world as workers of the world,
fashioned Third World solidarity as a form of international class politics,
and demanded redistribution on the basis that postcolonial states had in
fact produced the wealth the West enjoyed. Against this account of a historically produced dependence, and by analogizing international inequality to
domestic class politics, proponents of the NIEO recast the meaning of sovereign equality. While anticolonial nationalists had already universalized
formal equality and gestured toward equal decision-making by challenging institutions like the Security Council, in the NIEO sovereign equality
grounded a demand for an equitable share of the world's wealth. The view
that sovereign equality had material implications marked anticolonial nationalists' biggest departure from the postwar international legal order.

In describing the NIEO as a welfare world, I aim to capture both the
scale of the project and the ways it departed from the black Marxist roots
of anticolonial worldmaking. It will be clear to readers that we have traversed
a great deal of political and ideological distance since George Padmore's
and C.L.R. James's calls for a black internationalism that would serve as
the vanguard of a world revolution against both capital and empire. The
NIEO was, as we shall see, Marxist in its diagnosis of economic dependence, drawing on traditions of dependency and world systems theory. Ultimately, however, its prescriptions were articulated within the terms of a
liberal political economy, a contradiction dependency and world systems
theorists, whose critiques had in part inspired the NIEO, immediately recognized.[10] Moreover, even within the terms of its international welfarism,
the NIEO was not without its blind spots, which were revealed as Third
World solidarity frayed and the disanalogies between the domestic and international economies became visible.

But for all its limits, the NIEO, situated between the crisis of the
developmental-welfare state and anticipating the era of globalization, represented a compelling vision of what a just and egalitarian global economy

required. The innovations, as well as the political and normative significance of this vision, are revealed in contrasting the NIEO with the development model that preceded it and the structural adjustment programs
as well as the philosophical debates on global justice that would come to
displace it. The following section reconstructs the central coordinates of
the development model as articulated in the work of the St. Lucian economist Sir W. Arthur Lewis, who served as Nkrumah's first economic advisor
and contributed to Eric Williams's plan for a centralized West Indian Federation. As I show, the basic contours of developmental economists deeply
informed this first generation of anticolonial nationalists. The crisis of development economics in the 1960s as well as the collapse of the first phase
of anticolonial worldmaking, dramatically symbolized by the coup that
ousted Nkrumah in 1966, made way for a new generation of anticolonial
worldmakers and a rethinking of self-determination's political economy.
The welfare world of the NIEO emerged from this context and marked
the final phase of anticolonial worldmaking in the age of decolonization.

The Developmental Model in Crisis

In *Aspects of Tropical Trade*, published just as the declining terms of trade
were beginning to preoccupy postcolonial states, W. Arthur Lewis posed
once again the question that was at the center of his career as a development economist: "Why does a man growing cocoa earn one tenth of the
wage of a man making steel ingots?"[11] Unlike dependency theorists who
were asking why the price of cocoa was falling relative to steel ingots and
other manufactured goods, Lewis's formulation understood the relationship between prices for tropical primary goods and manufactured products to be stable and determined by factors outside of international trade.
As a result, Lewis's answer to this question had changed very little since
the publication of his path-breaking 1954 "Economic Development with
Unlimited Supplies of Labor," which would eventually win him a Nobel
Prize.[12] According to Lewis, the wage differentials of the cocoa farmer and
steelworker had little to do with the relative marginal utilities of the two
products. Instead, it depended on the difference in food production in the
tropical regions where cocoa is produced and in the temperate regions
where steel ingots are made. According to Lewis, "each of these men has
the alternative of growing food. Their relative incomes are therefore determined by their relative productivities in growing food; and the relative
prices of steel and cocoa are determined by these relative incomes and by
productivities in steel and cocoa."[13] The cocoa farmer and the steelworker

had to be paid wages that attracted them away from food production and toward these forms of employment. Because an agricultural revolution had already occurred in the temperate regions, wages would be higher.[14]

The absence of an agricultural revolution was thus one of the distinguishing features of underdeveloped countries. This meant that relatively low wages could attract workers away from food production and toward the production of cash crops like coffee and cocoa. Moreover, without a revolution in agricultural production, the economies of underdeveloped countries did not have the necessary surplus food and raw materials that could be consumed in an industrial sector. Additionally, the food producers, who remained subsistence farmers, could not become the consumers of industrialized goods.[15] With this account of underdevelopment, Lewis urged against increasing productivity in cash crops. Producing more coffee or cocoa would only further depress prices.[16] Instead, he recommended a program of development that simultaneously revolutionized agriculture to increase food production and initiated processes of industrialization. The precise balance of these two aims depended on the population size of the countries in question.[17]

In his reliance on the economic history of industrialization in the West and his account of the state's role in development, Lewis's model illustrates the central features of postwar development economics and modernization theory. The need for "a prior or simultaneous revolution" in agriculture to initiate and accompany industrialization as well as the theory of the release of "redundant" labor from agriculture to new industries were built on Lewis's interpretation of classical political economy and the example of industrialization in Britain.[18] In this view of a replicable trajectory of development where societies transition from traditional to modern, Lewis echoed W. W. Rostow's popular book *The Stages of Economic Growth*, which situated postcolonial states in a stadial history at a phase of development already superseded in the West. But while Lewis viewed development as a universal and replicable process, the state's role in initiating development distinguished twentieth-century development from its British precedent and gave late developers an advantage. Through state planning, innovations in agricultural production could be initiated, and the negative consequences of subsequent industrialization, especially inequality, could be mitigated.[19]

In his model of state-led development, Lewis tended to deemphasize the role of colonialism and international hierarchy. He rejected "political arguments," which suggested that imperialism had discouraged industrialization. Noting the example of Latin America, which had been independent for much of the nineteenth century, he argued that independence did not change the central features of tropical economies—limited agricultural productivity and unlimited supplies of labor.[20] By extension, he did not have an account of the structural dynamics of international trade and, thus, would be ambivalent about the demands included under the New International Economic Order. He concluded, "The most important item on the agenda of development is to transform the food sector and create the domestic basis for industry and modern services. If we can make this domestic change, we shall automatically have a new international economic order."[21]

It was this vision of development that Lewis championed during his role as Nkrumah's economic advisor and as an advocate of a centralized West Indian Federation. Nkrumah asked Lewis to write a report on industrialization in Ghana in 1952, a year after the Convention People's Party's sweeping electoral victory and five years before independence. His *Report on Industrialization and the Gold Coast Economy* reiterated the central themes of his theory of development, arguing that Ghana's first priority must be "a concentrated attack on the system of growing food in the Gold Coast, so as to set in motion as ever-increasing productivity." This, along with improvements in public services from infrastructure to education, would "provide the market, the capital, and the labor for industrialization" while reducing the costs of manufacturing in Ghana.[22] The legislative assembly accepted Lewis's report, and Lewis joined Nkrumah's administration as an economic advisor after independence. Lewis occupied this position for only fifteen months and resigned because of his acrimonious relationship with Nkrumah, who wanted to move quickly to the industrialization stage, a move that sidestepped what Lewis believed was the more important step of modernizing agricultural production.[23]

Yet despite their disagreements about the precise sequence of development, they agreed on its basic trajectory. Both Lewis and Nkrumah supported a policy in which the state would limit the prices paid to cocoa farmers so that it could accumulate surpluses that it would then invest in economic development.[24] In advocating for this policy, Nkrumah fully endorsed the central elements of development economics and modernization theory. For instance, in justifying the postcolonial state's central role in development, he approvingly cited Rostow's argument that postcolonial states were in need of "take-off" to move through the stages of growth.[25] He also quoted Myrdal's *Economic Theory and Underdeveloped Regions* to argue that "under-developed countries, utilizing their newly won independent status, can by purposive policy interferences manage to alter considerably the direction of the market processes under the impact of which they have hitherto remained backward."[26] Moreover, Nkrumah's critique of free trade and economic integration in the absence of political union during the federation debates drew on Myrdal's cumulative causation thesis, which holds that markets tend to favor well-endowed areas, which, in the absence of state intervention designed to generate "a created harmony," would exacerbate inequalities.[27]

In his vision for both the Ghanaian state and a Union of African States, Nkrumah remained committed to the development model as a universal and replicable process that the postcolonial state could direct at either the national or regional level. Strikingly, however, unlike Lewis, Nkrumah was also convinced that imperialism had played a constitutive role in the underdevelopment and dependence of postcolonial states. Thus, while Lewis viewed Latin America's continued underdevelopment after the end of formal empire as proof that colonialism had played no significant role in causing it, Nkrumah understood Latin America's postcolonial experience as an exemplary case of neocolonialism where economic exploitation and domination could be extended even in the absence of direct political control.[28] Taken to its logical conclusion, the anticolonial thesis that underdevelopment was the product of colonial domination and unequal integration cut against the view that development was a universal process. As dependency and world systems theorists would argue, the "development of underdevelopment" had generated a peripheral capitalism with its own logics.[29] On this view, the postcolonial world was not at a stage already superseded in the West. Instead, its underdevelopment was constitutive of Western development, and as a result, the postcolonial world could not replicate the development model.

Through a commitment to the postcolonial state as an agent of transformation, Nkrumah could hold that imperialism had produced dependence and distorted indigenous economies and, at the same time, insist that development could be replicated. In its national and regional iterations, the postcolonial state could undo the economic distortions of colonial rule and restart a blocked process of development. This faith in the postcolonial state made him skeptical about a welfare world. Despite citing him favorably on the role of postcolonial states in development, in his 1965 *Neocolonialism*, Nkrumah rejected Myrdal's internationalization of welfarism. In an implicit reference to Myrdal's 1960 *Beyond the Welfare State*, Nkrumah noted, "It has been argued that the developed nations should effectively assist the poorer parts of the world, and that the whole world should be turned into a Welfare State. However, there seems little prospect that anything of this sort could be achieved."[30] His rejection of the welfare world was on the one hand practical. Referring to the unwillingness of rich states to even consider increasing foreign aid, he remained pessimistic about securing more robust forms of international redistribution.

But beyond this practical consideration, his argument rehashed his contradictory faith in state-led development. On the one hand, he reiterated his view of development's universality, arguing that the postcolonial world occupied a stage that "present developed countries [had experienced] in the period prior to their development."[31] At the same time, recalling the critique that held an imperial economy responsible for producing dependence, he argued that anticolonial nationalists should limit the postcolonial states' interactions with an international economy. According to Nkrumah, "the less developed world will not become developed through the goodwill or generosity of the developed powers. It can only become developed through a struggle against the external forces which have a vested interest in keeping it undeveloped."[32] In this statement, the international economy remained a site of domination and dependence against which nationalists should ultimately aim to secure national and regional independence.

Thus, even as the declining terms of trade undermined a development program that at least initially required the export of cocoa, Nkrumah did not embrace a welfare world. Instead, he returned once again to federal solutions. Noting that both Nigeria and Ghana had increased their production of cocoa threefold but their gross earnings from this product had fallen from "125 million pounds to 117 million," Nkrumah argued that consumer states rather than producers were capturing the benefits of increased productivity. The NIEO's program of global redistribution specifically sought to correct this unfair distribution of global trade's benefits. However, rather than directly address this relationship of dependence, Nkrumah focused on African disunity and balkanization. He argued, "So long as African agricultural producers are disunited they will be unable to control the market price of their primary products." And the unity he had in mind went beyond an alliance or cartel of producer states. Returning again to the project of a centralized federation, he argued, "Any organization which is based on a mere commercial agreement between primary producers is insufficient to secure a fair world price. This can only be obtained when the united power of producer countries is harnessed by common political and economic policies and has behind it the united financial resources of the State concerned."[33]

The year after he wrote these words in *Neocolonialism* Nkrumah was ousted from office in a coup orchestrated while he was abroad. Although the coup was backed by the United States, it was not without popular support among Ghanaians reeling from economic crisis and political suppression. By 1966, declining cocoa prices, rising state expenditures, and increasing corruption had left Ghana with large debts, a balance of payments crisis, and a high rate of inflation.[34] The end of Nkrumah's government in Ghana marked the end of the first phase of anticolonial self-determination in the Black Atlantic. After the coup, the center of gravity in Pan-African circles shifted from Accra to Dar es Salaam, where Nyerere's government spearheaded a project of African socialism and provided resources to southern African freedom fighters still battling the last vestiges of alien rule. The ascendancy of Nyerere and the election of Michael Manley as prime minister of Jamaica in 1972 indicated the emergence of a new generation of anticolonial nationalists. Manley, the second son of Norman Manley, honed his political views and skills in journalism and trade union politics and came to power on a platform of democratic socialism. To the ire of the United States, and unlike Eric Williams in Trinidad, Manley had a close relationship with Fidel Castro and more thoroughly embraced the radical politics of the Third World. Friends and interlocutors since their student days in the United Kingdom, Manley and Nyerere shaped a new vision of anticolonial worldmaking that culminated in the NIEO's welfare world.

A New Political Economy of Self-Determination

By the mid-1960s, statesmen and social scientists were wrestling with the limited economic gains of the first two decades of decolonization and began to question the ways in which the ideal of a universal process of development failed to correspond to the conditions of postcolonial states. Writing just as he came to power and capturing a growing skepticism of the Lewis model, Manley argued that "the politics of [postcolonial] change" and more broadly the "subject of political method is best approached in terms of preferences rather than absolutes and more safely discussed in the language of analysis than dogma." For Manley, those who sought transformation had to keep in mind "the natural sociological tendency of a particular people at a particular point in time" as well as the "question of objectives."[35] The expectation that postcolonial societies would conform to Western models or trajectories substituted dogma for the work of creating a social theory that would both capture the consequences of colonialism and delineate models of transformation specific to the legacies of empire. This was not a rejection of development, but an effort to build a model of development from the ground up. Manley's politics of change thus began with an examination of "the condition of a newly independent society encumbered with the economic, social, and psychological consequences of three hundred years of colonialism and [would explore] how far the notion of equality can supply the key to an economic, social, political—indeed, a national strategy."[36]

This sociologically grounded politics of change drew on a broader debate in Jamaica and elsewhere in the postcolonial world about the theoretical agenda of an emerging Third World social science. Beginning a decade before Manley's election, the New World Group, a cohort of political economists at the University of the West Indies in Mona, Jamaica, rejected the central tenets of development economics and followed dependency theorists in outlining the specificity of peripheral economies.[37] Lloyd Best, the founder of the New World Group, and his colleagues theorized the Caribbean as a distinctive "plantation society" and traced the ways in which the institutional form of the colonial plantation had created similar political and economic dynamics in parts of Africa and Asia.[38] At the University of Dar es Salaam, social scientists also rejected the underlying assumptions of development economics and modernization theory. Loosely described as the "Dar es Salaam school," this cohort of intellectuals, which briefly included Giovanni Arrighi, John S. Saul, and Walter Rodney, sought to trace the logics and legacies of the colonial economy in southern and eastern Africa.[39] These intellectual formations had close ties with the governments of Manley and Nyerere. For instance, Manley's economic advisor, Norman Girvan, was part of the New World Group, while Nyerere's 1967 Arusha Declaration, which outlined the program of African socialism, prompted the reorganization of the social sciences at the University of Dar es Salaam.[40]

Situated within this broader intellectual milieu, Manley and Nyerere sharpened the anticolonial critique of dependence through an emphasis on the international division of labor imperialism had engendered. The global economy was, Manley argued, the product of an imperialism in which large parts of the globe were "geared to produce, not what was needed for themselves or for exchange for mutual advantage, but rather... compelled to be the producers of what others needed."[41] The forced external orientation of colonial economies had either fully transplanted indigenous social forms or substantially distorted them. In Jamaica, the violence of colonial conquest had fully displaced native society with a plantation economy, the logics of which continued to reverberate in the economic and political conditions of postcolonial Jamaica. Organized as an appendage to the imperial economy, Jamaica had imported its relations of hierarchy and dependence, which structured the domestic sphere. While colonial plantations had not completely dominated Tanzania's economy, their institutionalization in the late nineteenth century as well as the introduction of cash crops had significantly restructured peasant societies. Thus "social phenomena seemingly reminiscent of pre-colonial Africa [had] acquired an entirely new meaning in a colonial context."[42]

The legacies of colonial rule were such that postcolonial states had to pioneer new models of development that took seriously the distortions of the colonial economy and the international division of labor it engendered. Both Manley and Nyerere mobilized the language of self-reliance to describe their domestic and international economic projects. Emerging from dependency theory, self-reliance is often viewed as a version of autarky. In its usage among dependency theorists, it involved strategies of delinking and dissociation from the international economy. By slowly withdrawing as much as possible from an international order that had facilitated relations of dependence, peripheral countries could begin a process of internal "autocentric" or "self-reliant" development.[43] This model rejected industrialization and instead advocated for an emphasis on the rural sector with the goal of ensuring food security, more egalitarian land distribution, and a stable equilibrium between the rural and urban sectors of the economy.[44] Delinking and self-reliance could involve horizontal links between postcolonial states of the kind that Nkrumah envisioned under the rubric of regional federation. But its orientation to the global economy was ultimately one of exit.

Because of its emergence within dependency theory and its connection to the aspiration of delinking, self-reliance is often perceived as synonymous with protectionism. This account tends to emphasize the nationalization policies postcolonial states pursued and imagines the NIEO primarily as an effort to legitimize a strong claim to economic sovereignty. Through the guarantee of permanent sovereignty over natural resources and by allowing for the expropriation of private corporations according to national standards of compensation, the NIEO did aim to strengthen the postcolonial state, especially against the claims of multinational corporations.[45] Both Manley and Nyerere endorsed this kind of state intervention and control.[46] But to delimit their aspirations for a new economic order to this aim of strengthening state sovereignty overlooks the more expansive internationalism of this iteration of anticolonial worldmaking and minimizes the overarching concern with domestic and international equality.

Both Manley and Nyerere rejected the notion that self-reliance entailed exit from the global economy. Instead, they argued that postcolonial self-reliance must begin with the entrenched dependencies of the colonial economy and seek to undo hierarchical relations that facilitated domination. This vision of overcoming dependence was to be realized domestically through socialist policies and internationally in the New International Economic Order. Conceived as parallel projects, socialist nationbuilding and anticolonial worldmaking sought to simultaneously create an independent self-reliant postcolonial citizen and a self-reliant national community. This interlocked account of the individual citizen, the domestic economy, and international economy highlights the ways that anticolonial nationalists viewed the aims of overcoming dependence and securing postcolonial independence through concentric and interdependent circles of intervention designed to realize political and economic equality at each level.

Domestically, the concern with inequality directed Nyerere's attention to the dominant rural sectors of Tanzania's economy. Unlike Nkrumah, Nyerere rejected the equation of development with industrialization. The emphasis on industrialization, he argued, exacerbated international and national inequality, as it favored the urban over rural sectors of the country and required foreign investments that entrenched the dependence of the postcolonial state.[47] Nyerere's African socialism thus viewed the peasant and the village as its primary object, but this was not because the rural sector was free from hierarchy. While Nyerere's rhetoric of kinship and his rejection of class as a meaningful category within African societies often represented his project in a romantic and utopian light, he remained alert to the hierarchies that attended rural life. The colonial introduction of plantations and cash crops had transformed many peasants into wage laborers and in turn created inequalities among peasants. Nyerere worried that the country would be divided into a "farmer's class and a laborer's class, with the latter being unable either to work for themselves or to receive a full return for the contribution they are making to the total output." While having a farmer's class of entrepreneurial peasants might generate growth as this cohort increased their property, enhanced their productivity, and employed more workers, this would result in the emergence of a "rural proletariat depending on the decisions of other men for their existence, and subject in consequence to all the subservience, social and economic inequality, and insecurity, which such a position involves."[48]

For Nyerere, the problem with this wage relation was not just that it left the wage earner unable to meet his basic needs. Instead, Nyerere focused on the ways that the dependence and inequality it created threatened to erode equal citizenship. While "democracy based on political equality is a necessary part of human dignity," Nyerere maintained that political equality did not "just mean that every citizen diseased and ignorant, [could] be made politically equal by constitutional niceties, with a man who controls the price of his food, who is educated, and who is in good health."[49] In the absence of more egalitarian economic relations, the guarantees of equal citizenship could be undermined as those at the top of the economic hierarchy mobilized their standing to secure their dominance.[50] With this problem of hierarchy in mind, Nyerere's domestic program of self-reliance thus aimed to generate the material conditions for democratic equality in the postcolonial state. In this vision, the domestic economy centered on "rural economic and social communities where people live together and work together for the good of all." These local communities were "interlocked so that all of the different communities also work together in cooperation for the common good of the nation as a whole."[51] Within the cooperative framework, peasants were linked through horizontal and egalitarian relations rather than vertical and hierarchical ones.

This vision of a rural postcolonial economy, organized through local collectivities, sought to create a self-reliant peasantry. In a preview of Nyerere's account of self-reliance at the international level, the peasant's self-reliance and equality were to be secured through collaboration in collective farming rather than independent production. Known as *ujamaa*, Nyerere's villagization policies blended a modernizing ambition that viewed the centralized village as an object of state intervention with an approach in which the village was figured as a site of experimentation and popular initiative.[52] In its modernist ambition, settlement in villages allowed the state to modernize farming practices, extract taxes, and organize the provision of social services, especially health care and education.[53] In the more decentralized experimental vision, the village was a site of "autonomous social relations" and a space of voluntarism in which the ethics of a primitive communism could be recreated and preserved.[54]

Across the Atlantic, Manley drew comparisons between his politics of change and Nyerere's African socialism. On the one hand, he argued that colonial rule had left postcolonial states on both sides of the Atlantic with unprecedented levels of inequality as local elites and multinational corporations dominated the economy. Like Nyerere, Manley was concerned that concentrated wealth would undermine postcolonial citizenship. While

equality before the law was a foundational principle of the Jamaican constitution, it was eroded in practice. According to Manley, "inherent in the
adversary system is the fact that wealth has a better chance of victory than
poverty." Moreover, elites were positioned to legislate, and as such the legal
system inherited from the colonial state "reflect[ed] a savage bias in favor
of property as distinct from people."[55] But while Nyerere could harken
back to a model of primitive communism as the basis of a postcolonial socialism, this was not an available option in Jamaica. Transatlantic slavery
and the long history of colonial rule, Manley noted, "had severed Afro-
Jamaicans' connections and ties to tribal society."[56]

The democratic socialism that Manley espoused was thus articulated
within the terms of a colonial modernity.[57] At the center of this project was
an effort to democratize economic access and decision-making. In the agricultural sector, this involved a restructuring of land ownership through
cooperatives of farmers and workers that would participate in ownership
and decision-making.[58] In addition to reforming land ownership, Manley argued that farmers should also have ownership stakes in the secondary industries that process their agricultural products. He argued that as
"long as the farmer is seen as a planter and reaper pure and simple, . . . he
[will] tend to be condemned to the low end of the 'value added' scale."[59]
Restructuring the ownership of secondary industries would make the "agricultural sector and the farmers who are its foundations the beneficiaries
of the more sophisticated processes that are increasingly derived from
the basic activity of farming."[60] To address the growing power of multinational corporations, Manley advocated policies that protected laborers
and restructured the relationship between the state and the multinational
corporation. First, his government instituted labor laws that set minimum
wages, required pensions, expanded labor unions, and mandated workers'
participation in decision-making.[61] Second, he hoped to bring bauxite and
other key industries under partial local control. Manley argued that while
Jamaica could not do without foreign capital, it had to operate on the basis
of joint ventures with the government and the local private sector. The aim
of this policy was to ensure that "no economic decisions affecting Jamaica
are taken in foreign board rooms."[62]

In Manley's view, the multinational corporation illustrated the limits
of socialist nation-building. While he thought that the state should be empowered to regulate private actors, the transnationalism of the corporation evaded the nation-state's capacity for economic regulation. Instead
of viewing the multinational corporation, and the challenges it posed, as
novel or unprecedented, Manley framed it as a twentieth-century heir to

the imperial-era trading company. In doing so, he harkened back to the imperial origins of the global economy. Decolonization, he argued, had transformed political power in the international order, but the global economy remained "a structure of economic control whose roots went as far back as the seventeenth century."[63] Thus, while the growing power of multinational corporations revealed the contradictions between "international economy and the nation-state," which had consequences for all states, the disaggregation of economic activity from the site of political contestation and regulation distinctively encumbered postcolonial states that were already in relations of structural dependence.

For states like Jamaica and Tanzania, which produced primary goods and stood in relations of dependence with North Atlantic states, this structural dependence undermined the socialist nation-building Manley and Nyerere envisioned. They understood the vulnerability of their nation-building to the dictates of the global economy in two ways. First, they echoed Nkrumah's classic statement of neocolonialism where external actors, including private corporations, exploit the extraversion and dependence of postcolonial economies to indirectly ensure political conditions favorable to their interests.[64] Second, they argued that even when external actors did not interfere in this way, the structural logics of the global economy ensured that their projects of nation-building were vulnerable to the fluctuations of the international markets and, as a result, would remain unrealized. According to Nyerere, the declining terms of trade meant that "however great our efforts to reorganize our national economies so that they produce the goods our people need, and these goods are distributed less unequally, Third World countries are, and will be, distributing poverty." Postcolonial states were "working to create justice in [an international] sieve," as the structural inequalities of the global economy consistently undermined efforts to achieve domestic equality.[65]

The international sieve required transforming international dependence into an economic interdependence that removed the conditions of domination and allowed postcolonial states to realize their projects of nation-building. As I noted above, this orientation to the global economy departed from the dependency theorists' calls for delinking. On the one hand, this was a strategic calculation about the specific conditions of small states like Jamaica and Tanzania, whose economies emerged from imperial relations and were deeply tied to the global economy. Neither Manley nor Nyerere believed delinking was a viable political option for their countries.[66] There was in this argument a certain fatalism about the entrapment of postcolonial states within a global economy. In the aftermath of regional federations, both Manley and Nyerere concluded that however unequal and violent economic integration had been, the global economy imperialism had produced was here to stay and could not be escaped.

At the same time, accepting the global economy as an indelible feature of political and economic life made possible its reimagining. The claim that imperialism had produced an uneven but integrated global economy allowed proponents of the NIEO to represent the international arena as a site for demands of redistribution that extended far beyond aid and charity. This was not pitched as a backward-looking argument for historical redress and remedy of colonial exploitation of the kind that contemporary reparations projects have articulated. Instead, it was a demand based on the claim that the structural conditions of the global economy persistently transferred the gains of productivity to the global north. On this view, the rejection of delinking was not so much an argument about feasibility but an opportunity to stage a political demand for international redistribution. Rather than withdrawing from the relations of structural inequality, postcolonial states could restructure these relations to create a more equitable distribution of both the profit and employment global trade generated. The international division of labor might not be escaped, but it could be remade into an egalitarian economy that could undo the relations of dependence and secure the economic dimensions of international nondomination.

To make the case for international redistribution, Nyerere and Manley analogized the international division of labor to its domestic counterpart. In this analogy, postcolonial states were cast as the workers and farmers of the world. According to Nyerere, the "poor nations are now in the position of a worker in nineteenth century Europe." Both the industrial workers and the poor nations had to sell labor "at whatever price he could obtain for it." The only difference was that the poor nations did not directly sell their labor power, but instead provided primary goods in the international market.[67] For Manley, this position of postcolonial states as producers of raw materials was more analogous to the rural sectors and farmers of the global north.[68] In these analogies to the internal divisions of the bourgeois and working classes as well as to urban and rural sectors, they envisioned the global economy as one economic unit and highlighted the deep connection between poverty in the postcolonial world and the wealth of metropolitan states.[69] Just as the exploitation of the working class and rural sectors generated the wealth of industrializing societies, the exploitation of the colonial periphery and the persistence of relations of dependence after formal colonial rule ended made possible the global dominance of the Western world.

This view that the world constituted one economic unit was untimely in the context of the economic nationalism that dominated the postwar era. As we shall see, Myrdal pitched his welfare world in the context of what he described as international economic disintegration. Beginning in the interwar period, European states withdrew from international trade, developed protectionist policies, and established domestic welfarism. Against this experience, the thesis of an international division of labor and the analogy to its domestic counterpart both recalled an earlier moment of imperial integration and anticipated a new era of economic globalization. In its backward-looking orientation, this argument cast the underdevelopment of the postcolonial world as the product of an imperial global economy. In its forward-looking vision, it conceived of an egalitarian globalization with international mechanisms of distribution that would offset the structural inequalities of trade and provide the necessary international context for self-government.

Situated between a past of imperial dependence and a future of global interdependence, invocations of the domestic analogy buttressed the claim that resolving international inequality ought to resemble the domestic solutions industrialized countries had eventually accepted. Nyerere argued that when faced with domestic inequality, "nations do not deal with the problem . . . by relying upon charity." Aid and charity reproduced relations of dependence and cast the recipients as suppliants who were subject to the goodwill of the donors. Nyerere argued that within the domestic welfare state, redistribution stems from the view that "poverty and wealth are linked together, that each depends upon the other and that the well-being of the whole society requires action to equalize the opportunity and the welfare of the poorer areas and people." As a result, welfare states do not depend on the beneficence of the wealthy and instead "all transfer resources from their rich to their poor by taxation."[70] Manley added to this account of redistributive taxation that the welfare states also instituted protectionist policies for their agricultural sectors. "The whole existence of European agriculture," Manley argued, "rests upon a carefully worked out set of political arrangements that ensures that the farmer, say within France, does not fall behind as a lost victim of French economic development."[71]

Through these domestic analogies, Manley, Nyerere, and other proponents of the NIEO offered a distinctive politics of the global economy. Their demand for redistribution was not based on claims of benevolent charity or moral duties of assistance, but instead on an argument for the postcolonial world's fair share of the wealth they had helped to produce. The postcolonial world would not supplicate the developed world. Instead, it was positioned to fight an "international class war." In this context, the choice available to the developed world was "an economic revolution effected in an orderly and planned manner, or violent revolution."[72] This economic revolution would internationalize the redistributive, regulative, and protectionist ambitions of the welfare state. As the culmination of that revolution, the NIEO entailed "a real and automatic . . . transfer of resources from the rich to the poor, instead of the other way round as at present . . . fair representation on international bodies which affect [the world's] economic future . . . [and] a real commitment to the development of the world as one unit, which it is, with a deliberate discrimination in favor of the poor and disadvantaged, when they operate in the same area as the rich and the powerful."[73]

Making a Welfare World

Although neither Manley nor Nyerere cited Gunnar Myrdal in their arguments for an egalitarian global economy, his idea of a welfare world captures their vision. The welfare world emerged in a series of works Myrdal published between 1956 and 1960 where he traced the contradictions of the postwar economic order, pointing in particular to the international consequences of the economic nationalism and autarky that had accompanied the rise of the welfare state in Europe.[74] For Myrdal, twentieth-century innovations in technology, transportation, and communications should have led to greater economic integration at the international level. However, the postwar era was one of economic disintegration and closure. This economic nationalism, Myrdal argued, had created the conditions in which the principles of liberty, equality, and fraternity could be fully realized within the nation-states of Europe. Through national redistribution, Western states had avoided the "Marxian catastrophe" in which capitalism self-destructs under the weight of its own contradictions.[75] But while violent class antagonism had been successfully sublimated in European welfare states, economic nationalism exacerbated international inequality and foreclosed the possibility of mitigating the "international class gap."[76]

Invoking a domestic analogy similar to Nyerere's, Myrdal argued that from the perspective of the developing world the rise of economic nationalism in the West was experienced as "a protective 'rich men's club'" that further deepened the inequalities generated by imperial domination.[77] For Myrdal, the division and clash between the developed and developing nations resembled "the fluid and uncertain internal conditions in the rich countries of the Western world during that early stage when political democracy was only 'in the air' as an ideal and a hope, and when trade unionism was on the march."[78] As in the European domestic context of the late nineteenth century, the unjust division of wealth and power could lead to instability, conflict, and violence. If the rise of welfare states had stemmed the threat of domestic class warfare, Myrdal argued that the internationalization of welfarism could similarly overcome the protracted inequality of the world order. This internationalization of welfarism involved both postcolonial states adopting the welfare state as their model for domestic economic policy and the creation of a welfare world that expanded and supplemented welfare states at the international level. This new internationalism, which Myrdal distinguished from the nineteenth-century internationalism of free trade, aimed at the "harmonizing, coordinating, and unifying of national economic policy structures internationally."[79]

Myrdal did not offer an extended discussion of the institutional interventions needed to inaugurate the welfare world.[80] And while Myrdal hoped to influence and redirect American foreign policy just as the Kennedy administration assumed political power, his proposal received little attention from the political establishment.[81] Ignored by the United States, postcolonial states would take up the struggle for a welfare world in the United Nations. Two years after the publication of Myrdal's *Beyond the Welfare State*, postcolonial states passed a resolution in the General Assembly to constitute the United Nations Conference of Trade and Development (UNCTAD), which was founded in 1964.[82] Against the objections of the United States and Western European states, postcolonial states once again used their majority coalition in the General Assembly to place the Argentinian economist Raúl Prebisch at the helm of UNCTAD. Myrdal's colleague at the UN, Prebisch was long concerned with international inequality and the problem of declining terms of trade for primary goods–producing states.[83] In the immediate postwar period, he had initially argued that postcolonial states should pursue import substitution industrialization and more protectionist economic policies. But by the late 1950s, Prebisch was worried that import substitution would not break the relations of dependence in the global economy. In his leadership of UNCTAD, he redirected his attention to the regulation of international trade and gave shape to the postcolonial world's vision of international welfarism. Prebisch coined the phrase "New International Economic Order" in 1963 and for the next decade set the foundations for what would be the 1974 Declaration on the Establishment of a New International Economic Order and the Charter of Economic Rights and Duties of States.[84]

When Myrdal accepted the 1974 Nobel Prize in Economics, he delivered a lecture entitled "The Equality Issue in World Development." In a defense of the NIEO, he endorsed developing nations' demands for "fundamental changes of international economic relations" and criticized the limited availability of multilateral aid for development. However, he did not identify the NIEO with his prior conceptualization of a welfare world. Instead, anticipating some of the NIEO's critics, Myrdal highlighted the "inequality problem" within developing countries and argued for the prioritization of land reform.[85] But while Myrdal himself did not link the NIEO to his internationalization of welfare, both critics and sympathizers took up this perspective. For instance, the neoliberal economist Ernst-Ulrich Petersmann, who played an important role in spearheading reforms of the General Agreement on Tariffs and Trade, rejected the NIEO for its "internationalized welfare world."[86] On the opposite end, the international lawyer Bernard Röling celebrated the egalitarian ambitions of the NIEO and described it as an effort to transform the UN from a peace to a welfare organization.[87]

In describing the NIEO as an internationalization of the welfare state, both Petersmann and Röling sought to capture the ways that this project of anticolonial worldmaking marked a radical departure from the postwar international order. As if to mark this transformation, postcolonial states set aside the standard General Assembly resolution once more and announced the NIEO with a declaration and a charter. On the one hand, these documents were linked to the founding documents of the United Nations. For instance, the 1974 declaration affirmed "the spirit, purposes and principles of the Charter of the United Nations to promote the economic advancement and social progress of all peoples."[88] In doing so, proponents of the NIEO sought legal justification for their ambitious program in the established principles of international law.[89] But these documents also suggested a refounding of international society. Like the 1960 Declaration on the Granting of Independence discussed in chapter 3, which sought to establish the right to self-determination as the foundation of a postimperial world order, the NIEO's charter and declaration were attempts to refashion international law in order to align it with the aims of anticolonial worldmaking. These documents and subsequent resolutions were to function as new "bases of economic relations between all peoples and all nations" and were perceived by the developed nations of the global north as "fundamental departures from the traditional rules of international law."[90]

The NIEO's reformulation of sovereign equality was central to this transformation of the postwar international legal order. Through the 1960 passage of UN General Assembly resolution 1514, anticolonial nationalists had universalized formal equality and gestured toward a view of sovereign equality that entailed equal decision-making power in the international sphere. In the NIEO's charter and declaration, postcolonial states laid claim to this principle of equality and fashioned the General Assembly as a legislative body that had the power to issue legally binding international economic policy—an account that critics of the NIEO vociferously disputed. Central to this view was a procedural argument that international economic rules should be decided within the UN General Assembly, which represented all states and gave each one a vote. According to the Declaration on the Establishment of the New International Economic Order, the UN was "a universal organization ... capable of dealing with problems of international economic cooperation in a comprehensive manner and ensuring equally the interests of all countries."[91] The NIEO charter further extended this claim by reference to the principle of sovereign equality. Article 10 noted that the juridical equality of all states and their equal status as members of the international community grant them "the right to participate fully and effectively in the international decision-making process in the solution of world economic, financial, and monetary problems."[92]

This claim of legislative equality would be mobilized to further expand the meaning of sovereignty equality. While formal equality historically relegated social and economic inequality to territorial states as domestic matters rather than to international institutions, anticolonial critics argued that the standard view of legal equality masked the material inequality through which powerful states reproduced their dominance. To say that Jamaica or Tanzania and the United States were equal members of the international order obfuscated the outsized economic dominance that the United States exercised and could deploy to compel dependent states.[93] In this critique of formal equality, Nyerere extended his domestic critique of the limits of equality before the law. Just as equal political citizenship within the state does not undo the "dependence and dominance" of the "man who needs to sell his labor in order to buy bread," formal sovereign equality left intact the dependence of postcolonial states.[94] Echoing his vision of socialist nation-building, which called for equalizing the material conditions of postcolonial citizenship, Nyerere argued that the discrepancies between formal equality and substantive inequality had to be rectified if sovereign equality was to be a meaningful principle of the international order.[95]

This critique of formal equality and the radicalization of the meaning of sovereign equality in the demand for economic redistribution emerged from a critique of "the dominant philosophy of international exchange . . . that of a 'Free Market.' "[96] A 1964 UNCTAD report called attention to the limits of this philosophy as it was embodied in the 1947 General Agreement on Tariffs and Trade. GATT was premised on the idea "that the free play of international economic forces by itself leads to the optimum expansion of trade and the most efficient utilization of the World's productive resources." But there were two problems with this view. First, the commitment in principle to free trade was thwarted in practice as developed nations instituted high protective tariffs and import quotas that protected domestic markets (particularly in agriculture) from the exports of developing nations. This was detrimental to the developing countries since they could not sell their goods to the developed countries.[97] Thus, while formal equality required all states to comply with GATT's requirement, wealthy and powerful states could break the rules with impunity.

Secondly, the "free play of economic forces" was modeled on the assumption that comparative advantage and specialization entailed equally beneficial trade for all. However, as the problem of declining terms of trade illustrated, international trade did not follow a pattern of equal exchange.[98] Here, the problem was that even if all states did play by the same rules, the distribution of the benefits of trade would be uneven and follow the hierarchical ordering of states. According to Manley, like the Bretton Woods system more generally, GATT was the product of a Eurocentric international order. While it sought to "create an international system of political management for the world economy," an effort the NIEO hoped to emulate, it did so before most of the world could participate in international decision-making. As a result, it privileged the interests of the Western world and thus continued to reproduce inequality.[99]

In light of these critiques of the postwar global economy, the NIEO sought two broad transformations of the postwar trade regime. First, UNCTAD recommended a coordinated liberalization that sought to gear the benefits of freer international trade toward the developing nations. This would involve a General System of Preferences (GSP) that granted poor nations preferential access to the markets of developing nations. GSP would replace the prevailing "Most Favored Nation" standard in which these kinds of preferences were not allowed.[100] From the perspective of developing nations, free and fair trade entailed "unrestricted and duty-free access to the markets of all the developed countries for all manufactures and semi-manufactures from all developing countries."[101] Granting preferences to developing nations ensured that international trade not only would support development but also would increase the capacity of developing nations to import from their trading partners.[102]

This model of regulated liberalization required developed and developing nations to undergo a series of "structural adjustments" so that the increased international trade did not adversely affect domestic economies.[103] While structural adjustment is now associated with IMF-led policies directed at indebted nations, Johanna Bockman has recently argued that it was initially mobilized as a strategy for securing an egalitarian global economy—what she terms socialist globalization.[104] Here, structural adjustment suggested a process by which developed and developing nations would readjust their domestic economies to create "conditions of international trade conducive, in particular, to the achievement of a rapid increase in the export earnings of developing countries and, more generally, to the expansion and diversification of trade between all countries."[105] Such a restructuring suggested that the emergence of a new international economic order required a thoroughgoing transformation of all national economies.[106]

At the international level, structural adjustment required economic planning to avoid or mitigate the regressive redistribution of income.[107] From the perspective of the NIEO, the international community had "a clear responsibility towards developing countries that have suffered a deterioration in their terms of trade in the same way as governments recognize a similar responsibility towards their domestic primary producers."[108] Through compensatory financing to make up for unexpected price drops in commodities, commodity agreements that regulated prices for primary products and a Common Fund for Commodities to help developing countries diversify their economies, the NIEO organized a system of "special and differential treatment" for postcolonial states. These interventions aimed to ensure that postcolonial states, as the farmers and workers of the world, received a fair share of the wealth they produced. In "the absence of a world government" that could institute international taxation, the NIEO relied on these indirect mechanisms to create a welfare world in which international trade was structured by interdependence rather than dependence.[109]

In the addition of part 4 to GATT in 1966, which paved the way for preferences in favor of developing nations, and exemptions to the most favored nation standard secured in 1971, postcolonial states won important concessions in the international trade regime that laid the groundwork for this welfare world. These victories institutionalized the view that international economic rules must attend to the differentially positioned statuses of states in the global economy and prioritize the needs of the developing world. In making the case for this kind of preferential treatment, the NIEO deployed the language of equity. Both the charter and declaration identify equity along with sovereign equality and interdependence as the principles underlying the new global economy.[110] The declaration further notes as one of its principles "the broadest co-operation of all the State members of the international community, based on equity, whereby the prevailing disparities in the world may be banished and prosperity secured for all."[111]

While sovereign equality was invoked to justify equal legislative power in formulating international economic law and was the basis of the demand for a fair share in the distribution of international wealth, the principle of equity framed the substance of this law as a site where the structurally unequal positions of states were taken into consideration. This was not the first time that equity was mobilized alongside equality. As I argued in chapter 2, Jan Smuts transposed equity onto equality and concluded that both the British Empire and the League of Nations realized the principles of freedom and equality. In his formulation, equity was a mechanism of preserving hierarchy and rewriting self-determination as a racially adjusted principle. Equity signaled that international standing reflected the political, economic, and racial position of states. By contrast, in the NIEO, the principle of equity was employed to mitigate the hierarchy of the global economy by tilting the rules that governed it in favor of developing nations. Thus whereas Smuts's mobilization of equity encumbered states like Ethiopia and Liberia with a burdened membership in which their obligations to international society were onerous and their rights limited, the NIEO's vision of equity entailed a redistribution of rights and obligations in the international order such that the most powerful states shouldered greater burdens for the creation of an egalitarian global economy.[112]

But while equitable globalization entailed preferential treatment for postcolonial states, proponents of the NIEO argued that it was in service of the global economy more broadly. For instance, in endorsing policies like compensatory financing and commodity agreements, UNCTAD argued that such measures maintained the purchasing power of developing states, which in turn allowed them to buy manufactured goods from developed states. Economic planning to mitigate the declining terms of trade was thus necessary both to increase the incomes of developing nations and increase international trade between developed and developing nations. In the absence of such protective measures, the declining terms of trade would lead to a contraction of world trade that would have negative consequences for all states.[113] As was the case for the NIEO more broadly, this argument for the international management of national purchasing power was drawn directly from the analogy to the domestic division of labor and the welfare state that had rectified its inequalities. Within the domestic context, states addressed the inequality between industrial and agricultural sectors by taking measures to support prices of or income from agricultural products. In similar fashion, policy interventions at the international level were required to avoid or mitigate the regressive redistribution of income.[114]

Taken to its logical conclusion, this analogy looked forward to the "world unity and federation" that Pan-Africanists believed was the telos of the project of decolonization they were just starting in 1945.[115] While the NIEO also championed a strong account of postcolonial sovereignty, in its more ambitious vision, it provided an outline of an internationally managed global economy that was structured by equitable interdependence rather than hierarchical dependence. This project marked the highpoint of anticolonial worldmaking. In the NIEO, overcoming dependence was imagined as possible only in a context of equalized political and economic power. This radically reimagined mode of sovereign equality would supply the condition of international nondomination in which postcolonial nation-building could realize the principle of equality domestically.

But despite its compelling vision of a global economy organized as a welfare world, the NIEO contained a number of tensions at the center of which was the analogy between domestic and international economic relations. First, while the formulation of postcolonial states as the workers and farmers of the world reframed and politicized the global economy, it evaded the question of the workers and farmers within postcolonial states. As I have suggested above, the program of a welfare world drew on a long-standing Marxist critique of colonial dependence but was also a departure from the black Marxist internationalism that had informed an earlier moment of anticolonial worldmaking. For instance, at the Fifth Pan-African Congress organized in 1945, Nkrumah had penned a Declaration of the Colonial Workers, Farmers, and Intellectuals, which called on the "workers and farmers of the Colonies" to use their weapons "the Strike and the Boycott" in the fight against colonial rule.[116] In keeping with George Padmore's vision of a Black International, Nkrumah positioned colonial workers and farmers as the vanguard of the impending anticolonial revolutions and of an international class war.

Just two and a half decades later, postcolonial states were themselves analogized to workers and farmers in the demand for an egalitarian global economy, and it was not clear how this formulation related to the domestic division of labor in postcolonial states. Though Nyerere conceived of the G77 as a trade union for the poor, postcolonial states were increasingly limiting the rights of independent organized labor within their countries. In Ghana, for example, the trade union movement was nationalized and folded into the state apparatus, making it almost a requirement that workers join state-sanctioned unions.[117] This absorption of unions into the state and party coincided with nationalists' rejection of class as a useful category of analysis and mobilization within postcolonial states. For instance, Nyerere grounded his version of African socialism not on the domestic class struggle, but on a conception of socialization in the family and the village. On this view, the nation was understood through the metaphors of kinship, while class conflict was displaced onto the international stage.[118]

For socialists like Nyerere and Manley, the demand for a New International Economic Order was always viewed as an international corollary to the effort to institute socialism at home. According to Nyerere, "the fight for equality . . . has to be waged both within our nations, and on a world basis."[119] But ultimately, the NIEO proposals formulated within the UN had nothing to say about the domestic distribution of wealth and resources. The question of distribution at home was entirely a matter for the state to adjudicate. Critics of the NIEO on both the left and the right pointed to this silence on internal inequality as a sign of the hypocritical nature of postcolonial demands for an egalitarian global economy. For Marxists like Samir Amin, the NIEO's integrationist orientation to the global economy would only exacerbate economic dependence and further empower the postcolonial bourgeoisie and the urban sector, while marginalizing the larger rural sector.[120] From the opposite ideological perspective, the conservative Robert Tucker sought to distance the proponents of the NIEO from their liberal supporters in the West by arguing that the former were unconcerned with inequality at the individual level so long as they achieved equality between states.[121]

Aside from its abstraction from individual workers and farmers within the postcolonial state, the domestic analogy obscured the obvious disanalogy between the national and the international—the absence of a state with the coercive power and processes of legitimation that had enabled the emergence of national welfarism. Unlike its domestic counterpart, the welfare world was to be secured without a world state. While the NIEO gestured toward the inevitable world unity and federation announced at the 1945 Pan-African Congress, its proponents did not take on the task of envisioning a statist or federal institutional structure for this future.

Instead, Nyerere and others turned to existing international institutions such as the UN General Assembly and argued that they could provide the necessary political structure to constitute a welfare world.[122] As I discussed in chapter 3, this commitment to refashioning the United Nations system was always a key element of anticolonial internationalism. As an aspirational vision of the UN, it looked forward to an egalitarian international society that supported the anticolonial right to self-determination. However, proponents of the NIEO underestimated the ways in which international institutions remained antagonistic to demands for greater equality.[123]

Thus, while postcolonial states operated as if the General Assembly were the legislature of the new international order, there was no real effort to outline a process by which postcolonial states might mobilize their majority to initiate this transformation of the UN system. The contrast between the regional federations described in the last chapter and the NIEO illuminates this point. The debates in the West Indies and Africa gave sustained attention to the kinds of political institutions required for supranational redistribution. From the perspective of federalists like Eric Williams and Kwame Nkrumah, regional integration and redistribution demanded a strong federal state. When the question of interstate redistribution was posed on the global stage, the hierarchies embedded in the UN system limited the range of institutional possibilities. As a result, proponents of the NIEO provided no clear guidelines for how commitments in documents like the declaration and charter were to become obligations in the absence of stronger political institutions.

The link between domestic trade unionism and the solidarity politics of the Third World was also unstable and unraveled in the course of the NIEO's short lifespan. The idea that the developing world was akin to the working class of the world that could organize as a trade union ignored the political and economic schisms between developing nations. According to Amin, rather than speak of a united Third World, the postcolonial states should be divided into third and fourth worlds, with the latter constituting a protoperiphery of the former. The policies of the NIEO, Amin argued, were likely to benefit the more economically powerful states while exacerbating relations of dependence within the postcolonial world.[124] The differences among the Third World states became starkly visible at the height of the oil crisis. While OPEC functioned in important ways as a model for the kinds of commodity associations other developing nations hoped to create and signaled what the power of collective action in the international sphere might accomplish, the hike in oil prices and the accompanying spike in food prices proved to be particularly painful for the developing world.[125] Relatedly, the kinds of trade liberalization advocated by the NIEO were more likely to benefit larger, more industrialized countries like Brazil rather than predominantly rural economies.[126] The language of a trade union for the poor nations thus tended to mask the differentiated nature of the developing world.

Beset with these limitations of the domestic analogy, the NIEO also embodied the central contradiction of anticolonial worldmaking in the age of decolonization, caught as it was between reinforcing state sovereignty and recommending internationalist solutions to the postcolonial predicament. In a very general way, these two commitments were expressed in the declaration and charter. These documents affirmed the principles of sovereign equality and nonintervention and expanded sovereignty to include permanent sovereignty over natural resources, a claim that had been dropped in the redefinition of self-determination as a right. At the same time, the NIEO outlined robust international economic interventions and suggested in its invocation of structural adjustment that even domestic economic policy had to follow the prescriptions of the NIEO. In this light, the charter's article 14 notes that each state has the "duty to co-operate in promoting a steady and increasing expansion and liberalization of world trade" and by extension to move "towards the progressive dismantling of obstacles to trade and the improvement of the international framework for the conduct of world trade."[127]

To be clear, the commitments to both independence and internationalism are not incompatible. Indeed, throughout this book, I have argued that what made anticolonial nationalism distinctive as a project of worldmaking was not only that it imagined nationalism and internationalism as compatible commitments but, more importantly, that anticolonial nationalists believed national independence could be achieved only through internationalist projects. But as I suggested in chapter 1, this combination of nationalism and internationalism took two different forms. In the first iteration, international institutions were mobilized to secure and underwrite the nation-state, while in the second account, international institutions were to transcend the state, a vision that anticolonial nationalists articulated at the 1945 Pan-African Congress and sought to realize through regional federations.

The NIEO combined both of these approaches, and the precise combination of national independence and internationalist interdependence proved to be a difficult balance. Nowhere was this more apparent than in attempts to address the growing power of multinational corporations by championing states' rights and insisting on international regulation. In these two proposals, divergent visions of the relationship between the national and international were imagined. In the first, international law was called on to affirm and strengthen the rights of states against private corporations. In contrast, the turn to international regulation of multinationals implied that state sovereignty was a limited bulwark against ever more complex transnational economic flows, and thus international law was employed to supplement and transcend the state as the site of political regulation.[128] Within the NIEO, these visions of the international as a supplement to and transcendence of the nation-state were neither fully reconciled with each other nor decisively adjudicated in one direction or the other. However, by the 1970s, nationalists had abandoned the efforts to delegate and disperse sovereignty embodied in the federal moment for the more minimal internationalism of defending the nation-state.

Displacing the NIEO

These internal limitations and inconsistencies do not in themselves explain the collapse of the NIEO, as external challenges ensured that the project never had the opportunity for its internal contradictions to unfold. Its demise is thus a story of ideological and political displacement that occurred in a context where postcolonial states' economic and political standing was weakened and undermined. By calling it a displacement, I want to suggest a strategic and concerted effort to dislodge the demands for a new economic order, which took advantage of the political weakness of postcolonial states and capitalized on the NIEO's internal contradictions. As postcolonial states worked to achieve the goals of the new economic order within the United Nations, the grounds were shifting under their feet in the aftermath of the 1973 oil embargo. In a context where balance of payments crises and rising levels of indebtedness subjected postcolonial states to the dictates of international financial institutions, the NIEO's critics, which ranged from First World statesmen to neoliberal economists, found the political stage on which they could launch their displacement.[129]

Jamaica was one of the first countries to experience the consequences of these economic shocks. Between 1973 and 1974, bauxite production was at its height in Jamaica, and the Manley government extracted greater rents from the industry in order to offset the effects of the higher oil prices and to fund its ambitious social programs. During his administration, spending on public education and health care increased from 24 to

27 percent of the budget, infant mortality rates declined from 32.5 percent in 1970 to 11.3 percent by 1980, and labor's share of income increased from 61 percent to 69 percent between 1971 and 1976.[130] By the mid-1970s, in retaliation for the higher rents, bauxite companies cut production just as bauxite producers in Australia, Brazil, and West Africa edged out Jamaica in international markets with lower prices. By 1976, government expenditure outgrew revenues, resulting in deficits of about 15 percent that were largely financed by central bank credit.[131] When Manley was reelected in 1976, his government was forced to negotiate a stabilization program with the International Monetary Fund. The 1977 agreement, the first in a series of structural adjustments, required a 30 percent devaluation of the currency; major cuts in public expenditures, especially in the wages of public sector workers; and the privatization of state assets. As a further condition for assisting Jamaica, the IMF required regular "performance tests" to ensure that its benchmarks were met.[132] The deleterious effects of the economic crisis and the IMF agreement on Manley's democratic socialism were immediately visible as labor's share of income fell 5 percent between 1977 and 1978, wiping out in a year the achievements of his first term.[133] Under similar economic and financial pressure, Nyerere's government also found itself turning to international financial institutions in the late 1970s. Like Manley's policies, Nyerere's brand of African socialism had made significant progress on social indicators such as illiteracy, infant mortality, and primary school attendance.[134] However, by 1977 increasing social spending, coupled with declining terms of trade, left Nyerere's government dependent on IMF loans to close budget deficits. Nyerere initially rejected the IMF and World Bank conditionality, which included reductions in expenditures and liberalization of the economy as a requirement for further loans.[135]

In 1980, a year after breaking negotiations with the international financial institutions, Nyerere organized a conference on the IMF and the Third World in Arusha—the city where in 1967 he had announced his program of African socialism. Manley did not attend in person but sent his economic advisor and a letter outlining Jamaica's experience with the IMF. He critiqued the punitive attitude that informed structural adjustment, highlighted the deterioration of living conditions as social welfare programs were cut, and called for a new approach to international finance commensurate with the aims of the NIEO.[136] The IMF's early interventions in Jamaica and Tanzania were thus at the center of the South-North Conference on the International Monetary System and the New International Order. In response to both the breakdown of the Bretton Woods system and the exclusion of developing nations from the IMF and World Bank, the Arusha initiative called for a new democratic and universal monetary system that would be attentive to economic development in the global south and that established an international currency unit independent of the US dollar.[137] For Nyerere and Manley, the economic crisis at home and internationally was an opportunity to advance the "struggle for the New International Order."[138]

But far from initiating a new phase of debates about the NIEO and revealing the limits of the NIEO's initial preoccupation with trade, the Arusha initiative would be one of the last attempts to revive the postcolonial demand for a welfare world. As more developing nations fell prey to the debt crisis and began to default on loans, structural adjustment programs were a ubiquitous feature of postcolonial politics in the 1980s. In this context, structural adjustment, which UNCTAD understood as a coordinated project of economic reforms in both developing and developed nations, was now limited to the reform and disciplining of indebted nations, largely in the global south. In this new language of structural adjustment, we see a clear instance of displacement by appropriation, whereby the IMF and other actors sought to reinterpret the idea of "structural reform" in light of supply-side economics. As UNCTAD continued to insist that structural adjustment had to include transformations in the developed economies designed to open markets in the global north to the developing world, the IMF now argued that structural adjustment entailed "the elimination of structural imbalance and rigidities in the economies of the poorer countries."[139]

This delimitation of structural adjustment to "the poorer countries" was tellingly accompanied by a rejection of the UN General Assembly as the appropriate site for international economic decision-making. Proponents of the NIEO had argued that the General Assembly was a more representative, and thus more democratic, institution to legislate on questions of trade, inequality, and underdevelopment. However, for critics of the NIEO, locating decisions about economic policy within the General Assembly dangerously politicized the economy and allowed Third World states to leverage their majorities against more powerful actors in the global economy. By giving greater prominence to international financial institutions in the aftermath of the debt crisis, economic questions could be insulated from majoritarianism and depoliticized. Economic decision-making was thus no longer a site of political contestation but an arena of technical and legal expertise, better left to economists and lawyers rather than politicians.

The rise of neoliberal economics, which extended far beyond the halls of international institutions, gave ideological shape to this displacement of the NIEO and launched a counterrevolution against the aspiration for an egalitarian global economy. For neoliberal economists associated with the Mont Pèlerin Society, the demand for equality threatened the "self-equilibrating system of the world economy."[140] While order had meant a global economy that aimed toward redistributive justice for the NIEO's proponents, from the perspective of neoliberals order entailed a fluctuating system in which actors respond to market stimuli without a preconceived end state in mind.[141] In reforms to GATT and international investment law, the neoliberal counterrevolution prevailed against the NIEO. While the NIEO paired equity with equality and envisioned a form of regulated globalization with preferential treatment for developing postcolonial states, neoliberal reformers returned to formal equality as the basis of the global economy. The "idea of one rule for all in the world economy" came to displace the NIEO's effort to redistribute rights and obligations in such a way that powerful states shouldered greater burdens. Moreover, as subjects to the regulative rules of the world economy, states could no longer claim the capacity to transform the international order. State sovereignty, from the neoliberal perspective, was not only compatible with but also required subjection to the disciplining mechanisms of the market.

This marked a wholesale rejection of the key tenets of the NIEO—an interconnected account of nation-building and worldmaking that recognized the consequences of economic dependence on self-government, politicized international inequality to ground a claim of redistribution, and was committed to sovereign states as the agents and subjects of the welfare world. In the aftermath of the NIEO's demise, its call for global justice would be taken up in altered form among Anglo-American philosophers. Beginning with the pioneering work of Charles Beitz in the late 1970s, philosophers, working in the shadow of John Rawls's 1971 *A Theory of Justice* and confronted with the NIEO's internationalization of welfarism, engaged in their own worldmaking by theorizing the moral foundations of global justice.[142] With individuals as the subject of global justice, this cosmopolitan reframing highlighted the morally arbitrary nature of state borders and called into question the deeply ingrained antidistributional preferences of the richest countries. This critical orientation to the state also entailed rejecting the NIEO's conception of postcolonial states as the workers of the world. Inequality between states could not serve as a useful proxy for identifying and rectifying inequality between individuals. For Beitz, global justice required an international difference principle such that it is "the globally least advantaged representative person (or group of persons) whose position is to be maximized."[143]

The shift from the state to the individual as the subject of global justice coincided with the emergence of a basic needs approach that prioritized sufficiency. While Beitz retained the NIEO's egalitarian ambitions, a range of political actors—from development economists at the World Bank to nongovernmental organizations—shifted attention to absolute poverty over relative inequality.[144] In the immediate aftermath of the global food crisis and famines in Bangladesh, Ethiopia, and elsewhere, alleviating human suffering and meeting the basic needs of individuals took center stage for policy makers and philosophers alike. At the core of this shift from equality to subsistence was on the one hand the view that global equality was either too far off or impractical, and on the other hand, an intuition that in the absence of a minimal standard, a Rawlsian difference principle could still leave the basic needs of the worst-off individuals unmet.[145]

As the neoliberal counterrevolution instilled market fundamentalism in economic practice, social justice was globalized, individualized, and minimized in moral and political theory.[146] In this context, returning to the NIEO's welfare world reminds us of the anti-imperial origins of contemporary debates about global justice. As one observer noted in the late 1970s, "whatever the other consequences of the demands by the Third World for a new, more egalitarian economic order, one thing is clear: those demands have given rise to an unprecedented debate on the subject of global distributive justice."[147] Just as striking, however, are the departures of this contemporary debate from the Third World's vision of a welfare world. As the last and most ambitious project of anticolonial worldmaking, the NIEO offered a radically different account of global justice—one that situated injustice in a shared imperial history, located individuals as citizens of unequally positioned states, connected the achievement of global justice to realizing the principle of international nondomination necessary for the exercise of self-government, and reimagined the meaning of international equality. Its demise marked the beginning of self-determination's fall, while its critique of the global economy continues to reverberate in new postcolonial visions of global justice.[148]

Epilogue

THE FALL OF SELF-DETERMINATION

IN MARCH 1975, less than a year after the United Nations General Assembly passed the Charter of Economic Rights and Duties of States, Daniel Patrick Moynihan wrote a scathing critique of the demands for a New International Economic Order. Having completed a two-year post as the United States ambassador to India, and before his brief stint later that year as representative to the United Nations, Moynihan expressed indignation that "a vast majority of the nations of the world feel there are claims which can be made on the wealth of individual nations that are both considerable and threatening." Moynihan accepted that the world was predicated on interdependence, and he credited the United States, as founder of the United Nations, for having birthed the "notion of a world society." But for Moynihan, the NIEO's vision of interdependence reflected the "tyranny of a new majority" that undermined the United States' vision of a liberal international order.[1]

According to Moynihan, this new majority posed a challenge to American leadership that was distinct from the one posed by the Soviet Union. He traced its demands for international redistribution to former British colonial subjects who had imbibed the doctrines of the Fabian socialist tradition and were now seeking to internationalize the lessons of British welfarism. This radical demand for international equality, Moynihan argued, required that the United States forgo its policy of appeasement and assert a politics of opposition. Leading a minority party of liberty against the majority's demands for equality, Moynihan outlined three strategies of opposition. First, he argued that the United States should defend a liberal internationalism where policies "are limited in their undertaking, concrete in their means, representative in their mode of adoption, and definable in terms of the results." Second, he urged the United States to assert that the economic conditions of the Third World are "of their own making and no one else's," such that "no claim on anyone else arises in consequence." Finally, he recommended that American spokesmen call attention to the hypocrisies of the Third World agenda by turning "their own standards" of equality and liberty against them. Rather than "apologize for an imperfect democracy," Moynihan hoped the United States would "speak for and in the name of political and civil liberty."[2]

Moynihan's strategy of opposition drew on a growing sense among Western observers that the promises of decolonization were exhausted and had led to a series of moral and political dead ends. As chapter 3 illustrated, liberals like Isaiah Berlin, Clyde Eagleton, and Louis Henkin were already suspicious of the anticolonial reinvention of self-determination in the 1950s and 1960s. By the mid-1970s, this chorus of criticism grew louder as the trajectories of postcolonial states appeared to confirm their early skepticism. Surveying the political crises of secession, famine, and state repression, observers concluded that the right to self-determination, with its collectivist and statist claims, was now passé.[3] Critics argued that anticolonial nationalists had made self-determination entirely an external and negative principle, concerned solely with the absence of alien rule and disconnected from democratic self-government.[4] According to Rupert Emerson, by critiquing alien rule as a denial of fundamental freedoms and human rights, and yet instituting forms of government that undermined the "basic tenets of the western democratic system," anticolonial nationalists engaged in a form of bad faith.[5]

The problem was not just that opportunistic postcolonial elites had hijacked self-determination and human rights in the service of their own agenda, but also that the kinds of states decolonization had created appeared to lack the necessary sociological preconditions for self-government. Returning to a Wilsonian-era delimitation of self-determination based on "preparation for self-rule," critics argued that the universalization of self-determination had carried the principle to "a logical, but absurd extreme." The result was "a society of nations composed of two hundred or more members, half of which would be less populous than Lancaster (Pennsylvania) and some one hundred cities in the United States."[6] Dismissing the anticolonial insistence that international political and economic relations were deeply implicated in domestic politics, this critique framed questions of political and economic crisis as matters of internal capacity. With the question of capacity back on the table, unequal forms of membership in international society could once again be entertained. Echoing the debates about membership in the League of Nations, Emerson argued, "If full membership in the United Nations is to be denied to peoples whose numbers and such other attributes as may be internationally specified fall below some agreed standard, there remain a variety of other possibilities," including membership in only specialized agencies, which directly affected new states or associate membership without voting privileges.[7] This call for undoing the universal principle of sovereign equality would have wider circulation and practical effects in the aftermath of the Cold War as categories such as "failed" and "rogue" states justified unequal standing, legitimized military intervention, and allowed for the reintroduction of trusteeship.[8]

The 1970s critique of self-determination also coincided with a gradual American abandonment of the United Nations and other multilateral institutions of the postwar international order. While in 1945 the UN was a quintessentially American creation that sought to institutionalize a liberal international order, thirty years after its founding American policy makers and statesmen were confronted with an international organization that anticolonial nationalists had transformed into an arena for the politics of decolonization. After World War II, they capitalized on the openings the emerging discourse of human rights offered and captured the United Nations through their growing majority in the General Assembly. At the same time, fears about Cold War competition ensured at least a policy of restraint and appeasement from North Atlantic states. In the 1960s, as postcolonial states deployed the new right to self-determination to challenge the remnants of alien rule, and in particular the apartheid regime in South Africa, the gulf and conflict between anticolonial nationalists' refashioning of the UN as a site of "postcolonial revolution" and the United States' view of the international organization as "a forum for cooperation, collective security, and American-centered consensus" was clear.[9]

In formulating his strategy of opposition, Moynihan had hoped that the United States would recapture the UN and reassert a liberal rule-based international order. However, owing in part to the backlash against this anticolonial appropriation and the loosening of the Cold War's restraints, what gradually followed was an American defection from postwar international institutions. Rather than reclaim international institutions, American policy makers embraced "a new sovereigntism" that rejected the incorporation of international norms and advocated military intervention without international authorization.[10] This ideological orientation reached its height after September 11, 2001, as the threat of terrorism, a resurgent nationalism, and an assertive executive branch justified preemptive war; encouraged the arrogation of international conventions on war, torture, and detention; and strengthened unrepresentative and exclusionary institutions like the Security Council to advance American interests.[11]

Seen in this light, the fall of self-determination and the origins of our contemporary international order can be found in the ideological and institutional transformations that began in the 1970s. The rejection of self-determination and the growing dismissal of international institutions marked the closure of the historical and political moment that had made anticolonial worldmaking possible. These developments also set the foundations for a new era of unrestrained American imperialism, where the principle of sovereign equality was curtailed and the United States was freed from even a rhetorical commitment to a rule-bound international order. If the thirty years after the Second World War were characterized by the anticolonial quest for a domination-free international order that radicalized the meaning of sovereign equality, the three decades that followed the end of the Cold War gave rise to a striking return to and defense of a hierarchical international order.

This revival and reconstitution of an imperial world occurred as anticolonial nationalism, faced with its own internal crises and limits, could no longer mount an effective challenge. In the decade and a half after the height of decolonization in 1960, the idea of the postcolonial state as the site of a politics of citizenship that could accommodate racial, ethnic, and religious pluralism was called into question as movements from below resisted and repudiated the majoritarian, homogenizing, and exclusionary tendencies that appeared embedded in the structure of the nation-state. At the same time, anticolonial worldmaking, which began as an effort to rethink sovereignty, culminated in projects that reinforced the nation-state. Nowhere was this reversal more apparent than in the resolution of the federal debates where efforts to delegate sovereignty to a federation gave way to regional organizations that zealously guarded the sovereign rights of member states. The preoccupation with the precarious nature of postcolonial independence had inspired demanding projects of worldmaking to secure international nondomination. But as these projects faltered and nationalists faced domestic opposition and international criticism, they increasingly embraced a more defensive posture toward the state.

Owing to these political crises and the shifting coordinates of international politics, which were only magnified with the fall of the Soviet Union, the language of self-determination and the institutional form of the state appeared to no longer animate political visions within the postcolonial world. Self-determination as worldmaking and nation-building and the postcolonial state imagined as the agent of international and domestic transformation were central to building a world after empire. As the conditions that had made these commitments viable dissipated, their political purchase also declined. Emblematic of this emptying of the promise of self-determination was Michael Manley's return to the position of prime minister.[12] Having lost his 1980 reelection as Jamaica still reeled from the consequences of the debt crisis and structural adjustment, Manley assumed the office again in 1989. Converted to the neoliberalism he had resisted in the late 1970s, the erstwhile democratic socialist now insisted, "If you want a really dynamic, effective economy, the only damn thing you can do is to pursue the market logic completely. . . . That means you have to divest what was brought under state control . . . and [expose] the economy to the shock of competition, knowing full well that some of what has been built up will be lost in order to create a leaner but more enduring process of development."[13]

While Manley himself maintained that he was rethinking and not abandoning democratic socialism, the about-face was undeniable and exemplified the political closure that characterized the fall of self-determination. In a revealing correspondence with Kari Polanyi Levitt, a member of the New World Group at the University of West Indies, Manley reflected on the tragedy this closure entailed.[14] At the height of his despair, he concluded that the NIEO was "predicated on a fantasy—namely that anyone in international politics will respond to an argument built on ethics."[15] When Levitt reminded him, "The NIEO agenda was not based on 'ethics' but on the sovereign rights of developing countries over natural resources, on the need for codes of conduct for transnationals, and international measures to stabilize commodity prices," Manley changed his tune.[16] In response, he argued that the "failure to unite OPEC and other developing countries," which he called the "real tragedy," and the rise of Ronald Reagan and Margaret Thatcher, who "buried" the Third World's demands for equality, had led to the collapse of the NIEO.[17] But if this second assessment captured the contingent political conditions that contributed to the NIEO's displacement, it did not give Manley any hope that anticolonial worldmaking might be resuscitated.

Like the Manley of the 1990s, we live in the shadow of self-determination's fall. The vision of a postimperial world order that gave rise to three decades of anticolonial worldmaking appears far removed from our political present. Looking back from our vantage point and with a clear view of the forces arrayed against this project, the fall of self-determination might appear inevitable. We might even believe, as Manley briefly did, that those projects were fantastical and unrealistic. But to come to this set of conclusions is to evade reckoning with the ways that we inhabit as our present the promises and ruins of anticolonial worldmaking. The incomplete decolonization that culminated in a world of unequal nation-states, the regional organizations that emerged from the dream of federation, and the visions of global justice that stand in the place of the NIEO's welfare world indicate the scale of both expectations and disappointments that characterized anticolonial worldmaking. Examining this present, it would be a mistake to collapse the partiality and eventual decline of a set of languages and strategies for making a world after empire with the demise of the moral and political vision that looked forward to an egalitarian and domination-free world.

Emerging from the imperial integration and differentiation that has structured the modern world, this vision of an anti-imperial world had different articulations before the rise of self-determination and might yet be remade in new languages and modes. Part of the task of this book has been to show that even instances that appeared as moments of closure—first the decline of interwar internationalisms and the consolidation of a system of nation-states, and later the political and economic limits of the postcolonial state—were occasion for reformulating the contours of an anti-imperial future and enacting new strategies to realize this vision. On this view, the fall of self-determination marks not only a dead end but also a staging ground for reimaging that future. In the Black Atlantic world, from which the worldmakers of this book emerged, intimations of a new language are afoot in the Movement for Black Lives, the Caribbean demand for reparations for slavery and genocide, and South African calls for a social and economic decolonization. Like the worldmakers of decolonization, these political formations have returned to the task of rethinking our imperial past and present in the service of imagining an anti-imperial future.

Introduction: Worldmaking after Empire

1. Kwame Nkrumah, "Speech at the Independence of Ghana, March 6, 1957," in *I Speak of Freedom: A Statement of African Ideology* (New York: Frederick A. Praeger, 1961), 107.

2. Kevin Gaines, *American Africans in Ghana: Black Expatriates and the Civil Rights Era* (Chapel Hill: University of North Carolina Press, 2006), 77–82.

3. W.E.B. Du Bois, "A Future for Pan-Africa: Freedom, Peace, Socialism," in *The World and Africa and Color and Democracy*, ed. Henry Louis Gates Jr. (New York: Oxford University Press, 2007), 187–90.

4. Michel-Rolph Trouillot, "North Atlantic Universals: Analytic Fictions, 1492–1945," *South Atlantic Quarterly* 101 (Fall 2002): 839–58. Lisa Lowe, *The Intimacies of Four Continents* (Durham, NC: Duke University Press, 2015).

5. Hannah Arendt, *The Origins of Totalitarianism* (1951; New York: Harcourt Books, 1994), 124–25. Although Arendt emphasizes the unprecedented scale of imperialism in the late nineteenth century, historians of political thought have recently illustrated the ways that beginning in the early modern period, Europe's imperial encounters played a constitutive role in the ways canonical political thinkers imagined domestic political possibilities. For this argument, see Karuna Mantena, "Review Essay: Fragile Universals and the Politics of Empire," *Polity* 38 (October 2006): 543–55, 544–45. See, for example, Richard Tuck, *The Rights of War and Peace: Political Thought and the International Order from Grotius to Kant* (Oxford: Oxford University Press, 1999); Sankar Muthu, *Enlightenment against Empire* (Princeton, NJ: Princeton University Press, 2003); Jennifer Pitts, *A Turn to Empire: The Rise of Imperial Liberalism in Britain and France* (Princeton, NJ: Princeton University Press, 2005); Isaac Nakhimovsky, *The Closed Commercial State: Perpetual Peace and Commercial Society from Rousseau to Fichte* (Princeton, NJ: Princeton University Press, 2011); and Richard Whatmore, *Against War and Empire: Geneva, Britain, and France in the Eighteenth Century* (New Haven, CT: Yale University Press, 2012).

6. On the relationship between democratization and liberal imperialism, see Pitts, *Turn to Empire*, 163–240, 247–54. For an exploration of the ways that Victorian thinkers reconsidered the relationship between national and imperial politics and envisioned a range of international institutions to manage and harmonize this tension, see Duncan Bell, *Reordering the World: Essays on Liberalism and Empire* (Princeton, NJ: Princeton University Press, 2016).

7. Mark Mazower, *Governing the World: The History of an Idea, 1815 to the Present* (New York: Penguin, 2012), 55–64.

8. Karl Marx and Friedrich Engels, *The Communist Manifesto* (1848; London: Penguin Classics, 2002), 220–24; Karl Marx, *Capital*, vol. 1, *The Critique of Political Economy* (1867; London: Penguin Classics, 1976), 914–40.

9. Marx, *Capital*, 1: 915.

10. Marx and Engels, *Communist Manifesto*, 915.

11. Manu Goswami, *Producing India: From Colonial Economy to National Space* (Chicago: University of Chicago Press, 2004), 26–27.

12. Manu Goswami, "Imaginary Futures and Colonial Internationalisms," *American Historical Review* 117 (December 2012): 1461–85.

13. Michelle Ann Stephens, *Black Empire: The Masculine Global Imaginary of Caribbean Intellectuals in the United States, 1914–1962* (Durham, NC: Duke University Press, 2005); Holger Weiss, *Framing a Radical African Atlantic: African American Agency, West African Intellectuals and the International Trade Union Committee of Negro Workers* (Leiden: Brill, 2014).

14. Chartering the processes by which this triumph was consolidated remains an ongoing project. On the contingent and contested processes by which the triumph of the nation-state was consolidated, see Frederick Cooper, *Decolonization and African Society: The Labor Question in French and British Africa* (New York: Cambridge University Press, 1996); Frederick Cooper, "Labor, Politics and the End of Empire in French Africa," in *Colonialism in Question: Theory, Knowledge, History* (Berkeley: University of California Press, 2005), 204–30; Frederick Cooper, *Citizenship between Empire and Nation: Remaking France and French Africa, 1945–1960* (Princeton, NJ: Princeton University Press, 2014); Gary Wilder, *Freedom Time: Negritude, Decolonization, and the Future of the World* (Durham, NC: Duke University Press, 2015); Karuna Mantena, "Popular Sovereignty and Anti-colonialism," in *Popular Sovereignty in Historical Perspective*, ed. Richard Bourke and Quentin Skinner (New York: Cambridge University Press, 2016), 297–319.

15. Brent Hayes Edwards, *The Practice of Diaspora: Literature, Translation, and the Rise of Black Internationalism* (Cambridge, MA: Harvard University Press, 2003).

16. Ibid., 284. As Edwards puts it, at the end of the war, "the central interwar [Francophone] figures are almost all deceased, imprisoned, or no longer in France." For instance, by 1945, Césaire and Nardal were back in Martinique, while Senghor returned to Senegal after serving a sentence in a Nazi prison camp.

17. Wilder, *Freedom Time*.

18. For popular histories of these broader formations, see Vijay Prashad, *The Darker Nations: A People's History of the Third World* (New York: New Press, 2007); and Vijay Prashad, *The Poorer Nations: A Possible History of the Global South* (New York: Verso, 2012).

19. W.E.B. Du Bois, "To the Nations of the World," in *W.E.B. Du Bois: A Reader*, ed. David Levering Lewis (New York: Henry Holt, 1995), 639.

20. Eric Williams, *Inward Hunger: The Education of a Prime Minister* (London: Andre Deutsch, 1969), 54. For an account of the idea of generations as a salient concept in the recovery and reconstruction of intellectual history with specific attention to the Anglophone Caribbean, see David Scott, "The Temporality of Generations: Dialogue, Tradition, Criticism," *New Literary History* 45 (Spring 2014): 157–81.

21. Robert Vitalis, *White World Order, Black Power Politics: The Birth of American International Relations* (Ithaca, NY: Cornell University Press, 2015), 11–12. See, for example, Alain Locke, *Race Contacts and Interracial Relations: Lectures on the The-*

ory and Practice of Race, ed. Jeffrey Stewart (Washington, DC: Howard University Press, 1992); Ralph Bunche, *A Worldview of Race* (Washington, DC: Associates in Negro Folk Education, 1936); Rayford Logan, *The African Mandates in World Politics* (Washington, DC: Public Affairs, 1948); Merze Tate, "The War Aims of World War I and II and Their Relation to the Darker Peoples of the World," *Journal of Negro Education* 12 (Summer 1943): 521–32.

22. Jason C. Parker, " 'Made-in-America Revolutions'? The 'Black University' and the American Role in the Decolonization of the Black Atlantic," *Journal of American History 96* (December 2009): 727–50.

23. Nnamdi Azikiwe, *My Odyssey: An Autobiography* (London: C. Hurst, 1970), 123, 145–48, 156–57.

24. Nnamdi Azikiwe, *Liberia in World Politics* (London: Arthur H. Stockwell, 1934). Just three years later, he offered a broader account of imperialism in Africa. See Nnamdi Azikiwe, *Renascent Africa* (1938; London: Frank, Cass, 1968).

25. Kwame Nkrumah, *Ghana: The Autobiography of Kwame Nkrumah* (London: Thomas Nelson and Sons, 1957), 27.

26. George Padmore, *How Britain Rules Africa* (London: Wishart Books, 1936).

27. George Padmore, *Africa and World Peace* (1937; London: Frank Cass, 1972).

28. Marika Sherwood, *Kwame Nkrumah: The Years Abroad 1935–1947* (Legon, Ghana: Freedom, 1996).

29. Nkrumah, *Ghana*, 44; Sherwood, *Kwame Nkrumah*, 76–81.

30. Kwame Nkrumah, *Towards Colonial Freedom: Africa in the Struggle against World Imperialism* (1947; London: Heinemann, 1962); George Padmore, *The Gold Coast Revolution: The Struggle of an African People from Slavery to Freedom* (London: D. Dobson, 1953); George Padmore, *Pan-Africanism or Communism? The Coming Struggle for Africa* (1956; Garden City, NY: Doubleday, 1971).

31. On Manley's generation as the second in a twentieth-century tradition of anticolonial political thought, see David Scott, *Refashioning Futures: Criticism after Postcoloniality* (Princeton, NJ: Princeton University Press, 1999), 222.

32. Thomas Molony, *Nyerere: The Early Years* (Suffolk: James Currey, 2014), 147–61; Priya Lal, *African Socialism in Postcolonial Tanzania: Between the Village and the World* (New York: Cambridge University Press, 2015), 49; Darrell E. Levi, *Michael Manley: The Making of a Leader* (London: Andre Deutsch, 1989), 65.

Chapter One: A Political Theory of Decolonization

1. United Nations General Assembly Resolution 1514 (XV), "Declaration on the Granting of Independence to Colonial Countries and Peoples," A/RES/1514/XV, December 14, 1960, http://wpik.org/Src/unga1514.html, accessed June 13, 2012.

2. Yassin El-Ayouty, *The United Nations and Decolonization: The Role of Afro-Asia* (The Hague: Martinus Nijhoff, 1971).

3. Rupert Emerson, *From Empire to Nation: The Rise to Self-Assertion of Asian and African Peoples* (Cambridge, MA: Harvard University Press, 1960); John Plamenatz, *On Alien Rule and Self-Government* (London: Longman's, 1960).

4. Plamenatz, *On Alien Rule*, 16.

5. Emerson, *From Empire to Nation*, 16–17.

6. Michael W. Doyle, *Empires* (Ithaca, NY: Cornell University Press, 1986), 12.

7. Anna Stilz, "Decolonization and Self-Determination," *Social Philosophy and Policy* 32 (October 2015): 1–24, 16; Lea Ypi, "What's Wrong with Colonialism," *Philosophy and Public Affairs* 41 (Spring 2013): 158–91, 158.

8. Hedley Bull and Adam Watson, eds., *The Expansion of International Society* (Oxford: Clarendon, 1984).

9. Doyle, *Empires*, 20.

10. Bull and Watson, eds., *Expansion of International Society*, 1–9. See also Adam Watson, *The Evolution of International Society: A Comparative Historical Analysis* (New York: Routledge, 1992).

11. Contemporary historians and political theorists reiterate this account of the global diffusion of the nation-state. See, for example, Jürgen Habermas, "The European Nation-State: On the Past and Future of Sovereignty and Citizenship," in *The Inclusion of the Other: Studies in Political Theory*, ed. Ciaran Cronin and Pablo De Greiff (Cambridge, MA: MIT Press, 1998), 105–6; David Armitage, *The Declaration of Independence: A Global History* (Cambridge, MA: Harvard University Press, 2007), 103–4; Jean Cohen, *Globalization and Sovereignty: Rethinking Legality, Legitimacy, and Constitutionalism* (New York: Cambridge University Press, 2012), 80.

12. Harold Macmillan, "Prime Minister's Speech at the Joint Meeting of Both Houses of Parliament in Cape Town," February 3, 1960, http://www.africanrhetoric .org/pdf/J%20%20%20Macmillan%20-%20%20the%20wind%20of%20change .pdf, accessed June 15, 2016.

13. Stuart Ward, "The European Provenance of Decolonization," *Past and Present* 230 (February 2016): 227–60.

14. Ibid., 229, 258.

15. Kwame Nkrumah, "Address to the Nationalists Conference," in *12 Key Speeches of Kwame Nkrumah* (London: African Publication Society, 1970), 6.

16. Kwame Nkrumah, "Undated Speech," in *Axioms of Kwame Nkrumah* (London: Thomas Nelson and Sons, 1967), 55.

17. Kwame Nkrumah, *Africa Must Unite* (New York: International, 1963), 50.

18. For an account of the politics of postcolonial citizenship in Nkrumah's Ghana, see Jeffrey Ahlman, *Living with Nkrumahism: Nation, State, and Pan-Africanism in Ghana* (Athens: Ohio University Press, 2017).

19. See, for example, David Lake, *Hierarchy in International Relations* (Ithaca, NY: Cornell University Press, 2009).

20. Antony Anghie, *Imperialism, Sovereignty and the Making of International Law* (New York: Cambridge University Press, 2005), 2–3.

21. Ibid., 22.

22. Richard Tuck, "Alliances with Infidels in the European Imperial Expansion," in *Empire and Modern Political Thought*, ed. Sankar Muthu (New York: Cambridge University Press, 2012), 76.

23. Ibid., 83.

24. Anghie, *Imperialism*, 70.

25. L.F.L. Oppenheim quoted in ibid., 81–82.

26. Martti Koskenniemi, *The Gentle Civilizer of Nations: The Rise and Fall of International Law, 1870–1960* (New York: Cambridge University Press, 2001), 127–31.

27. Siba N'Zatioula Grovogui, *Sovereigns, Quasi-sovereigns, and Africans: Race and Self-Determination in International Law* (Minneapolis: University of Minnesota Press, 1996), 77.

28. Anghie, *Imperialism*, 105.

29. Ibid., 4.

30. Du Bois, "To the Nations of the World," 639; W.E.B. Du Bois, *The Souls of Black Folk*, ed. David W. Blight and Robert Gooding-Williams (1903; Boston: Bedford Books, 1997), 45.

31. Thomas Holt, *The Problem of Freedom: Race, Labor, and Politics in Jamaica and Britain, 1832–1938* (Baltimore: Johns Hopkins University Press, 1991); Saidiya V. Hartman, *Scenes of Subjection: Terror, Slavery, and Self-Making in Nineteenth-Century America* (New York: Oxford University Press, 1997); Frederick Cooper et al., eds., *Beyond Slavery: Explorations of Race, Labor, and Citizenship in Postemancipation Societies* (Chapel Hill: University of North Carolina Press, 2000); Catherine Hall, *Civilising Subjects: Metropole and Colony in the English Imagination, 1830–1867* (Chicago: University of Chicago Press, 2002).

32. Karuna Mantena, *Alibis of Empire: Henry Maine and the Ends of Liberal Imperialism* (Princeton, NJ: Princeton University Press, 2010), 30–39.

33. Marilyn Lake and Henry Reynolds, *Drawing the Global Colour Line: White Men's Countries and the International Challenge of Racial Equality* (New York: Cambridge University Press, 2008), 67.

34. Andrew Zimmerman, *Alabama in Africa: Booker T. Washington, the German Empire, and the Globalization of the New South* (Princeton, NJ: Princeton University Press, 2010).

35. Duncan Bell, *The Idea of Greater Britain: Empire and the Future of World Order, 1860–1900* (Princeton, NJ: Princeton University Press, 2007); Duncan Bell, "Beyond the Sovereign State: Isopolitan Citizenship, Race and Anglo-American Union," *Political Studies* 62 (June 2014): 418–34; Lake and Reynolds, *Drawing the Global Colour Line*, 49–94; Bell, *Reordering the World*.

36. W.E.B. Du Bois, "The Souls of White Folk," in *Darkwater: Voices within the Veil* (1920; Mineola, NY: Dover, 1999), 17.

37. Vitalis, *White World Order, Black Power Politics*. For instance, while China was historically imagined as an ancient civilization, by the late nineteenth century it was reduced to a "Negro state of secondary importance" with some international lawyers recommending "international administration on the model of the Congo" for China. Teemu Ruskola, "Raping Like a State," *UCLA Law Review* 57 (June 2010): 1477–536, 1523–25.

38. Michael Adas, "Contested Hegemony: The Great War and the Afro-Asian Assault on the Civilizing Mission Ideology," *Journal of World History* 15 (March 2004): 31–63.

39. On the Japanese demand for racial equality, see Lake and Reynolds, *Drawing the Global Colour Line*, 284–309.

40. A. J. Balfour quoted in ibid., 11.

41. On Haiti, see James Weldon Johnson, *Self-Determining Haiti* (New York: Nation, 1920). On Liberia, see Azikiwe, *Liberia in World Politics*. As we shall see in chapter 2, the Italian invasion of Ethiopia spurred anticolonial protest across the

Black Atlantic world. It would be analyzed and taken up in a number of texts, including Padmore, *Africa and World Peace*; and Nkrumah, *Towards Colonial Freedom*.

42. Nkrumah, *Towards Colonial Freedom*, xv.

43. Ibid.

44. Kwame Nkrumah, *Neocolonialism: The Last Stage of Imperialism* (New York: International, 1965), 33.

45. Ibid., xv.

46. On the centrality of external nondomination to republican political thought, see Quentin Skinner, *Liberty before Liberalism* (New York: Cambridge University Press, 1998), 49–50; Quentin Skinner, "On the Slogans of Republican Political Theory," *European Journal of Political Theory* 9 (January 2010): 95–102, 100–101.

47. Eric Williams, "The Economic Development of the Caribbean Up to the Present," in *The Economic Future of the Caribbean*, ed. Franklin Frazier and Eric Williams (Washington, DC: Howard University Press, 1944), 19–25; Michael Manley, "Overcoming Insularity in Jamaica," *Foreign Affairs* 49 (October 1970): 100–110.

48. Michael Manley, *The Poverty of Nations: Reflections on Underdevelopment and the World Economy* (London: Pluto, 1991), 32–36.

49. For examples, see Charles Carnegie, "Garvey and the Black Transnation," *Small Axe* 5 (March 1999): 48–71; Edwards, *Practice of Diaspora*; Stephens, *Black Empire*; Goswami, "Imaginary Futures and Colonial Internationalisms."

50. As historians and political scientists have noted, to call the modern international order "Westphalian," a reference to the 1648 Treaty of Westphalia, is a misnomer. In its own time, the treaty and its aftermath were not experienced as a radical rupture in domestic and international politics. Moreover, from the seventeenth through the nineteenth century, the Treaty of Westphalia carried many meanings, including interpretations that saw the treaty as limiting sovereignty—a project that is now associated with the "post-Westphalian" moment. The idea of an international order with sovereignty, equality, and nonintervention as its structuring principles is better credited to Emer De Vattel. Its association with Westphalia is a relatively recent development—one that can be traced to developments in the field of international relations after World War II. During this period, what was once a historical event open to a diverse set of meanings and implications for the international order was transformed into a construct against which contemporary developments of globalization and supranational institutions are measured and evaluated. Stephen Krasner, "Rethinking the Sovereign State Model," in *Empires, Systems and States: Great Transformations in International Politics*, ed. Michael Cox et al. (New York: Cambridge University Press, 2001), 17–43; Benno Teschke, *The Myth of 1648: Class, Geopolitics, and the Making of Modern International Relations* (New York: Verso, 2003); Sebastian Schmidt, "To Order the Minds of Scholars: The Discourse of the Peace of Westphalia in International Relations Literature," *International Studies Quarterly* 55 (September 2011): 601–23; Jennifer Pitts, "Intervention and Sovereign Inequality: The Legacy of Vattel," in *Just and Unjust Military Intervention: European Thinkers from Vitoria to Mill*, ed. Stefano Recchia and Jennifer M. Welsh (New York: Cambridge University Press, 2013), 134–35.

51. Emerson, *From Empire to Nation*, 289; Plamenatz, *On Alien Rule*, 28.

52. The language "derivative discourse" and critique of this account is drawn from Partha Chatterjee, *Nationalist Thought and the Colonial World: A Derivative Discourse?* (Minneapolis: University of Minnesota Press, 1986).

53. Partha Chatterjee, *Lineages of Political Society: Studies in Postcolonial Democracy* (New York: Columbia University Press, 2011), 8–11.

54. Elie Kedourie, *Nationalism* (London: Hutchinson, 1960).

55. Ibid., 112.

56. Ibid.

57. Ibid., 109.

58. Chatterjee, *Nationalist Thought and the Colonial World*, 3–4; Margaret Canovan, *Nationhood and Political Theory* (North Hampton, MA: Edward Elgar, 1996), 2.

59. Habermas, "European Nation-State," 115.

60. Canovan, *Nationhood and Political Theory*, 139–40; Joan Cocks, *Passion and Paradox: Intellectuals Confront the National Question* (Princeton, NJ: Princeton University Press, 2002), 8, 48.

61. Cocks, *Passion and Paradox*, 9.

62. Chatterjee, *Nationalist Thought and the Colonial World*, 1–30.

63. Ibid., 10, 30.

64. Ibid., 30.

65. Scholars of the postcolonial state have already offered an extensive exploration of the crisis and decline of postcolonial nation-building, pointing to the ways in which anticolonial nationalism failed to attend to internal pluralism and sanctioned authoritarianism in the name of the nation. See, for example, Chatterjee, *Nationalist Thought and the Colonial World*; Partha Chatterjee, *The Nation and Its Fragments: Colonial and Postcolonial Histories* (Princeton, NJ: Princeton University Press, 1993); Goswami, *Producing India*; Mahmood Mamdani, *Citizen and Subject: Contemporary Africa and the Legacy of Late Colonialism* (Princeton, NJ: Princeton University Press, 1996); Mahmood Mamdani, *When Victims Become Killers: Colonialism, Nativism, and the Genocide in Rwanda* (Princeton, NJ: Princeton University Press, 2002).

66. For an account of this trajectory with specific reference to Algerian decolonization, see Jeffrey James Byrne, *Mecca of Revolution: Algeria, Decolonization and the Third World Order* (New York: Oxford University Press, 2016).

67. For instance, in the reintroduction of preventive detention, a colonial-era measure, Julius Nyerere acknowledged that "few things are more dangerous to the freedom of a society than" restricting the liberty of citizens whom the state had not proven guilty beyond reasonable doubt. Yet he justified the practice as necessary in a context where "a handful of individuals can still put our nation into jeopardy" because it has "neither the long tradition of nationhood, nor the strong physical means of national security." Meredith Terretta, "From Below and to the Left? Human Rights and Liberation Politics in Africa's Postcolonial Age," *Journal of World History* 24 (June 2013): 389–416, 404–5.

68. Martin Wight, "Why Is There No International Political Theory?," in *Diplomatic Investigations*, ed. Herbert Butterfield and Martin Wight (London: George Allen and Unwin, 1966), 21; Kenneth Waltz, *Theory of International Politics* (London: Addison-Wesley, 1979), 113.

69. Charles Beitz, "Justice and International Relations," *Philosophy and Public Affairs* 4 (Summer 1975): 360–89, 373.

70. For the phrase "fortress-like conception of state sovereignty," see Gregory Fox, "The Right to Political Participation in International Law," *Yale Journal of International Law* 17 (Summer 1992): 539–607, 545. On the legal and institutional constraints that limit state sovereignty, see David Held, "Democratic Accountability and Political Effectiveness from a Cosmopolitan Perspective," *Government and Opposition* 39 (March 2004): 364–91; Seyla Benhabib, "Twilight of Sovereignty or the Emergence of Cosmopolitan Norms? Rethinking Citizenship in Volatile Times," *Citizenship Studies* 11, no. 1 (2007): 19–36; and Jürgen Habermas, "The Constitutionalization of International Law and the Legitimation Problems of a Constitution for World Society," *Constellations* 15 (December 2008): 444–55.

71. Jürgen Habermas, "Does the Constitutionalization of International Law Still Have a Chance?," in *The Divided West*, ed. and trans. Ciaran Cronin (Cambridge: Polity, 2006), 124.

72. Ibid., 135–39; Habermas, "Constitutionalization of International Law," 445–48. For accounts that stress the constitutional character of existing international organizations, see Bardo Fassbender, "'We the Peoples of the United Nations': Constituent Power and Constitutional Form in International Law," in *The Paradox of Constitutionalism: Constituent Power and Constitutional Form*, ed. Martin Loughlin and Neil Walker (Oxford: Oxford University Press, 2008); Bardo Fassbender, *The United Nations Charter as the Constitution of the International Community* (Boston: Martinus Nijhoff, 2009). For a critique of this turn to constitutionalization and an alternative pluralist approach, see Cohen, *Globalization and Sovereignty*. More recently, Türküler Isiksel has traced the specific form that constitutionalism takes in international settings. Türküler Isiksel, *Europe's Functional Constitution: A Theory of Constitutionalism beyond the State* (New York: Oxford University Press, 2016).

73. Cohen, *Globalization and Sovereignty*, 80.

74. Ibid., 1–2.

75. Trouillot, "North Atlantic Universals," 839.

76. James Tully, "On Law, Democracy and Imperialism," in *Public Philosophy in a New Key*, vol. 2, *Imperialism and Civic Freedom* (New York: Cambridge University Press, 2008), 133.

77. Grovogui, *Sovereigns, Quasi-sovereigns, and Africans*, 179–88. Anghie, *Imperialism*, 239–44.

78. For a defense of conditional or limited membership, see Robert Jackson, *Quasi-states: Sovereignty, International Relations and the Third World* (Cambridge: Cambridge University Press, 1990); Anne-Marie Slaughter, "Security, Solidarity, and Sovereignty: The Grand Themes of UN Reform," *American Journal of International Law* 99 (July 2005): 619–31; Robert Keohane, "Political Authority after Intervention: Gradations in Sovereignty," in *Humanitarian Intervention: Ethical, Legal and Political Dilemmas*, ed. J. L. Holzgrefe and Robert O. Keohane (New York: Cambridge University Press, 2003). For a critical account of the new modes of unequal membership, see Gerry Simpson, *Great Powers and Outlaw States: Unequal Sovereigns in the International Legal Order* (Cambridge: Cambridge University Press, 2004); Koskenniemi, *Gentle Civilizer of Nations*, 480–509; Tully, "On Law, Democracy and Imperialism," 136.

79. Martti Koskenniemi, "The Police in the Temple Order, Justice and the UN: A Dialectical View," *European Journal of International Law* 6, no. 1 (1995): 325–48; Anne Orford, *International Authority and the Responsibility to Protect* (Cambridge: Cambridge University Press, 2011).

80. I adapt the language of "critical and diagnostic" as well as "normative and uto-pian" from Seyla Benhabib's account of the two dimensions of critical theory, which she calls "explanatory-diagnostic" and "anticipatory-utopian." See Seyla Benhabib, *Critique, Norm, Utopia: A Study of the Foundations of Critical Theory* (New York: Columbia University Press, 1986), 142.

81. For example, developing countries have challenged the intellectual property rights regime agreed to under the auspices of the World Trade Organization by argu-ing that the protections offered to pharmaceutical companies prevented states from protecting the right to health. Cristina Lafont, "Sovereignty, Human Rights and the Responsibility to Protect," *Constellations* 22 (March 2015): 68–78, 72–73; Cristina Lafont, "Sovereignty and the International Protection of Human Rights," *Journal of Political Philosophy* 24 (December 2016): 427–45, 434–36. Moreover, as recent work on cosmopolitanism from below illustrates, human rights can be the basis for col-lective political projects. For example, see Ayten Gündoğdu, *Rightlessness in the Age of Rights: Hannah Arendt and the Contemporary Struggles of Migrants* (New York: Oxford University Press, 2015).

82. Cohen, *Globalization and Sovereignty*, 24.

83. John Rawls, *The Law of Peoples with the Idea of Public Reason Revisited* (Cambridge, MA: Harvard University Press, 2001), 37.

84. Alexander Wendt and Michael Barnett, "Dependent State Formation and Third World Militarization," *Review of International Studies* 19 (October 1993): 321–47.

85. Pitts, "Intervention and Sovereign Equality," 138.

86. Philip Pettit, "A Republican Law of Peoples," *European Journal of Political Theory* 9 (January 2010): 70–94, 77–78; Philip Pettit, "The Globalized Republican Ideal," *Global Justice: Theory Practice Rhetoric* 9, no. 1 (2016): 47–68, 56–57.

87. Pettit, "Globalized Republican Ideal," 61.

88. Ibid., 63–64. For a similar critique and effort to expand the reach of interna-tional nondomination, see Dorothea Gädeke, "The Domination of States: Towards an Inclusive Republican Law of Peoples," *Global Justice: Theory Practice Rhetoric* 9, no. 1 (2016): 1–27.

89. Catherine Lu, "Colonialism as Structural Injustice: Historical Responsibility and Contemporary Redress," *Journal of Political Philosophy* 19 (September 2011): 261–81, 279.

Chapter Two: The Counterrevolutionary Moment

1. V. I. Lenin, "The Tasks of the Proletariat in the Present Revolution," in *Collected Works of V. I. Lenin (CWL)*, trans. and ed. Bernard Isaacs (Moscow: Progress, 1964), 24: 19–33, 21. Note that the April 4 date of Lenin's theses is based on the old Russian calendar.

2. Second All Russian Congress of Soviets of Workers' and Soldiers' Deputies, "Decree on Peace," in *CWL*, trans. Yuri Sdobnikov and George Hanna, ed. George Hanna, 26: 249–53, 250.

3. V. I. Lenin, "The Right of Nations to Self-Determination," in *CWL*, trans. Bernard Isaacs and Joe Fineberg, ed. Julius Katzer, 20: 393–454, 397.

4. Ibid., 399–400.

5. Ibid., 406.

6. V. I. Lenin, "The Socialist Revolution and the Right to Self-Determination," in *CWL*, trans. Yuri Sdobnikov, ed. George Hanna, 22: 143–56, 151–52.

7. V. I. Lenin, "The Revolutionary Proletariat and the Right of Nations to Self-Determination," in *CWL*, trans. and ed. Julius Katzer, 21: 407–14, 407.

8. Adam Tooze, *The Deluge: The Great War, America and the Remaking of the Global Order, 1916–1931* (New York: Viking, 2014), 115.

9. V. I. Lenin, "Declaration of the Rights of the Working and Exploited People," in *CWL*, 26: 423–26, 424.

10. Arno J. Mayer, *Political Origins of the New Diplomacy, 1917–1918* (New Haven, CT: Yale University Press, 1959), 31.

11. Secretary of State to President Wilson, January 2, 1918, *Papers Relating to the Foreign Relations of the United States: The Lansing Papers; 1914–1920*, vol. 2 (Washington, DC: Government Printing Office, 1940), 347–48.

12. Lenin, "Declaration of the Rights of Working and Exploited People," 424.

13. W.E.B. Du Bois, "The African Roots of War," *Atlantic Monthly* (May 1915): 707–14, 708, 711.

14. Adas, "Contested Hegemony."

15. Erez Manela, *The Wilsonian Moment: Self-Determination and the International Origins of Anticolonial Nationalism* (New York: Oxford University Press, 2007).

16. Ibid., 39.

17. Woodrow Wilson, "Address to a Joint Session of Congress, February 11, 1918," in *The Papers of Woodrow Wilson* (*PWW*), ed. Arthur S. Link (Princeton, NJ: Princeton University Press, 1984) 46: 318–24, 321.

18. For accounts that locate self-determination as a central principle in Wilson's rhetoric and postwar plans, see Arthur S. Link, *Woodrow Wilson: Revolution, War and Peace* (Arlington Heights, IL: AHM, 1979); and Thomas Knock, *To End All Wars: Woodrow Wilson and the Quest for a New World Order* (New York: Oxford University Press, 1992). For accounts that decenter self-determination, see Trygve Throntveit, "The Fable of the Fourteen Points: Woodrow Wilson and National Self-Determination," *Diplomatic History* 35 (June 2011): 445–81; and Tooze, *Deluge*, 17–18, 119.

19. For instance, Erez Manela highlights Wilson's late turn to self-determination and insists on its ambiguity in his political thought. Yet he characterizes the rise of self-determination and its later appropriation by nationalists in the colonized world as the "Wilsonian moment." In this moment between 1918 and 1919, Wilson had become associated with a peace plan that required the founding of an international organization, rejected annexation, insisted on the equality of nations, and was committed to the consent of the governed. Manela, *Wilsonian Moment*, 16.

20. For a recent comprehensive study of the mandates system, see Susan Pedersen, *The Guardians: The League of Nations and the Crisis of Empire* (New York: Oxford University Press, 2015).

21. "The Covenant of the League of Nations," in *The Avalon Project: Documents in Law, History and Diplomacy*, http://avalon.law.yale.edu/20th_century/leagcov.asp, accessed February 19, 2016.

22. Manela, *Wilsonian Moment*, 60–61.

23. Stephen Skowronek, "The Reassociation of Ideas and Purposes: Racism, Liberalism, and the American Political Tradition," *American Political Science Review* 100 (August 2006): 385–401.

24. Carl Schmitt, *The* Nomos *of the Earth in the International Law of the* Jus Publicum Europaeum, trans. G. L. Ulmen (1950; New York: Telos, 2003), 214–42.

25. Hedley Bull, "A Universal International Society," in *The Expansion of International Society*, ed. Hedley Bull and Adam Watson, 123.

26. "Covenant of the League of Nations."

27. Michele L. Louro, "At Home in the World: Jawaharlal Nehru and Global Anti-imperialism" (PhD diss., Temple University, 2011), 16–17.

28. League of Nations Second Assembly, "Report of the First Committee on the Position of Small States," September 21, 1921, League of Nations Admissions, League of Nations Documents (hereafter LofN Doc), Box 1453, 1547/1547.

29. Anghie, *Imperialism*, 116.

30. Robert Lansing, *The Peace Negotiations: A Personal Narrative* (Boston: Houghton Mifflin, 1921), 97.

31. Theodore Hazeltine Price to Woodrow Wilson, May 9, 1917, in *PWW*, 42: 255, 255; Jan Smuts, "Speech to the Legislative Council of the Transvaal Colony," April 3, 1909, *Selections from the Smuts Papers* (*SSP*) (London: Cambridge University Press, 1966), 2: 551–62, 556.

32. Woodrow Wilson, "Abraham Lincoln: A Man of the People," in *PWW*, 19: 33–47, 33.

33. Woodrow Wilson, "The Reconstruction of the Southern States," in *Woodrow Wilson: Essential Writings and Speeches of the Scholar-President*, ed. Mario Dinunzio (New York: New York University Press, 2006), 207.

34. Ibid., 206.

35. Ibid., 209.

36. Woodrow Wilson, *History of the American People*, vol. 5 (New York: Harper and Brothers, 1902), 300.

37. Woodrow Wilson, "Introduction," in *Conciliation with the Colonies: The Speech by Edmund Burke*, ed. Robert Anderson (Boston: Houghton Mifflin, 1896), xviii.

38. Woodrow Wilson, "Character of Democracy in the United States," in *An Old Master and Other Political Writings* (New York: Charles Scribner's Sons, 1893), 114.

39. Ibid., 104.

40. Woodrow Wilson, "A Calendar of Great Americans," *PWW*, 8: 368–81, 374. According to Wilson, "Jefferson was not a thorough American because of the strain of French philosophy that permeated and weakened all his thought" (373).

41. Wilson, "Character," 117.

42. Ibid., 118.

43. Ibid., 295.

44. J. R. Seeley, *The Expansion of England* (1883; Cambridge: Cambridge University Press, 2010), 8.

45. Wilson, "Democracy and Efficiency," in *PWW*, 12: 6–21, 18.

46. Woodrow Wilson, "Remarks to the Associated Press in New York," in *PWW*, 33: 37–41, 39.

47. On the passive voice as a recurring strategy of liberal imperialism, see Jeanne Morefield, *Empires without Imperialism: Anglo-American Decline and the Politics of Deflection* (New York: Oxford University Press, 2014), 17.

48. Wilson, "Remarks to Associated Press in New York," 39.

49. Woodrow Wilson, "The Ideals of America," in *PWW*, 12: 208–27, 223.

50. Ibid.

51. Wilson, "Democracy and Efficiency," 12, 14.

52. Wilson, "Ideals of America," 221.

53. Wilson, "Democracy and Efficiency," 16.

54. Wilson, "Ideals of America," 225.

55. Edmund Burke quoted in ibid., 211. For a history of English character, see Peter Mandler, *The English National Character: The History of an Idea from Edmund Burke to Tony Blair* (New Haven, CT: Yale University Press, 2006).

56. Wilson, "Democracy and Efficiency," 17.

57. Jan Smuts, "Speech to the De Beers Consolidated Political and Debating Association in Kimberley," October 30, 1895, in *SSP*, 1: 80–100, 93.

58. Ibid.

59. Ibid., 94.

60. Ibid., 95.

61. Ibid.

62. Ibid., 93, 95. Changes to the Cape Colony franchise in 1892 raised the salary and property requirements for exercising the vote. Though not explicitly racial, it disenfranchised most Africans. This was followed in 1894 with the Glen Grey Act, which instituted individual (rather than communal) land tenure as well as a labor tax directed at natives, particularly the Xhosa. Crucially, land ownership through this act could not be used to fulfill the property qualifications for the parliamentary franchise.

63. Ibid., 94–95.

64. Jan Smuts, "Native Policy in Africa," in *Africa and Some World Problems* (Oxford: Clarendon, 1930), 77.

65. Smuts, "Speech to the De Beers Consolidated Political and Debating Association in Kimberley," 96.

66. Ibid.

67. On the development of the ideology of indirect rule, see Mantena, *Alibis of Empire*; "General Act of the Conference of Berlin concerning the Congo," *American Journal of International Law Supplement: Official Documents* 3 (January 1909): 7–25, article 6.

68. Smuts, "Native Policy in Africa," 78.

69. Smuts, "South and Central Africa," in *War-Time Speeches: A Compilation of Public Utterances in Great Britain* (London: Hodder and Stoughton, 1917), 79.

70. Smuts, "Native Policy in Africa," 83–84.

71. Smuts, "South and Central Africa," 80.

72. Ibid.

73. Ibid. Significantly, this policy of separate development did not prevent black workers from working for whites. Smut noted: "The natives will, of course, be free to go and to work in the white areas." Separate development disguised the political economy of apartheid South Africa, which required this movement of black labor from the Bantustans to mines and fields owned by whites.

74. Jan Smuts, *League of Nations: A Practical Suggestion* (New York: Nation, 1919), 11.

75. Ibid., 8, 27.

76. Jan Smuts, "The War and Some Empire Problems," in *War-Time Speeches*, 6.

77. Morefield, *Empires without Imperialism*, 190.

78. Smuts, *League of Nations*, 10.

79. Ibid., 13.

80. Ibid., 12.

81. Ibid.

82. Timothy Mitchell, *Carbon Democracy: Political Power in the Age of Oil* (New York: Verso, 2011), 80.

83. Grovogui, *Sovereigns, Quasi-sovereigns, and Africans*, 80.

84. Woodrow Wilson, "An Address to the Senate, January 22, 1917," in *PWW*, 40: 533–39, 536.

85. Ibid.

86. Woodrow Wilson, "An Address to a Joint Session of Congress, January 8, 1918," in *PWW*, 45: 534–39, 537–38.

87. Ibid., 538.

88. Ibid.

89. "Extracts from the Theses on the International Situation and the Policy of the Entente Adopted by the First Comintern Congress," in *The Communist International: 1919–1943 Documents*, ed. Jane Degras (New York: Frank Cass, 1917), 1: 31–36, 33–34.

90. "Manifesto of the Communist International to the Proletariat of the Entire World," in *The Communist International: 1919–1943 Documents*, 1: 38–47, 42–43.

91. "Extracts from the Theses on the International Situation and the Policy of the Entente Adopted by the First Comintern Congress," 35.

92. Clarence G. Contee, "Du Bois, the NAACP, and the Pan-African Congress of 1919," *Journal of Negro History* 57 (January 1972): 13–28, 24.

93. W.E.B. Du Bois, "Let Us Reason Together," *Crisis* 18 (September 1919): 231–35.

94. League of Nations, Motion Proposed by Sir Arthur Steel-Maitland, Delegate for New Zealand, on September 7, 1922, Third Assembly of the League of Nations, September 7, 1922, A/47/1922, LofN Doc, Box 61 23253/23253. Note that all League of Nations sources in this chapter are drawn from the League of Nations archives at the United Nations Library in Geneva, Switzerland.

95. Jean Allain, "Slavery and the League of Nations: Ethiopia as a Civilised Nation," *Journal of the History of International Law* 8 (November 2006): 213–44, 224.

96. Zimmerman, *Alabama in Africa*, 198–204.

97. Hartman, *Scenes of Subjection*, 121.

98. Rawls, *Law of Peoples*, 106.

99. Ibid., 111.

100. John Harris, *Slavery and the Obligations of the League* (London: Antislavery and Aborigines Protection Society, 1922).

101. Ibid.

102. Ibid.

103. John Harris to William E. Rappard, March 23, 1923, LofN Doc, Box R61, 27439/23252.

104. Frederick Lugard, "Slavery in Abyssinia," November 6, 1922, LofN Doc, Box R61, 24628/23252.

105. Ibid.

106. Ibid.

107. League of Nations, *Request for Admission to the League of Nations from Abyssinia*, September 6, 1923, A.55.923.VI, LofN Doc, Box R1454, 30357/29888.

108. League of Nations, *Record of the Fourth Assembly, Meetings of the Committee, Minutes of the Sixth Committee (Political Questions)*, September 19, 1923, 15.

109. Arnulf Becker Lorca, *Mestizo International Law: A Global Intellectual History 1842–1933* (Cambridge: Cambridge University Press, 2014), 277–78.

110. League of Nations, *Record of the Fourth Assembly, Meetings of the Committee, Minutes of the Sixth Committee (Political Questions)*, Report of the Second Sub-committee of the Sixth Committee, Abyssinia's Application for Admission to the League, Annex 5, September 14, 1923, 34.

111. Ibid.

112. Ibid., 35.

113. Ibid., 18.

114. M.H.A. Grimshaw, "Memorandum on the Questions of Slavery," April 15, 1925, LofN Doc, Box R66, 4456/23252.

115. "Slavery Convention," signed at Geneva, September 25, 1926, http://www.ohchr.org/EN/ProfessionalInterest/Pages/SlaveryConvention.aspx, accessed December 17, 2015.

116. Pedersen, *Guardians*, 257.

117. Ibid., 259.

118. The reasons for US interest in the question of slavery in Liberia are complex. The American Colonization Society created Liberia in order to resettle former slaves and free blacks. Liberia declared its independence in 1847, which the United States recognized in 1862. Despite its independence, Liberia had significant economic and political ties to the United States. The Firestone Rubber Company, a US corporation, was the largest private company operating in Liberia. The historian Ibrahim Sundiata argues that concerns about the Firestone Company's labor needs as well as worries that international scrutiny would lead to criticism of American investments prompted the note of protest to the league. I. K. Sundiata, *Black Scandal: America and the Liberian Labor Crisis, 1929–1936* (Philadelphia: Institute for the Study of Human Issues, 1980), 42.

119. "The 1930 Enquiry Commission to Liberia," *Journal of the Royal African Society* 30 (July 1931): 277–90, 278–80.

120. "Communication from the Government of Liberia Transmitting the Report of the International Commission of Enquiry in Liberia," December 15, 1930, C.658.M.272.1930.VI, *Publications of the League of Nations*, VI.B Slavery, 1930, 87.

121. Eric Drummond, "Interview with Mr. Gilbert," November 11, 1930, LofN Doc, Box R2356 22321/14352.

122. "Communication from the Government of Liberia Transmitting the Report of the International Commission of Enquiry in Liberia," 84–85.

123. Ibid., 45.

124. Eric Drummond, "Record of Interview with M. Quinones de Leon," December 4, 1930, LofN Doc, Box R2356, 22321/14352.

125. "Communication from the Government of Liberia Transmitting the Report of the International Commission of Enquiry in Liberia," 82.

126. Ibid., 84.

127. Sundiata, *Black Scandal*, 59–67.

128. Lord Noel-Buxton, "Report on Abyssinia," April 26, 1932, LofN Doc, Box R2353, 21243/2053.

129. Lord Noel-Buxton, "Slavery in Abyssinia," *International Affairs* 11 (July 1932): 512–26, 519.

130. Ibid., 518.

131. Rose Parfitt, "*Empire des Nègres Blancs*: The Hybridity of International Personality in the Abyssinia Crisis of 1935–1936," *Leiden Journal of International Law* 24 (December 2011): 849–72, 851.

132. Anghie, *Imperialism*, 180.

133. Pedersen, *Guardians*, 285.

134. Lugard quoted in Sundiata, *Black Scandal*, 74–75.

135. Lorca, *Mestizo International Law*, 280.

136. Parfitt, "*Empire des Nègres Blancs*," 849–50.

137. Schmitt, Nomos *of the Earth*, 243.

138. Ibid.

139. Ibid., 242–43.

140. "Memorandum by the Italian Government on the Situation in Ethiopia," September 11, 1935, C.340.M.171.1935.VII, in League of Nations, *Official Journal*, 88th and 89th Council Sessions, 66.

141. Ibid., 52.

142. Ibid., 8–11.

143. Ibid., 63.

144. Ibid., 36.

145. Ibid., 52.

146. Ibid., 36.

147. Ibid., 63.

148. Ibid., 57.

149. Ibid., 59.

150. Ibid., 62–63.

151. Ibid.

152. "Report of the Committee of Five to the Council," September 24, 1935, C.379.M.191.1935.VII.

153. Baron Aloisi, Representative of Italy at Fifteenth Plenary Meeting, October 10, 1935—Records of the 16th Assembly, Plenary Meetings and Index in *League of Nations Official Journal Supplements 1935*, 103–4.

154. League of Nations, "Slavery Report of the Advisory Committee of Experts," May 15, 1936, C.189(1).M.145.1936.VI, *Publications of the League of Nations*, VI.B Slavery, 1936.

155. Colonel C. E. Callwell, *Small Wars: Their Principles and Practice* (London: Harrison and Sons, 1906), 21.

156. Dominik Schaller and Jürgen Zimmerer, "Settlers, Imperialism, Genocide: Seeing the Global without Ignoring the Local—Introduction," *Journal of Genocide Research* 10 (June 2008): 191–99, 192.

157. Alberto Sbacchi, "Poison Gas and Atrocities in the Italo-Ethiopian War," in *Italian Colonialism*, ed. Ruth Ben-Ghiat and Mia Fuller (New York: Palgrave Macmillan, 2005), 47–56.

158. W.E.B. Du Bois, "The League of Nations," *Crisis* 18 (May 1919): 10–11.

159. W.E.B. Du Bois to Secretary General Eric Drummond, September 16, 1921, LofN Doc, Box R39, 15865/13940.

160. W.E.B. Du Bois, "Liberia, the League and the United States," *Foreign Affairs* 11 (July 1933): 682–95, 684.

161. Ibid., 695.

162. W.E.B. Du Bois, "Inter-racial Implications of the Ethiopian Crisis: A Negro View," *Foreign Affairs* 14 (October 1935): 82–92, 92.

163. Ibid., 84.

164. C.L.R. James, "Slavery Today: A Shocking Exposure," in *Toussaint L'Ouverture: The Story of the Only Successful Slave Revolt in History*, ed. Christian Høgsbjerg (Durham, NC: Duke University Press, 2013), 209–10.

165. Ibid., 211.

166. C.L.R. James quoted in Christian Høgsbjerg, *C.L.R. James in Imperial Britain* (Durham, NC: Duke University Press, 2014), 100.

167. Ibid., 99. C.L.R. James, "Is This Worth a War? The League's Scheme to Rob Abyssinia of Its Independence," in *At the Rendezvous of Victory: Selected Writings* (London: Allison and Busby, 1984), 15–16.

168. C.L.R. James, *World Revolution, 1917–1936: The Rise and Fall of the Communist International* (London: Martin Secker and Warburg, 1937), 387–88.

169. Ibid., 37, 421.

170. After Padmore resigned, the Comintern expelled him, citing essays he had written about Liberia and the league as examples of his sympathies to bourgeois nationalism. George Padmore, "An Open Letter to Earl Browder," *Crisis* 43 (October 1935): 302, 315.

171. For an examination of the collaboration between Padmore and Kouyaté, see Edwards, *Practice of Diaspora*, chapter 5.

172. Padmore quoted in ibid., 279.

173. Padmore quoted in ibid., 279–80.

Chapter Three: From Principle to Right

1. Antonio Cassese, *Self-Determination of Peoples: A Legal Appraisal* (New York: Cambridge University Press, 1995), 37. Churchill would famously declare in 1941 that he had not become "the King's First Minister in order to preside over the liquidation

of the British Empire." Ashley Jackson, *The British Empire and the Second World War* (London: Hambledon Continuum, 2006), 26.

2. Charter of the United Nations, http://www.un.org/en/sections/un-charter/introductory-note/index.html, accessed June 15, 2017.

3. West African Press Delegation, *The Atlantic Charter and British West Africa: Memorandum on Post-war Reconstruction of the Colonies and Protectorates of British West Africa* (London: West Africa Press Delegation to Britain, 1943).

4. Ibid., 3.

5. Ibid.

6. These comments appeared in the April 25, 1945, editorial of Azikiwe's newspaper the *West African Pilot* and are quoted in Marika Sherwood, "'There Is No New Deal for the Blackman in San Francisco': African Attempts to Influence the Founding Conference of the United Nations, April–July, 1945," *International Journal of African Historical Studies* 29 (April 1996): 71–94, 82.

7. For a discussion of Smuts's role in the United Nations, see Mark Mazower, *No Enchanted Palace: The End of Empire and the Ideological Origins of the United Nations* (Princeton, NJ: Princeton University Press, 2009), 28–65; Saul Dubow, "Smuts, the United Nations and the Rhetoric of Race and Rights," *Journal of Contemporary History* 43 (January 2008): 45–74.

8. W.E.B. Du Bois, "The World and Africa: An Inquiry into the Part Which Africa Has Played in World History," in *The World and Africa and Color and Democracy*, ed. Henry Louis Gates Jr. (New York: Oxford University Press, 2007), 154.

9. W.E.B. Du Bois, quoted in Mazower, *No Enchanted Palace*, 63.

10. "The Challenge to the Colonial Powers," in *History of the Pan-African Congress: Colonial and Coloured Unity; A Program of Action*, ed. George Padmore (1947; London: Hammersmith Bookshop, 1963), 5.

11. "Declaration of the Colonial Workers, Farmers, and Intellectuals," in Padmore, *History of the Pan-African Congress*, 7.

12. Kwame Nkrumah, *Osagyefo at the United Nations* (Accra: Government Printers, 1960), 6.

13. General Assembly Resolution 1514 (XV), "Declaration on the Granting of Independence to Colonial Countries and Peoples," A/RES/1514/XV, December 14, 1960, http://wpik.org/Src/unga1514.html, accessed June 13, 2012.

14. Alex Quaison-Sackey quoted in Steven L. B. Jensen, *The Making of International Human Rights: The 1960s, Decolonization, and the Reconstruction of Global Values* (New York: Cambridge University Press, 2016), 65.

15. Léon Maka quoted in ibid., 65n55.

16. Amilcar Cabral, "Anonymous Soldiers for the United Nations," in *Revolution in Guinea: An African People's Struggle* (London: Love and Malcomson, 1969), 40–41.

17. See, for example, Mary Ann Glendon, *A World Made New: Eleanor Roosevelt and the Universal Declaration of Human Rights* (New York: Random House, 2001); Samantha Power, *A Problem from Hell: America and the Age of Genocide* (New York: Basic Books, 2002); Elizabeth Borgwardt, *A New Deal for the World: America's Vision for Human Rights* (Cambridge, MA: Belknap Press of Harvard University Press, 2005); and Jay Winter, *Dreams of Peace and Freedom: Utopian Moments in the Twentieth Century* (New Haven, CT: Yale University Press, 2006).

18. Borgwardt, *New Deal for the World*; Elizabeth Borgwardt, "'When You State a Moral Principle, You Are Stuck with It': The 1941 Atlantic Charter as a Human Rights Instrument," *Virginia Journal of International Law* 46 (2006): 501–62.

19. On the continuities, see Mazower, *No Enchanted Palace*, chapters 1 and 2.

20. Emerson, *From Empire to Nation*; Plamenatz, *On Alien Rule*; Bull and Watson, *Expansion of International Society*.

21. Clyde Eagleton, "Excesses of Self-Determination," *Foreign Affairs* 31 (July 1953): 592–604.

22. Ibid., 602.

23. Isaiah Berlin, "Two Concepts of Liberty," in *Liberty: Incorporating Four Essays on Liberty*, ed. Henry Hardy (Oxford: Oxford University Press, 2002), 206–7.

24. James Tully argues that for Berlin, "the central division of the Cold War is between the negative liberty ideal of a highly civilised and self-conscious minority in the West and the relatively mindless self-assertive paganism of the majority in the Third World." James Tully, "'Two Concepts of Liberty' in Context," in *Isaiah Berlin and the Politics of Freedom: "Two Concepts of Liberty" 50 Years Later*, ed. Bruce Baum and Robert Nichols (New York: Routledge, 2013), 36. For a critique of Berlin's dismissal of anticolonial demands for self-government, see Barnor Hesse, "Escaping Liberty: Western Hegemony, Black Fugitivity," *Political Theory* 42 (June 2014): 288–313.

25. Padmore, *Pan-Africanism or Communism*, xiii.

26. Ibid., xix. For Padmore's dismissal of Garvey, see George Padmore, *The Life and Struggle of Negro Toilers* (London: Red International Labor Union Magazine, 1931), 6.

27. Padmore, *Pan-Africanism or Communism*, xix.

28. Ibid., xvi.

29. Scott, *Refashioning Futures*, 5–6; R. G. Collingwood, *An Autobiography* (Oxford: Oxford University Press, 1939), 30–33.

30. Cooper, *Decolonization and African Society*; Cooper, "Labor, Politics and the End of Empire in French Africa."

31. On the debates in the Francophone world, see Cooper, *Citizenship between Empire and Nation*; Wilder, *Freedom Time*.

32. Frederick Cooper, "Possibility and Constraint: African Independence in Historical Perspective," *Journal of African History* 49 (July 2008): 167–96.

33. Armitage, *Declaration of Independence*, 13–15, 21–22; Gündoğdu, *Rightlessness in the Age of Rights*, 165–66, 187.

34. W.E.B. Du Bois, "Color and Democracy: Colonies and Peace," in *World and Africa and Color and Democracy*, 248–49.

35. Roger B. Taney, "Opinion of the Court," in *Scott v. Sandford*, 60, U.S. 393, March 6, 1857, http://www.law.cornell.edu/supct/html/historics/USSC_CR_0060_0393_ZO.html, accessed October 31, 2012.

36. Aziz Rana has argued that in the Dred Scott decision, the defense of absolute authority over blacks was combined with an argument for constitutional limits on the federal government to protect the rights of frontier settlers. Taney defended despotic power over black subjects, while limiting the national government's prerogative authority over white citizens. Aziz Rana, *The Two Faces of American Freedom* (Cambridge, MA: Harvard University Press, 2010), 168–69.

37. Du Bois, *Souls of Black Folk*, 45.

38. C.L.R. James, *The Black Jacobins: Toussaint L'Ouverture and the San Domingo Revolution* (1938; New York: Vintage, 1989); Eric Williams, *Capitalism and Slavery* (1944; Chapel Hill: University of North Carolina Press, 1994); W.E.B. Du Bois, *Black Reconstruction in America, 1860–1880* (1935; New York: Free Press, 1992).

39. Williams, *Capitalism and Slavery*.

40. James, *Black Jacobins*, 376.

41. Williams, *Capitalism and Slavery*, 8; Nkrumah, *Africa Must Unite*, 1.

42. Padmore, *How Britain Rules Africa*, 386.

43. Azikiwe, *Renascent Africa*, 57.

44. Edmund Burke, "Speech on Mr. Fox's East India Bill," in *Select Works of Edmund Burke: Miscellaneous Writings* (Indianapolis: Liberty Fund, 1999), 101.

45. Azikiwe, *Renascent Africa*, 74.

46. Nkrumah, *Towards Colonial Freedom*, 26–27; Bunche, *Worldview of Race*, 38.

47. Nkrumah, *Towards Colonial Freedom*, 24–25.

48. Azikiwe, *Renascent Africa*, 68.

49. Nkrumah, *Towards Colonial Freedom*, xiv.

50. J. A. Hobson, *Imperialism: A Study* (1902; Indianapolis: Liberty Fund, 2004); V. I. Lenin, *Imperialism: The Highest Stage of Capitalism* (1917; Chippendale, Australia: Resistance Books, 1999).

51. W.E.B. Du Bois, "The Hands of Ethiopia," in *Darkwater*, 33.

52. Padmore, *How Britain Rules Africa*, 3.

53. Ibid., 53–54.

54. Nkrumah, *Africa Must Unite*, 37.

55. John Harris, *Dawn in Darkest Africa* (London: Smith, Elder, 1912), 153; Cooper, *Decolonization and African Society*, 27–28.

56. Nkrumah, *Africa Must Unite*, 12.

57. Padmore, *How Britain Rules Africa*, 386.

58. Nkrumah, *Africa Must Unite*, 36.

59. Du Bois, "Hands of Ethiopia," 36.

60. Padmore, *Gold Coast Revolution*.

61. Philip Pettit, *Republicanism: A Theory of Freedom and Government* (Oxford: Oxford University Press, 1997); Skinner, *Liberty before Liberalism*.

62. Alex Gourevitch, *From Slavery to the Cooperative Commonwealth: Labor and Republican Liberty in the Nineteenth Century* (New York: Cambridge University Press, 2015); William Clare Roberts, *Marx's Inferno: The Political Theory of Capital* (Princeton, NJ: Princeton University Press, 2017).

63. Nkrumah, *Africa Must Unite*, 66.

64. Du Bois, "Souls of White Folk," 23. Du Bois, "African Roots of War," 707–14, 707.

65. Du Bois, "African Roots of War," 708.

66. Padmore, *Africa and World Peace*, 43.

67. Ibid., 248.

68. Du Bois, "Color and Democracy," 304.

69. Padmore, *Africa and World Peace*, 248.

70. Du Bois, "Color and Democracy," 308.

71. Padmore, *Africa and World Peace*, 123–25.

72. W.E.B. Du Bois, "Prospect of a World without Race Conflict," *Journal of American Sociology* 49 (March 1944): 450–56, 454.

73. Ibid., 451.

74. I thank Aziz Rana and Robert Nichols for pushing me to consider this limitation.

75. Robert Nichols, "Theft Is Property! The Recursive Logic of Dispossession," *Political Theory*, April 2, 2017, 1–26, 9, https://doi.org/10.1177/0090591717701709, accessed April 15, 2017; Glen Coulthard, *Red Skin, White Masks: Rejecting the Colonial Politics of Recognition* (Minneapolis: University of Minnesota Press, 2014), 7; Audra Simpson, *Mohawk Interruptus: Political Life across the Borders of Settler States* (Durham, NC: Duke University Press, 2014), 74.

76. Nichols, "Theft Is Property!," 10.

77. Audrey Jane Roy, "Sovereignty and Decolonization: Realizing Indigenous Self-Determination at the United Nations and in Canada" (MA thesis, University of Victoria, 2001).

78. "Declaration of Rights of the Caribbean Peoples to Self-Determination and Self-Government," in *Richard B. Moore, Caribbean Militant in Harlem: Collected Writings 1920–1972*, ed. W. Burghardt Turner and Joyce Moore Turner (Bloomington: Indiana University Press, 1992), 264.

79. "Appeal to the United Nations Conference on International Organization on Behalf of the Caribbean Peoples," in *Richard B. Moore, Caribbean Militant in Harlem*, 270–76.

80. "Challenge to the Colonial Powers," 5.

81. Final Communiqué of the Afro-Asian Bandung Conference, April 24, 1955, http://www.cvce.eu/obj/final_communique_of_the_asian_african_conference_of _bandung_24_april_1955-en-676237bd-72f7-471f-949a-88b6ae513585.html, accessed May 15, 2012.

82. United Nations General Assembly Resolution 545 (VI), "Inclusion in the International Covenant or Covenants on Human Rights of an Article Relating to the Right of Peoples to Self-Determination," A/RES/545/VI, February 5, 1952, http:// www.un.org/depts/dhl/resguide/r6_en.shtml, accessed September 16, 2012.

83. United Nations General Assembly Resolution 637 (VII), "The Rights of Peoples and Nations to Self-Determination," A/RES/637/VII, December 16, 1952, http:// www.un.org/depts/dhl/resguide/r7.htm, accessed September 16, 2012.

84. *Yearbook of the United Nations, 1952* (New York: United Nations Organization, 1952), 441.

85. Ibid., 445.

86. Ibid., 442.

87. Ibid.

88. Ibid.

89. Daniel J. Whelan, *Indivisible Human Rights: A History* (Philadelphia: University of Pennsylvania Press, 2010), 139.

90. Ibid.

91. Ibid., 140. The deleted paragraph read, "The right of peoples to self-determination shall also include permanent sovereignty over their natural wealth and resources. In no case may a people be deprived of its own means of subsistence on the grounds of any

rights that may be claimed by other states." Fears that this language legalized nationalization and expropriation of private property led many European states and the United States to reject this paragraph.

92. International Covenant on Civil and Political Rights, http://www.ohchr.org /en/professionalinterest/pages/ccpr.aspx, accessed October 14, 2012; International Covenant on Economic, Social and Cultural Rights, http://www.ohchr.org/EN/Prof essionalInterest/Pages/CESCR.aspx, accessed October 14, 2012.

93. *Yearbook of the United Nations, 1960* (New York: United Nations Organization, 1960), 44.

94. United Nations General Assembly Resolution 1514 (XV), "Declaration on the Granting of Independence to Colonial Countries and Peoples."

95. Ibid.

96. *Yearbook of the United Nations, 1960,* 46.

97. Jensen, *Making of International Human Rights,* 65.

98. United Nations General Assembly Resolution 1514 (XV), "Declaration on the Granting of Independence to Colonial Countries and Peoples."

99. Samuel Moyn, *The Last Utopia: Human Rights in History* (Cambridge, MA: Belknap Press of Harvard University Press, 2010), chapter 3. See also Jan Eckel, "Human Rights and Decolonization: New Perspectives and New Questions," *Humanity: An International Journal of Human Rights, Humanitarianism, and Development* 1 (Fall 2010): 111–35.

100. Roland Burke, *Decolonization and the Evolution of International Human Rights* (Philadelphia: University of Pennsylvania Press, 2010); Jensen, *Making of International Human Rights.*

101. Jensen, *Making of International Human Rights,* chapters 3 and 4.

102. Bonny Ibhawoh, *Imperialism and Human Rights: Colonial Discourses of Rights and Liberties in African History* (Albany: State University of New York Press, 2007), 55–64.

103. Nnamdi Azikiwe, *Political Blueprint for Nigeria* (Lagos: African Books, 1943); Kwame Nkrumah, "Education and Nationalism in Africa," *Education Outlook* 18 (1943): 32–40, 32; Ibhawoh, *Imperialism and Human Rights,* 155–57.

104. Ibhawoh, *Imperialism and Human Rights,* 8, 157–58.

105. Nnamdi Azikiwe, *Zik: A Selection from the Speeches of Nnamdi Azikiwe* (Cambridge: Cambridge University Press, 1961), 159.

106. Nkrumah, *Africa Must Unite,* 50; Azikiwe, *Political Blueprint,* 56.

107. Nkrumah, *Towards Colonial Freedom,* 43.

108. Julius Nyerere, "Independence Address to United Nations, 14 December 1961," in *Freedom and Unity: A Selection from Writing and Speeches 1952–1965* (Dar es Salaam: Oxford University Press, 1967), 146.

109. Kwame Nkrumah, "Independence and Sovereignty of the African People" (unpublished paper 1960), in African Affairs Papers, Box ADM 16/14, Public Records and Archives Administration Department, Accra, Ghana.

110. Ibid.

111. United Nations General Assembly, *Universal Declaration of Human Rights,* A/217/III, December 10, 1948, http://www.un.org/en/documents/udhr/, accessed May 10, 2014.

112. Nkrumah, "Independence and Sovereignty of the African People."

113. Moyn, *Last Utopia*, 111.

114. Eagleton, "Excesses of Self-Determination," 604.

115. Louis Henkin, "The United Nations and Human Rights," *International Organization* 19 (Summer 1965): 504–17, 512.

116. Ibid., 513.

117. "Declaration of the Rights of the Negro People of the World," in *Selected Writings and Speeches of Marcus Garvey*, ed. Bob Blaisdell (Mineola, NY: Dover, 2004), 17.

118. Ibid., 18.

119. Marcus Garvey, "The True Solution to the Negro Problem," in *The Philosophy and Opinions of Marcus Garvey; or, Africa for the Africans*, vol. 1 (Dover, MA: Majority, 1986), 52–53.

120. "Speech by Marcus Garvey, in Philadelphia, PA, October 21, 1919," in *The Marcus Garvey and Universal Negro Improvement Association Papers*, vol. 2, ed. Robert Hill (Berkeley: University of California Press, 1983), 94.

121. Julius Nyerere, "Biafra, Human Rights and Self-Determination in Africa," April 13, 1968, http://biafrasay.com/p/327314/biafra-human-rights-and-self-determination-in-africa-by-pres#327314, accessed August 10, 2017.

122. Hannah Arendt, "Rights of Man: What Are They?," *Modern Review* 3 (1949): 25–37, 37. On the ways that Arendt's republicanism limited her anti-imperial critique and contributed to her silence on anticolonial movements, see A. Dirk Moses, "*Das römische Gespräch* in a New Key: Hannah Arendt, Genocide, and the Defense of Republican Civilization," *Journal of Modern History* 85 (December 2013): 867–913.

123. Arendt, "Rights of Man," 37.

124. Arendt, *Origins of Totalitarianism*, 291.

125. Ibid., 291–92.

126. Ibid., 296–97.

127. Jeffrey C. Isaac, "A New Guarantee on Earth: Hannah Arendt on Human Dignity and the Politics of Human Rights," *American Political Science Review* 90 (March 1996): 61–73.

128. Arendt, "Rights of Man," 34.

129. United Nations General Assembly Resolution 1514 (XV), "Declaration on the Granting of Independence to Colonial Countries and Peoples."

130. Ibid.

131. Cohen, *Globalization and Sovereignty*, 199.

132. Jörg Fisch, *The Right of Self-Determination of Peoples: The Domestication of an Illusion*, trans. Anita Mage (New York: Cambridge University Press, 2015), 57.

133. For accounts of decolonization as an extension of Westphalia and the United Nations Charter, see Bull and Watson, *Expansion of International Society*; Jackson, *Quasi-states*.

134. Benjamin Straumann, "Series Editors' Preface," in C. H. Alexandrowicz, *The Law of Nations in Global History*, ed. David Armitage and Jennifer Pitts (Oxford: Oxford University Press, 2017), vi.

135. C. H. Alexandrowicz, "The New States and International Law," in *Law of Nations in Global History*, 404–10.

136. Nkrumah, *Osagyefo at the United Nations*, 6; Alex Quaison-Sackey, *Africa Unbound: Reflections of an African Statesman* (New York: Frederick A. Praeger, 1963), 154.

137. United Nations General Assembly Resolution 1991 (XVIII), "Question of Equitable Representation on the Security Council and the Economic and Social Council," A/RES/1991/XVIII, December 17, 1963, http://www.un.org/documents/ga/res/18/ares18.htm, accessed June 10, 2014.

138. Nkrumah, *Osagyefo at the United Nations*, 8.

139. Nkrumah, *Neocolonialism*.

140. Nkrumah, *Osagyefo at the United Nations*, 9–10.

141. Kwame Nkrumah, *The Challenge of the Congo: A Case Study of Foreign Pressures in an Independent State* (New York: International, 1967), 268.

142. UN General Assembly Resolution 2131 (XX), "Declaration on the Inadmissibility of Intervention in the Domestic Affairs of States and the Protection of Their Independence and Sovereignty," A/RES/20/2131, December 21, 1965, https://documents-dds-ny.un.org/doc/RESOLUTION/GEN/NR0/218/94/IMG/NR021894.pdf?OpenElement, accessed June 28, 2017.

143. Ibid.

144. Ryan M. Irwin, "Sovereignty in the Congo Crisis," in *Decolonization and the Cold War: Negotiating Independence*, ed. Leslie James and Elisabeth Leake (New York: Bloomsbury, 2015), 205.

145. Mamdani, *Citizen and Subject*, 20.

146. Irwin, "Sovereignty in the Congo Crisis," 206.

147. Mamdani, *Citizen and Subject*, 287–91.

148. Nyerere, "Biafra, Human Rights and Self-Determination."

149. Ibid.

150. Brad Simpson, "The Biafran Secession and the Limits of Self-Determination," *Journal of Genocide Research* 16 (August 2014): 337–54, 343.

151. Nyerere, "Biafra, Human Rights and Self-Determination."

152. Simpson, "Biafran Secession," 341.

153. Michael Ignatieff quoted in Lassie Heerten and A. Dirk Moses, "The Nigeria-Biafra War: Postcolonial Conflict and the Question of Genocide," *Journal of Genocide Research* 16 (August 2014): 169–203, 176.

154. Simpson, "Biafran Secession," 337.

155. Mark Bradley, *The World Reimagined: Americans and Human Rights in the Twentieth Century* (New York: Cambridge University Press, 2016), 141–42.

156. Ibid., 149. According to Bradley, between 1972 and 1979, 86 percent of Amnesty International's reports and publications focused on the global south.

157. Rupert Emerson, "The Fate of Human Rights in the Third World," *World Politics* 27 (January 1975): 201–26, 223.

158. Ibid., 225.

159. These arguments became dominant only with the end of the Cold War, reaching their height in the debates about humanitarian intervention during the 1990s. See, for example, Jackson, *Quasi-states*; Gerald B. Helman and Steven R. Ratner, "Saving Failed States," *Foreign Policy* 89 (Winter 1992): 3–20. On the persistence of trusteeship, see William Bain, *Between Anarchy and Society: Trusteeship and the*

Obligations of Power (New York: Oxford University Press, 2003); William Bain, "The Political Theory of Trusteeship and the Twilight of International Equality," *International Relations* 17 (March 2003): 59–77; Ralph Wilde, *International Territorial Administration: How Trusteeship and the Civilizing Mission Never Went Away* (Oxford: Oxford University Press, 2008).

160. Didier Fassin, *Humanitarian Reason: A Moral History of the Present* (Berkeley: University of California Press, 2012), xiii. On the dissociation of liberalism from empire as a precondition for the rise of this humanitarianism, see Samuel Moyn, "Imperialism, Self-Determination, and the Rise of Human Rights," in *The Human Rights Revolution: An International History*, ed. Akira Iriye et al. (New York: Oxford University Press, 2012), 172. On the significance of the post–Cold War era, see Stefan-Ludwig Hoffmann, "Human Rights and History," *Past and Present* 232 (August 2016): 279–310.

161. For contemporary critiques along these lines, see Grovogui, *Sovereigns, Quasi-sovereigns, and Africans*, 179–88; Anghie, *Imperialism*, 239–44; Pitts, "Intervention and Sovereign Equality," 148–53.

Chapter Four: Revisiting the Federalists in the Black Atlantic

1. *Government Proposals for a Republican Constitution* (Accra: Government Printers, 1960).

2. Nkrumah, *Neocolonialism*, 31.

3. Ibid., 33.

4. Ibid., xv.

5. Lenin, "Socialist Revolution and the Right to Self-Determination," 145.

6. The term "postcolonial predicament" is borrowed from Rana, *Two Faces of American Freedom*, 135.

7. For a history of the West Indies Federation, see John Mordecai, *The West Indies: The Federal Negotiations* (London: George Allen and Unwin, 1968).

8. Sékou Touré and Modibo Keita of Mali turned toward this political formation after abandoning the creation of a French-African federation. Guineans voted no on the 1958 referendum to approve the constitution for the Fifth French Republic, which prompted Guinean independence. Mali emerged as an independent state in 1960 after the breakup of the Mali Federation with Senegal. For a detailed examination of the 1958 referendum and the politics of French African union, see Cooper, *Citizenship between Empire and Nation*, chapter 7.

9. Rupert Emerson, "Pan-Africanism," *International Organization* 16 (Spring 1962): 275–90; Immanuel Wallerstein, *Africa, the Politics of Unity: An Analysis of a Contemporary Social Movement* (New York: Vintage Books, 1969).

10. For instance, Jason Parker argues that the failure of the West Indian Federation, like other federal experiments in the postcolonial world, "foundered most of all on the rocks of the particularist racial-ethnic identities contained within them." On this view, "racial-ethnic nationalism in the Third World had thus helped drive the effort to end rule by imperial outsiders—and in many areas, subsequently prevented

the formation of a viable polity to take its place." Jason C. Parker, *Brother's Keeper: The United States, Race, and Empire in the British Caribbean, 1937–1962* (New York: Oxford University Press, 2008), 168–69. More generally, there is a tendency to read the post–World War II period as a moment in which nationalism and the nation-state eclipsed anticolonial internationalism. See, for example, Carnegie, "Garvey and the Black Transnation"; Stephens, *Black Empire*.

11. Williams, "Economic Development of the Caribbean Up to the Present."

12. Eric Williams, "1776 and 1943" (unpublished paper), in Eric Williams Memorial Collection, Box 151, University of West Indies–St. Augustine.

13. Nkrumah, *Africa Must Unite*, 27.

14. Ibid., 50.

15. Nkrumah, *Towards Colonial Freedom*, xv.

16. Williams, "1776 and 1943."

17. Armitage, *Declaration of Independence*, 103–4, 113.

18. In 1940, the Carnegie Endowment for International Peace published a bibliography on studies of regional and world federation. The collection of books, periodicals, pamphlets, and magazine articles focused on regional federation in Europe and arguments for reorganizing the League of Nations as a world federation: "The New World Order: Select List of References on Regional and World Federation with Some Special Plans for World Order after the War" (Washington, DC: Carnegie Endowment for International Peace, 1940). For an argument in favor of world federation on the model of 1787, see W. B. Curry, *The Case for Federal Union: A New International Order* (London: Penguin Books, 1939). For an invocation of American federalists in the case for European federation, see Altiero Spinelli, "The Growth of the European Movement since World War II," in *European Integration*, ed. C. Grove Haines (Baltimore: Johns Hopkins University Press, 1957), 38–41.

19. Fox, "Right to Political Participation in International Law."

20. Held, "Democratic Accountability and Political Effectiveness from a Cosmopolitan Perspective"; Habermas, "Constitutionalization of International Law"; Cohen, *Globalization and Sovereignty*.

21. Nkrumah, *Africa Must Unite*, 24–27.

22. As Manu Goswami had argued, anticolonial nationalists in India rejected the integration and differentiation of the imperial global economy and conceived of the "nation as a territorial-economic collective." Goswami, *Producing India*, 232.

23. "America Must Remember Her Past," *Voice of Africa* 5 (November–December 1965): 8–9, Bureau of African Affairs Papers, File BAA/RLAA/33—Voice of Africa and Other Publications, 1964/1965, George Padmore Research Library on African Affairs. Nkrumah's Bureau of African Affairs published the journal *Voice of Africa* and was responsible for coordinating Ghana's African policy. The line "America Must Unite" is a gloss on Nkrumah's book *Africa Must Unite*, first published in 1963.

24. Ibid. While identifying African anticolonialism with the historical experience of the United States, the article critiqued the emergence of the United States as an imperial power. The unidentified author argued that US intervention in the Congo and Vietnam indicated that America had forgotten its own anticolonial past.

25. Eric Williams, "The Implications of Federation," August 11, 1955, Eric Williams Memorial Collection, Box 812, University of West Indies–St. Augustine; Eric

Williams, "The Pros and Cons of Federation," in *Federation: Two Public Lectures* (Port-of-Spain: College Press, 1956), 3.

26. Eric Williams, "Speech Made by the Honorable the Chief Minister during the Debate on the Chaguaramas Joint Commission Report, 6 June, 1958" (Port-of-Spain: Government Printing Office, 1958), C.L.R. James Papers, Folder ICS40/F/5/8, Senate House Library.

27. "Give Us Political Union," *Ghanaian Times*, October 24, 1965, in Newspaper Collections, Folder NP 4/44, Public Records and Archives Administration Department (PRAAD).

28. John Jay, "No. 2 Concerning Dangers from Foreign Force and Influence," in *The Federalist Papers*, ed. Clinton Rossiter (New York: Signet Classics, 2003), 32; Williams, "Implications of Federation."

29. Williams, "Implications of Federation."

30. Ibid.

31. Ibid.

32. "Joint Declaration by His Excellency Dr. Kwame Nkrumah, Prime Minister of Ghana, and His Excellency Mr. Sékou Touré, President of the Republic of Guinea, Issued at Conakry on 1 May, 1959," Bureau of African Affairs Papers, Box 966 Originals—Declarations, Resolutions, Policy Statements, George Padmore Research Library on African Affairs. The inspiration of the thirteen American colonies in the founding of the Ghana-Guinea union is also mentioned in H. E. Nana Kena II, "United States of Africa," *Voice of Africa* 2 (March 1962): 6–8, Bureau of African Affairs Papers, File BAA/RLAA/13—Voice of Africa, undated: Newspaper Clippings, George Padmore Research Library on African Affairs.

33. Kwame Nkrumah, "Address to the Summit Conference of the O.A.U.," May 24, 1963, reprinted in *Voice of Africa* 5 (September–October 1965): 44–50, Bureau of African Affairs Papers, File BAA/RLAA/33—Voice of Africa and Other Publications, 1964/1965, George Padmore Research Library on African Affairs.

34. Kwame Nkrumah quoted in "Why African Unity?," *OAU Review* 1 (May 1964) in Files of Ex-Presidential Affairs, Folder RG/17/2/434 OAU Printed Publications, PRAAD.

35. Kwame Nkrumah, "Address to African Heads of State and Government Conference of the OAU at Cairo," July 19, 1964, reprinted as "Kwame in Cairo," in *Voice of Africa* 5 (September–October 1965): 51–56, Bureau of African Affairs Papers, File BAA/RLAA/33—Voice of Africa and Other Publications, 1964/1965, George Padmore Research Library on African Affairs. The argument that balkanization was a strategy to maintain colonial control over newly independent states was a mainstay for proponents of union. An article proposing a "United States of Africa" also published in *Voice of Africa* argued that postcolonial "states are designed to be so weak and unstable in the organization of their economies and administration that they will be compelled by internal as well as external pressures, to continue to depend upon the colonial powers who have ruled them for several years. The weaker and the less stable an African state is, the easier it is for the colonial power concerned to continue to dominate the affairs and fortunes of the new state, even though it is supposed to have gained independence." H. E. Nana Kena II, "United States of Africa."

36. Cooper, *Citizenship between Empire and Nation*; Wilder, *Freedom Time*.

37. Letter from Barbara Ward to Kwame Nkrumah, November 26, 1961, in Office of the Ex-Bureau of African Affairs Papers Box SC/BAA/98 European Common Market, PRAAD. "Speech on European Common Market" by Mr. F.K.G. Goka, Minister of Finance, Delivered on Behalf of Dr. Kwame Nkrumah, President of the Republic of Ghana at Commonwealth Prime Ministers' Conference in London on September 10, 1962, Bureau of African Affairs Papers, Box 1079 European Common Market, George Padmore Research Library on African Affairs.

38. Joshua Simon, "José Martí's Immanent Critique of American Imperialism," unpublished paper presented at the American Political Science Association Meeting, September 2015, San Francisco, CA.

39. Cooper, *Colonialism in Question*, 28–29.

40. Asli Bâli and Aziz Rana, "Constitutionalism and the American Imperial Imagination," *University of Chicago Law Review* 85 (March 2018): 257–92.

41. Martin Staniland, *American Intellectuals and African Nationalists, 1955–1970* (New Haven, CT: Yale University Press, 1991), 76–78; Ryan M. Irwin, *Gordian Knot: Apartheid and the Unmaking of the Liberal World Order* (New York: Oxford University Press, 2012), 76.

42. Eliga H. Gould, *Among the Powers of the Earth: The American Revolution and the Making of a New World Empire* (Cambridge, MA: Harvard University Press, 2012), 1–2.

43. Ibid., 211.

44. Rana, *Two Faces of American Freedom*, 134–35.

45. In an examination of why early postcolonial federations—the United States, Australia, and Canada—succeeded while twentieth-century versions failed, Thomas Franck identifies the absence of imperial expansion in the latter as an important contributing factor. According to Franck, "for the pioneers of Australia, Canada, and the United States, there were the great frontier lands to conquer. This was the center of the common vision, the common idea, so big that it could accommodate within its infectious, exciting ethos liberals and conservatives, slaveholders and abolitionists, French and English, Catholics, Anglicans and nonconformists. The vast, vacant, lucrative frontiers not only gave a common cause to the diverse, but provided the space and riches that make diversity easier to accommodate." Thomas M. Franck, "Why Federations Fail," in *Why Federations Fail: An Inquiry into the Requisites for Successful Federation*, ed. Thomas M. Franck (New York: New York University Press, 1968), 189.

46. Jay, "No. 2 Concerning Dangers from Foreign Force and Influence."

47. Nkrumah, *Ghana*, 240–53; Donald Rothchild, "The Limits of Federalism: An Examination of Political Institutional Transfer in Africa," *Journal of Modern African Studies* 4 (November 1966): 275–93. For a study of Asante nationalism, see Jean Marie Allman, *The Quills of the Porcupine: Asante Nationalism in an Emergent Ghana* (Madison: University of Wisconsin Press, 1993).

48. Nkrumah, *Africa Must Unite*, 62.

49. Selwyn Ryan, "East Indians, West Indians and the Quest for Political Unity," *Social and Economic Studies* 48 (December 1999): 151–84, 155.

50. Ibid., 165.

51. Nkrumah, *Neocolonialism*, 239–41.

52. Williams, "Speech Made by the Honorable the Chief Minister during the Debate on the Chaguaramas Joint Commission Report, 6 June, 1958"; Eric Williams, *From Columbus to Castro: The History of the Caribbean, 1492–1969* (1970; New York: Vintage Books, 1984) 408–27.

53. Joshua Simon, *The Ideology of Creole Revolution: Imperialism and Independence in American and Latin American Political Thought* (New York: Cambridge University Press, 2017); "America Must Remember Her Past," 8–9.

54. Eric Williams, "Federation in the World of Today: Lecture at the Extra-mural Department in Trinidad and Tobago of the University College of the West Indies," February 25, 1955, Eric Williams Memorial Collection, Box 813, University of West Indies–St. Augustine.

55. Nkrumah, *Africa Must Unite*, 148.

56. Kenneth Wheare, *Federal Government* (1946; London: Oxford University Press, 1963), 26.

57. Ibid., 2–3.

58. Ibid., 53.

59. Ibid., 93.

60. Daniel J. Elazaar, *Exploring Federalism* (Tuscaloosa: University of Alabama Press, 1987), 64; Cohen, *Globalization and Sovereignty*, 112.

61. Murray Forsyth, *Union of States: The Theory and Practice of Confederation* (Leicester: Leicester University Press, 1981), 7.

62. Cohen, *Globalization and Sovereignty*, 133.

63. Wheare, *Federal Government*, 238–39. Wheare's discussion of the growing powers of the federal government should be dated to the nineteenth century in the United States. The Civil War and Reconstruction had already expanded the powers of the federal government relative to the states. By the turn of the century, the transition from a federation of coordinate powers to a "federal state" was already taking place. The transformation is palpable in the shifting rhetoric of the late nineteenth century. Well into the 1860s, Abraham Lincoln referred to the United States as the "Confederated States," a phrase that recognized the independence of the states. However, after Reconstruction, the constitutional histories written by Woodrow Wilson and John Burgess referred to the United States as a "federal state" and nation. See Forsyth, *Union of States*, 41–42.

64. Wheare, *Federal Government*, 115.

65. Ibid., 113–14. Between 1930 and 1940, these grants increased by 300 percent, and while in 1930 half of the grants were for expenditures on highways and the National Guard, by 1940, 53 percent of grants were for social services.

66. Harold Laski, "The Obsolescence of Federalism," *New Republic* 98 (May 3, 1939): 367–69.

67. A. H. Birch, *Federalism, Finance and Social Legislation in Canada, Australia and the United States* (Oxford: Clarendon, 1955), 305. Birch expanded on the implications of his study in an article-length piece on finance in the new federations. A. H. Birch, "Inter-governmental Financial Relations in New Federations," in *Federalism and Economic Growth in Underdeveloped Countries*, ed. Ursula K. Hicks et al., 113–29 (London: George Allen and Unwin, 1961). These views were crystallized in the work of William Riker, the foremost political scientist working on federation in the 1960s.

In his seminal 1964 book, Riker argued that modern federations, beginning with the American federation in 1787, were necessarily institutions for the aggregation and centralization of authority. He thus celebrated Hamilton's appropriation of the federal form to argue for greater centralization as a critical departure from ancient and early modern confederations to modern centralized federations. William Riker, *Federalism: Origin, Operation, Significance* (Boston: Little, Brown, 1964), 5–10.

68. Williams, "Federation in the World of Today."

69. Ibid.

70. "Osagyefo Addresses Parliament: Political Independence Does Not End Colonialism," *Evening News*, April 19, 1961, Bureau of African Affairs Papers, Box 1007 President's Speeches, vol. 2, George Padmore Research Library on African Affairs.

71. Eric Williams, "Speech at the Revision of the Federal Constitution, Intergovernmental Conference," September 11, 1959, Eric Williams Memorial Collection, Box 2119, University of the West Indies–St. Augustine.

72. Ibid.

73. Office of the Premier and Ministry of Finance, *The Economics of Nationhood* (Port-of-Spain: Government of Trinidad and Tobago, 1959), Federation Records, Trinidad National Archives, Box 6.

74. David Lowenthal, "Two Federations," *Social and Economic Studies* 6 (June 1957): 185–240, 240. The smaller islands of the federation (Antigua, Barbados, Dominica, Grenada, St. Kitts, Nevis and Anguilla, St. Lucia, and St. Vincent), collectively referred to as the "small eight," were unwilling to agree to a customs union without uniform income tax, increased federal services, and a larger program of grants-in-aid. Ulric Simmonds, "Which Way West Indies? Confusion Marks Federation Talks," *Daily Gleaner, Overseas Edition*, February 11, 1956, Eric Williams Memorial Collection, Box 574, University of the West Indies–St. Augustine.

75. "Letter from [Secretary of the Colonies] Mr. [Alan Lennox] Boyd to Sir [Hugh] Foot on the Incompatibility between Political Independence and Financial Dependence," in *British Documents on the End of Empire*, series B, vol. 6, *The West Indies*, ed. S. R. Ashton and David Killingray (London: Stationery Office, 1999), 139–40.

76. Mordecai, *West Indies*, 124.

77. "Broadcast given by the Honorable N. W. Manley," June 12, 1960, Federal Archives, Folder FWI-PM-IS-148, University of the West Indies–Cave Hill.

78. "Broadcast by the Premier of Jamaica, the Hon. Norman Manley," June 18, 1961, Federal Archives, Folder FWI-PM-IS-148, University of the West Indies–Cave Hill.

79. Norman Manley, "Jamaica's Proposal for Federation," February 22, 1960, Federation Records, Trinidad National Archives, Box 6.

80. Ibid.

81. "Comment on the *Economics of Nationhood*," November 2, 1959, C.L.R. James Papers, Folder ICS40/A/1/4, Senate House Library.

82. T. O. Elias, *Federation v. Confederation and the Nigeria Federation* (Port-of-Spain: Government of the West Indies, 1960), Federation Record, Trinidad National Archives, Box 6.

83. Ibid.

84. Ibid.

85. On Manley's miscalculation, see Mordecai, *West Indies*, 223, 392–415.

86. "Excerpts from Premier's [Eric Williams] Press Conference, November 5, 1961," Federal Archives, Folder: FWI-GG-GA-249, University of West Indies–Cave Hill.

87. Ibid.

88. W. Arthur Lewis, "Secret Memorandum to Honorable Sir Grantley Adams: Situation Arising from Jamaica Referendum," November 9, 1961, Federal Archives Folder: FWI-PM-GA-27, University of West Indies–Cave Hill.

89. Nkrumah, *Africa Must Unite*, 112, 154; Nkrumah, *Neocolonialism*, 11; Williams, "Federation in the World of Today."

90. "Union Government Is Essential to Economic Independence and Higher Living Standards," Files of Ex-Presidential Affairs, Folder RG/17/2/1047 OAU Papers, PRAAD.

91. "Summary of Preparatory Conference on Organization of African Unity, May 1963, Addis Ababa, Ethiopia," Files of Ex-Presidential Affairs, Folder RG/17/2/1047 OAU Papers, PRAAD.

92. Ibid.

93. "Balewa's Plans for African Unity," *West African Pilot*, May 25, 1963, Newspaper Collection, British Library. Nigerian prime minister Abubakar Balewa endorsed the Ethiopian proposal. He called for economic integration at a regional level with some coordination through the continental organization, collaboration on anticolonial policy at the United Nations and in support of freedom fighters in southern Africa, as well as a continental effort on nuclear disarmament.

94. Even the disagreement about the name of the new organization was heated and took hours during the preparatory conference. The Ethiopian draft had named the new body Organization of African States to stress the independence of each state. Botsio (with the support of other delegations) rejected this in part because the acronym OAS was also that of the secret French army in Algeria, "Organisation armée secrète." More importantly, Botsio insisted that the word *union* had to be part of the organization's name. Most delegates rejected the name Union of African States for the compromise of Organization of African Unity. "Summary of Preparatory Conference on OAU, May 1963, Addis Ababa," Files of Ex-Presidential Affairs, Folder RG/17/2/1047—OAU Papers, PRAAD.

95. "Address by His Imperial Majesty Haile Selassie I at the Conference of African Heads of State and Governments, Addis Ababa, Ethiopia, May 22, 1963, Addis Ababa, Ethiopia," Files of Ex-Presidential Affairs, Folder RG/17/2/451—OAU Papers, PRAAD.

96. "Address by His Imperial Majesty Haile Selassie I at the Conference of Independent African States, June 16, 1960," Bureau of African Affairs Papers, Box 483 Conference on Independent African States, George Padmore Research Library on African Affairs.

97. Ibid.

98. "Kojo Botsio, Minister of Foreign Affairs, Ghana to the Provisional Secretary General, Organization of African Unity, April 21, 1964," SC/BAA/492 Committee on OAU Summit Conference, PRAAD.

99. "Union Government Is Essential to Economic Independence and Higher Living Standards," in Files of Ex-Presidential Affairs, Folder RG/17/2/1047 OAU Papers, PRAAD.

100. Nnamdi Azikiwe, *The Future of Pan-Africanism* (London: Nigeria High Commission, 1961), 13.

101. Address by His Imperial Majesty Haile Selassie I at the Conference of African Heads of State and Governments Addis Ababa, Ethiopia, May 22, 1963, Addis Ababa, Ethiopia, Files of Ex-Presidential Affairs, Folder RG/17/2/451 OAU Papers, PRAAD.

102. Azikiwe, *Future of Pan-Africanism*, 13.

103. "Speech by Osagyefo Dr. Kwame Nkrumah at the Opening of the Summit Conference of the OAU, Accra, October 21, 1965," Office of the Ex-Bureau of African Affairs Papers, SA/BAA/468 OAU-1965, PRAAD.

104. "Let Us Build a New Africa: Full Text of the Speech Delivered by Dr. Nnamdi Azikiwe Governor-General and Commander-in-Chief of the Federation of Nigeria at the Opening of the Conference of the Heads of African and Malagasy States," *West African Pilot*, January 26, 1962, Newspaper Collection, British Library.

105. Ibid.

106. Ibid.

107. Speech by Osagyefo Dr. Kwame Nkrumah at the Opening of the Summit Conference of the OAU, Accra, October 21, 1965, SA/BAA/468 OAU-1965, Papers of the Bureau of African Affairs, PRAAD.

108. Ibid.

109. Kwame Nkrumah, "Towards a United Africa," *Voice of Africa* 2 (March 1962): 20–21, Bureau of African Affairs Papers, File BAA/RLAA/13, "Voice of Africa, undated": Newspaper Clippings, George Padmore Library on African Affairs.

110. Nkrumah, *Africa Must Unite*, 148–49.

111. "Provisional Draft of the Principles of the Constitution of the Union of African States with Explanatory Note," Files of Ex-Presidential Affairs, Folder RG 17/2/553 A Union Government for Africa, PRAAD, 4.

112. Ibid., 101.

113. Ibid., 99–101.

114. Ibid., 68–71. Articles 22–26 detail civil and political rights while articles 11–14 outline social and economic rights under discussion of the union's social policy.

115. "Let Us Build a New Africa."

116. Ibid.

117. Ibid.

118. The Organization of African Unity, reorganized as the African Union in 2001, and the 1965 Caribbean Free Trade Association (CARIFTA), which became the Caribbean Community (CARICOM) in 1973, eschewed the creation of federal structure to instead secure collaboration on economic integration and functional coordination. European integration took a similar trajectory, and although it has gone further, it remains within the logic of functional integration. On the functionalism of the European Union, see Isiksel, *Europe's Functional Constitution*.

119. The term "federal moment" is borrowed from Michael Collins, "Decolonisation and the 'Federal Moment,'" *Diplomacy and Statecraft* 24 (February 2013): 21–40.

120. Wilder, *Freedom Time*, 3.

121. Nkrumah, *Africa Must Unite*, 158.

122. Julius Nyerere, "East African Federation," in *Freedom and Unity*, 89.

123. "Charter of the Organization of African Unity," https://au.int/sites/default/files/treaties/7759-sl-oau_charter_1963_0.pdf, accessed November 13, 2017.

124. Ibid.

125. Simpson, "Biafra Secession," 345.

126. Ibid., 344.

Chapter Five: The Welfare World of the New International Economic Order

1. Eric Williams, "A Small Country in a Big World" (1964), Eric Williams Memorial Collection, Box 736, University of West Indies–St. Augustine.

2. Eric Williams, "West Africa and West Indies" (1964), Eric Williams Memorial Collection, Box 813, University of West Indies–St. Augustine.

3. Julius Nyerere, "A Call to European Socialists," in *Freedom and Development: A Selection from Writings and Speeches, 1968–1973* (Dar es Salaam: Oxford University Press, 1973), 375. See also Mohammed Bedjaoui, *Towards a New International Economic Order* (Paris: UNESCO, 1979), 35–36.

4. Frederick Cooper, *Africa since 1940: The Past of the Present* (New York: Cambridge University Press, 2002), 85. Anticolonial nationalists had a complex relationship to the colonial inheritance of development. While nationalists insisted that development could not be a prerequisite for self-determination, they remained attached to projects of modernization. They argued that development should follow the establishment of self-governing postcolonial political communities. This double bind—the rejection of claims of colonial backwardness on the one hand and the insistence that the formerly colonized can and should modernize—was a central feature of anticolonial thought. Sundhya Pahuja, *Decolonising International Law: Development, Economic Growth and the Politics of Universality* (New York: Cambridge University Press, 2011), 54–55. For more on the commitment to development as a double bind, see Chatterjee, *Nationalist Thought and the Colonial World*.

5. Goswami, *Producing India*, 276.

6. Ibid. As Goswami argues, this view of representation regarded the nation "as an undifferentiated whole in class, caste, religious, and regional terms" and "entailed the marginalization of subaltern social groups and classes."

7. Nkrumah, *Africa Must Unite*, 110.

8. Cooper, *Africa since 1940*, 86.

9. Ibid., 92.

10. For dependency and world systems theorists' engagement with the NIEO, see Herb Addo, ed., *Transforming the World Economy? Nine Critical Essays on the New International Economic Order* (London: Hodder and Stoughton, 1984).

11. W. Arthur Lewis, *Aspects of Tropical Trade, 1868–1963* (Stockholm: Almqvist and Wicksell 1969), 17.

12. W. Arthur Lewis, "Economic Development with Unlimited Supplies of Labor" (1954), in *Selected Economic Writings of W. Arthur Lewis*, 139–91 (New York: New York University Press, 1983).

13. Lewis, *Aspects of Tropical Trade*, 17.

14. Robert L. Tignor, *W. Arthur Lewis and the Birth of Development Economics* (Princeton, NJ: Princeton University Press, 2006), 257.

15. W. Arthur Lewis, *The Evolution of the International Economic Order* (Princeton, NJ: Princeton University Press, 1978), 8–9.

16. Ibid.

17. Lewis is best known for his theory of "unlimited supplies of labor," which he argued characterized countries "where population is so large relative to capital and natural resources, that there are large sectors of the economy where the marginal productivity of labor is negligible, zero or even negative." In countries where unlimited supplies of labor did exist, such as India, Egypt, and Nigeria, industrialization could be more rapid. Without unlimited supplies of labor, as was the case in Ghana and the smaller Caribbean islands, industrialization would occur on a slower pace. Lewis, "Economic Development with Unlimited Supplies of Labor," 141.

18. Lewis, *Evolution of the International Economic Order*, 10; Tignor, *W. Arthur Lewis*, 83.

19. W. Arthur Lewis, *The Principles of Economic Planning: A Study Prepared for the Fabian Society* (London: D. Dobson, 1949).

20. Lewis, *Evolution of the International Economic Order*, 8–9. Lewis noted that in an effort to maintain low wages in mining and plantations, foreign capitalists and imperial governments did not invest in technological innovations or food production. Moreover, the expropriation of land, imposition of taxation, and implementation of forced labor impoverished the subsistence economy by moving peoples and resources toward the export economy. However, imperialism plays only a minor role in Lewis's account of underdevelopment. Lewis, "Economic Development with Unlimited Supplies of Labor," 149.

21. Lewis, *Evolution of the International Economic Order*, 75.

22. W. Arthur Lewis, *Report on Industrialization and the Gold Coast Economy* (Accra: Government Printers, 1953).

23. Tignor, *W. Arthur Lewis*, 169–76; Ahlman, *Living with Nkrumahism*, 80–81, 130.

24. Tignor, *W. Arthur Lewis*, 176.

25. Nkrumah, *Africa Must Unite*, 97.

26. Ibid., 110; Gunnar Myrdal, *Economic Theory and Underdeveloped Regions* (London: Gerald Duckworth, 1957), 66. Myrdal's *Economic Theory* was based on a series of lectures he had given to the National Bank of Egypt in 1955. The lectures were published as Gunnar Myrdal, *Development and Underdevelopment: A Note on the Mechanism of National and International Economic Equality* (Cairo: National Bank of Egypt, 1956).

27. Myrdal, *Development and Underdevelopment*, 42–43; Myrdal, *Economic Theory and Underdeveloped Regions*, 47–48; "Union Government Is Essential to Economic Independence and Higher Living Standards," in Files of Ex-Presidential Affairs, Folder RG/17/2/1047 OAU Papers, Public Records and Archives Department.

28. Nkrumah, *Neocolonialism*, 239.

29. Andre Gunder Frank, "The Development of Underdevelopment," *Monthly Review* 18 (September 1966): 17–31; Samir Amin, *Unequal Development: An Essay on the Social Formations of Peripheral Capitalism*, trans. Brian Pierce (New York: Monthly Review Press, 1976).

30. Nkrumah, *Neocolonialism*, xix.

31. Ibid.

32. Ibid.

33. Ibid., 11.

34. Ahlman, *Living with Nkrumahism*, 204–6. A similar constellation of economic factors led to a wave of coups across the global south. The twenty years between the mid-1960s and the 1980s marked a large spike in the number of successful military takeovers. See Aaron Benanav, "A Global History of Unemployment: Surplus Population in the World Economy, 1949–2010" (PhD diss., University of California, Berkeley, 2014), 173–74.

35. Michael Manley, *The Politics of Change: A Jamaican Testament* (1974; Washington, DC: Howard University Press, 1990), 24. For a critique of Rostow's modernization theory, see Manley, *Poverty of Nations*, 70.

36. Manley, *Politics of Change*, 18.

37. Lloyd Best, "The Mechanism of Plantation-Type Economies: Outlines of a Model of Pure Plantation Economy," *Social and Economic Studies* 17 (September 1968): 283–326.

38. Ibid.; George Beckford, *Persistent Poverty: Underdevelopment in Plantation Economies of the Third World* (New York: Oxford University Press, 1972).

39. Giovanni Arrighi and John Saul, *Essays on the Political Economy of Africa* (New York: Monthly Review Press, 1973); Giovanni Arrighi, "The Winding Paths of Capital: Interview by David Harvey," *New Left Review* 56 (March–April 2009): 61–94, 63–64; Walter Rodney, *World War II and the Tanzanian Economy* (Ithaca, NY: Cornell University Press, 1976); Walter Rodney et al., eds., *Migrant Labor in Tanzania during the Colonial Period—Case Studies of Recruitment and Conditions of Labor in the Sisal Industry* (Hamburg: Arbeiten aus dem Institut für Afrika-Kunde, 1983).

40. On the Dar es Salaam school, see Horace Campbell, "The Impact of Walter Rodney and Progressive Scholars on the Dar es Salaam School," *Social and Economic Studies* 40 (June 1991): 99–135. For a comparative study of the New World Group and Dar es Salaam school, see Adom Getachew, "The Plantation in Comparative Perspective: Toward a Theory of Colonial Modernity," in *The Oxford Handbook of Comparative Political Theory*, ed. Leigh Jenco et al. (New York: Oxford University Press), forthcoming.

41. Manley, *Poverty of Nations*, 13–14.

42. Walter Rodney, "Migrant Labor and the Colonial Economy," in Rodney et al., *Migrant Labor in Tanzania during the Colonial Period*, 5.

43. Samir Amin, *Delinking: Towards a Polycentric World* (London: Zed Books, 1990), 63.

44. Ibid., 66.

45. Anghie, *Imperialism*, 211–20; Vanessa Ogle, "States' Rights against Private Capital: The 'New International Economic Order' and the Struggle over Aid, Trade, and Foreign Investments, 1962–1981," *Humanity: An International Journal of Human Rights, Humanitarianism, and Development* 5 (Summer 2014): 211–34.

46. For instance, Manley repeatedly pointed to the dominance of foreign corporations and local elites. When Manley was elected, "foreign interests owned 100 percent of the bauxite and alumina industry, more than half of the sugar industry and much more than half of the tourist industry." Moreover, "2.2% of farms occupied 63.1% of

arable acres, while 97.8% of farms shared 36.9% of arable land." Michael Manley, *Jamaica: Struggle in the Periphery* (London: Third World Media, 1982), 40. On nationalization in Tanzania, see Bonny Ibhawoh and J. I. Dibua, "Deconstructing Ujamaa: The Legacy of Julius Nyerere in the Quest for Social and Economic Development in Africa," *African Association of Political Science* 8 (January 2003): 59–93, 64–65.

47. Julius Nyerere, "Arusha Declaration," in *Freedom and Socialism: A Selection from Writings and Speeches 1965–1967* (Dar es Salaam: Oxford University Press, 1968), 240; Lal, *African Socialism in Postcolonial Tanzania*, 31.

48. Julius Nyerere, "Socialism and Rural Development," in *Ujamaa: Essays on Socialism* (London: Oxford University Press, 1968), 114–15. Given his attention to the problem of hierarchy among peasants, one of the ironies of his villagization program was the ways it exacerbated domination between peasants. According to D. A. Low, villagization in Tanzania (and elsewhere) empowered "well to do peasants" who could use the institutional arrangements of the concentrated village to exercise greater control over their poorer, less powerful counterparts. The egalitarian impulses motivating villagization thus perversely created new hierarchies. D. A. Low, *The Egalitarian Moment: Asia and Africa, 1950–1980* (New York: Cambridge University Press, 1996), 49–55.

49. Julius Nyerere, "New Economic Order," in *Freedom and a New Economic Order: A Selection from Speeches, 1974–1999* (Dar es Salaam: Oxford University Press, 2011), 27.

50. Ibid.

51. Nyerere, "Socialism and Rural Development," 20.

52. Lal, *African Socialism in Postcolonial Tanzania*, 46–50, 53–54.

53. Ibid., 46–48. Viewed from the perspective of its modernizing ambitions, James Scott has argued that Nyerere's program was emblematic of twentieth-century projects of "authoritarian high modernism" that strengthened the state apparatus, resulted in violent displacements and ruptures of peasant life, and failed to realize the aims of eradicating poverty and instituting equality. Like its counterparts in the Soviet Union and China, the villagization program in Tanzania relied on an attachment to the ideas of planning and technical expertise that endowed state bureaucrats and economic advisors with a monopoly of useful knowledge, which only needed to be applied. James Scott, *Seeing Like a State: How Certain Schemes to Improve the Human Condition Have Failed* (New Haven, CT: Yale University Press, 1998), 224–48.

54. Lal, *African Socialism in Postcolonial Tanzania*, 48–49.

55. Manley, *Politics of Change*, 58–59.

56. Ibid., 28.

57. On colonial modernity in the Caribbean, see David Scott, *Conscripts of Modernity: The Tragedy of Colonial Enlightenment* (Durham, NC: Duke University Press, 2004), 125–29.

58. Manley, *Politics of Change*, 99.

59. Ibid., 100.

60. Ibid.

61. Manley, *Jamaica*, 43–44.

62. Manley, *Politics of Change*, 104–5.

63. Manley, *Poverty of Nations*, 24.

64. Ibid., 83.

65. Nyerere, "New Economic Order," 28.

66. Manley, *Poverty of Nations*, 111; Julius Nyerere, "Independence Address to United Nations," in *Freedom and Unity*, 145; Nyerere, "The Third World and the International Economic Structure," in *Freedom and a New Economic Order*, 44.

67. Nyerere, "Call to European Socialists," 375.

68. Manley, *Poverty of Nations*, 93.

69. Nyerere, "Third World and the International Economic Structure," 37–38.

70. Ibid., 37.

71. Manley, *Poverty of Nations*, 93.

72. Nyerere, "Third World and the International Economic Structure," 37.

73. Ibid., 37–38.

74. Gunnar Myrdal, *An International Economy: Problems and Prospects* (New York: Harper and Row, 1956); Gunnar Myrdal, *Rich Lands Poor Lands: The Road to World Prosperity* (New York: Harper and Row, 1957); Gunnar Myrdal, *Beyond the Welfare State: Economic Planning and Its International Implications* (New Haven, CT: Yale University Press, 1960). For recent assessments of these texts, see Jamie Martin, "Gunnar Myrdal and the Failed Promises of the Postwar International Economic Settlement," *Humanity: An International Journal of Human Rights, Humanitarianism, and Development* 8 (Spring 2017): 167–73; Samuel Moyn, "Welfare World," *Humanity: An International Journal of Human Rights, Humanitarianism, and Development* 8 (Spring 2017): 175–83; Isaac Nakhimovsky, "An International Dilemma: The Postwar Utopianism of Gunnar Myrdal's *Beyond the Welfare State*," *Humanity: An International Journal of Human Rights, Humanitarianism, and Development* 8 (Spring 2017): 185–94.

75. Myrdal, *Beyond the Welfare State*, 221–22.

76. Ibid., viii.

77. Ibid., 148. Myrdal's reference to the "rich men's club" was particularly directed at the project of European economic and political integration. According to Myrdal, the economic integration of Western Europe would overcome economic nationalism within the regional context but, from the perspective of the world order, would only "represent a further step towards compartmentalization of international economic relations."

78. Ibid., 217.

79. Ibid., 171.

80. Samuel Moyn, *Not Enough: Human Rights in an Unequal World* (Cambridge, MA: Harvard University Press, 2018), 116.

81. Nakhimovsky, "International Dilemma," 191.

82. United Nations General Assembly Resolution 1785 (XVII), "United Nations Conference on Trade and Development," A/RES/17/1785, December 8, 1962, https://documents-dds-ny.un.org/doc/RESOLUTION/GEN/NR0/192/93/IMG/NR019293.pdf?OpenElement, accessed December 20, 2017.

83. United Nations Economic Commission for Latin America, *The Economic Development of Latin America and Its Principal Problems* (Lake Success, NY: UN Department of Economic Affairs, 1950).

84. United Nations General Assembly Resolution 3201 (S-VI), "Declaration on the Establishment of a New International Economic Order," A/RES/S-6/3201, May 1,

1974, http://www.un-documents.net/s6r3201.htm, accessed November 15, 2014; United Nations General Assembly Resolution 3281 (XXIX), "Charter of Economic Rights and Duties of States," A/RES/29/3289, December 12, 1974, http://www.un -documents.net/a29r3281.htm, accessed November 15, 2014.

85. Gunnar Myrdal, "The Equality Issue in World Development," Nobel Prize Lecture, March 17, 1975, http://www.nobelprize.org/nobel_prizes/economic-sciences /laureates/1974/myrdal-lecture.html, accessed March 15, 2016.

86. Ernst-Ulrich Petersmann quoted in Quinn Slobodian, *Globalists: The End of Empire and the Birth of Neoliberalism* (Cambridge, MA: Harvard University Press, 2018), 246–47.

87. B.V.A. Röling, "The History and the Sociological Approach of the NIEO and the Third World," in *North-South Dialogue: A New International Economic Order* (Thessaloniki: Institute of International Public Law and International Relations of Thessaloniki, 1982), 209–24.

88. General Assembly Resolution 3201 (S-VI), "Declaration on the Establishment of a New International Economic Order."

89. Antony Anghie, "Legal Aspects of the New International Economic Order," *Humanity: An International Journal of Human Rights, Humanitarianism and Development* 6 (Spring 2015): 145–58, 147.

90. General Assembly Resolution 3201 (S-VI), "Declaration on the Establishment of a New International Economic Order." On the ways the charter was perceived as a fundamental departure, see Subrata Roy Chowdhury, "Legal Status of the Charter of Economic Rights and Duties of States," in *Legal Aspects of the New International Economic Order*, ed. Kamal Hossain (1980; New York: Bloomsbury, 2013), 81.

91. General Assembly Resolution 3201 (S-VI), "Declaration on the Establishment of a New International Economic Order."

92. General Assembly Resolution 3201 (XXIX), "Charter of Economic Rights and Duties."

93. Nyerere, "New Economic Order," 28.

94. Nyerere, "Third World and the International Economic Structure," 46.

95. Nyerere, "New Economic Order," 28.

96. Ibid.

97. Raúl Prebisch, *Towards a New Trade Policy for Development: Report by the Secretary-General of the United Nations Conference on Trade and Development* (New York: United Nations, 1964), 28.

98. Ibid., 29–30.

99. Manley, *Poverty of Nations*, 32–33, 110–11.

100. Ibid., 34–35; Anghie, "Legal Aspects," 148.

101. Group of 77 and United Nations Conference on Trade and Development, *Trends and Problems in World Trade and Development: Charter of Algiers* (Belgrade: Medunarodna štampa Interpress, 1968), 15.

102. Prebisch, *Towards a New Trade Policy for Development*, 34–35.

103. *Proceedings of the United Nations Conference on Trade and Development, March 23–June 16, 1964* (New York: United Nations, 1964), 10.

104. Johanna Bockman, "Socialist Globalization against Capitalist Neocolonialism: The Economic Ideas behind the New International Economic Order," *Humanity:*

An International Journal of Human Rights, Humanitarianism, and Development 6 (Spring 2015): 109–28.

105. *Proceedings of the United Nations Conference on Trade and Development*, 10.

106. Bockman, "Socialist Globalization," 118.

107. *Proceedings of the United Nations Conference on Trade and Development*, 43.

108. Ibid., 81.

109. Nyerere, "New Economic Order," 28–29.

110. General Assembly Resolution 3201 (S-VI), "Declaration on the Establishment of a New International Economic Order"; General Assembly Resolution 3201 (XXIX), "Charter of Economic Rights and Duties."

111. General Assembly Resolution 3201 (S-VI), "Declaration on the Establishment of a New International Economic Order."

112. Slobodian, *Globalists*, 243.

113. Prebisch, *Towards a New Trade Policy on Development*, 80.

114. Ibid., 43; Jagdish Bhagwati, *The New International Economic Order: The North-South Debate* (Cambridge, MA: MIT Press, 1977), 8; Victor McFarland, "The New International Economic Order, Interdependence and Globalization," *Humanity: An International Journal of Human Rights, Humanitarianism, and Development* 6 (Spring 2015): 217–33.

115. "Challenge to the Colonial Powers," 5.

116. Ibid., 6–7.

117. Ahlman, *Living with Nkrumahism*, 130.

118. Issa Shivji, *The Silent Class Struggle* (Dar es Salaam: Tanzania House, 1974). Shivji was a member of the "Dar es Salaam school" and participated in the debates about social theory with Giovanni Arrighi, Walter Rodney, and others. Ibhawoh and Dibua, "Deconstructing Ujamaa," 62.

119. Nyerere, "New Economic Order," 26.

120. Samir Amin, "Self-Reliance and the New International Economic Order," *Monthly Review* 29 (July–August 1977): 1–21, 14–15.

121. Robert Tucker, *The Inequality of Nations* (New York: Basic Books, 1977), 19–72.

122. Nyerere, "New Economic Order," 25.

123. Anghie, "Legal Aspects," 146.

124. Amin, "Self-Reliance and the New International Economic Order," 15.

125. Mazower, *Governing the World*, 303–4.

126. Ogle, "States' Rights," 215.

127. General Assembly Resolution 3201 (XXIX), "Charter of Economic Rights and Duties."

128. On these tensions, see Anghie, "Legal Aspects," 150–55.

129. The shifting reception of NIEO among United States officials highlights the ways that the economic crisis unfolding in postcolonial world emboldened a more critical and confrontational approach to the Third World's demands. While skeptical of the NIEO, Henry Kissinger, for instance, pioneered a conciliatory strategy of appeasement toward the Third World. See Daniel Sargent, "North/South: The United States Responds to the New International Economic Order," *Humanity: An Inter-*

national Journal of Human Rights, Humanitarianism, and Development 6 (Spring 2015), 201–16; and Daniel Sargent, *A Superpower Transformed: The Remaking of American Foreign Relations in the 1970s* (New York: Oxford University Press, 2014), 177–82. However, by 1981, under the leadership of Ronald Reagan, the United States explicitly rejected any demands for greater economic equality. See Ogle, "States' Rights," 211, 224.

130. Kari Polanyi Levitt, *The Origins and Consequences of Jamaica's Debt Crisis 1970–1990* (Mona: Consortium Graduate School of the Social Sciences, 1991), 13. See also Manley, *Jamaica*, 151.

131. Levitt, *Origins and Consequences*, 14.

132. Norman Girvan et al., "The Third World and the IMF: The Case of Jamaica, 1974–1980," *Development Dialogue* 2 (1980): 113–65, 113.

133. Levitt, *Origins and Consequences*, 14.

134. Ibhawoh and Dibua, "Deconstructing Ujamaa," 71.

135. Duncan Holtom, "Reconsidering the Power of IFIs: Tanzania and the World Bank, 1978–1985," *Review of African Political Economy* 32 (December 2005): 549–67.

136. Michael Manley, "Message from the Prime Minister of Jamaica, Hon. Michael Manley, to the South-North Conference on the International Monetary System and the New International Order," *Development Dialogue* 2 (1980): 5–6.

137. "The Arusha Initiative: A Call for a United Nations Conference on International Money and Finance," *Development Dialogue* 2 (1980): 10–23.

138. Manley, "Message from the Prime Minister of Jamaica," 5–6.

139. Bockman, "Socialist Globalization," 121–22.

140. Slobodian, *Globalists*, 241. See also Umut Özsu, "Neoliberalism and the New International Economic Order: A History of 'Contemporary Legal Thought,'" in *Searching for Contemporary Legal Thought*, ed. Justin Desautels-Stein and Christopher L. Tomlins (Cambridge: Cambridge University Press, 2017), 330–47.

141. Slobodian, *Globalists*, 221.

142. Samuel Moyn, "The Political Origins of Global Justice," in *The Worlds of American Intellectual History*, ed. Joel Isaac et al. (New York: Oxford University Press, 2016), 133–52; Moyn, *Not Enough*, 172–79.

143. Charles Beitz, *Political Theory and International Relations* (Princeton, NJ: Princeton University Press, 1979), 152.

144. On the emergence of a basic needs approach and the ways it was articulated against the demands of the NIEO, see Moyn, *Not Enough*, chapter 6.

145. Ibid., 145, 186.

146. Ibid., 185, 189.

147. Robert Amdur, quoted in ibid., 166. See also Robert Amdur, "Global Distributive Justice: A Review Essay," *Journal of International Affairs* 31 (Spring/Summer 1977), 81–88, 81.

148. Recent calls for reparations especially in the Caribbean have returned to the framing impulse of the NIEO that the wealth of the global north was made possible through the violent domination and exploitation of the global south. But while invoking a similar history of an imperial global economy, they ground their claims not

in the welfarist language of redistribution but in a reparatory framework associated with contemporary transitional justice. Hilary McD. Beckles, *Britain's Black Debt: Reparations for Caribbean Slavery and Genocide* (Kingston: University of West Indies Press, 2013); David Scott, "Preface: Debt, Redress," *Small Axe* 43 (March 2014): vii–x; David Scott, "On the Moral Justification of Reparations for New World Slavery," in *Freedom and Democracy in an Imperial Context: Dialogues with James Tully*, ed. Robert Nichols and Jakeet Singh (New York: Routledge, 2014), 100–120. On the relationship between reparations and the philosophical literature on global justice, see Katrina Forrester, "Reparations, History and the Origins of Global Justice," in *Empire, Race and Global Justice*, ed. Duncan Bell (Cambridge: Cambridge University Press, forthcoming).

Epilogue: The Fall of Self-Determination

1. Daniel P. Moynihan, "The United States in Opposition," *Commentary* 59 (March 1975): https://www.commentarymagazine.com/articles/the-united-states-in-opposition/, accessed February 15, 2018.

2. Ibid.

3. S. Prakash Sinha, "Is Self-Determination Passé?," *Columbia Journal of Transnational Law* 12, no. 2 (1973): 260–73. Sinha's own answer to this question was circumspect. While he argued that the form self-determination had taken during decolonization might be coming to an end, he maintained that at its core self-determination was concerned with securing "justice for the individual" and as such would have a life beyond decolonization. For other observers of the period, "justice for the individual" required abandoning the collectivist right to self-determination in favor of individual human rights. Moyn, *Last Utopia*, 118–19.

4. Rupert Emerson, "Self-Determination," *American Journal of International Law* 65 (July 1971): 459–75, 466; Elmer Plischke, "Self-Determination: Reflections on a Legacy," *World Affairs* 140 (Summer 1977): 41–57, 51.

5. Emerson, "Fate of Human Rights," 223. See also Daniel Patrick Moynihan, "The Politics of Human Rights," *Commentary* 64 (August 1977): https://www.commentarymagazine.com/articles/the-politics-of-human-rights/, accessed February 15, 2018; Louis Henkin, *The Rights of Man Today* (Boulder, CO: Westview, 1978).

6. Plischke, "Self-Determination," 52.

7. Emerson, "Self-Determination," 471.

8. Jackson, *Quasi-states*; G. Simpson, *Great Powers and Outlaw States*.

9. Irwin, *Gordian Knot*, 132.

10. Bâli and Rana, "Constitutionalism and the American Imperial Imagination," 276.

11. Ibid., 280–84; Jean Cohen, "A Global State of Emergency or the Further Constitutionalization of International Law: A Pluralist Approach," *Constellations* 15 (December 2008): 456–84.

12. Scott, *Refashioning Futures*, 221–24.

13. "Michael Manley: A Man for All Times," *Daily Gleaner: A Special Gleaner Feature*, September 18, 1992, 21, West Indian Newspapers Collection, University of West Indies–St. Augustine.

14. Spanning seven months between December 1995 and July 1996, the correspondence was published in the inaugural issue of *Small Axe*. See Kari Levitt and Michael Manley, "The Manley/Levitt Exchange," *Small Axe* 1 (February 1997): 81–115.

15. Michael Manley quoted in ibid., 87. See also "Michael Manley: A Man for All Times," 8.

16. Levitt and Manley, "Manley/Levitt Exchange," 87.

17. Ibid., 92.

1. Archival Collections

Accra, Ghana
  Bureau of African Affairs Papers, George Padmore Research Library for African Affairs
  Files of the Ex-Bureau of African Affairs, Public Record and Archives Administration
  Files of Ex-Presidential Affairs, Public Record and Archives Administration
  Newspaper Collections, Public Record and Archives Administration
Cave Hill, Barbados
  Federal Archives Fonds, University of West Indies, Cave Hill
Geneva, Switzerland
  Papers of the Mandate Section, League of Nations Archives, United Nations Library
  Papers of the Political Section, League of Nations Archives, United Nations Library
  League of Nations Official Journal, United Nations Library
London, United Kingdom
  C.L.R. James Papers, Senate House Library
  British Library Newspaper Collection
Port-of-Spain and St. Augustine, Trinidad
  C.L.R. James Collection, University of the West Indies–St. Augustine
  Eric Williams Memorial Collection, University of the West Indies–St. Augustine
  Trinidad National Archives, Port-of-Spain, Trinidad
  West Indian Newspapers Collection, University of the West Indies–St. Augustine

2. Published Sources

"The 1930 Enquiry Commission to Liberia." *Journal of the Royal African Society* 30 (July 1931): 277–90.

Adas, Michael. "Contested Hegemony: The Great War and the Afro-Asian Assault on the Civilizing Mission Ideology." *Journal of World History* 15 (March 2004): 31–63.

Addo, Herb, ed. *Transforming the World Economy? Nine Critical Essays on the New International Economic Order*. London: Hodder and Stoughton, 1984.

Ahlman, Jeffrey. *Living with Nkrumahism: Nation, State, and Pan-Africanism in Ghana*. Athens: Ohio University Press, 2017.

Alexandrowicz, C. H. *The Law of Nations in Global History*, edited by David Armitage and Jennifer Pitts. Oxford: Oxford University Press, 2017.

Allain, Jean. "Slavery and the League of Nations: Ethiopia as a Civilised Nation." *Journal of the History of International Law* 8 (November 2006): 213–44.

Allman, Jean. "Nuclear Imperialism and the Pan-African Struggle for Peace and Freedom: Ghana, 1959–1962." *Souls: A Critical Journal of Black Politics, Culture, and Society* 10 (June 2008): 83–102.

Allman, Jean Marie. *The Quills of the Porcupine: Asante Nationalism in an Emergent Ghana*. Madison: University of Wisconsin Press, 1993.

Amdur, Robert. "Global Distributive Justice: A Review Essay." *Journal of International Affairs* 31 (Spring/Summer 1977): 81–88.

Amin, Samir. *Delinking: Towards a Polycentric World*. London: Zed Books, 1990.

———. *Re-reading the Postwar Period: An Intellectual Itinerary*. New York: Monthly Review Press, 1994.

———. "Self-Reliance and the New International Economic Order." *Monthly Review* 29 (July–August 1977): 1–21.

———. *Unequal Development: An Essay on the Social Formations of Peripheral Capitalism*. Translated by Brian Pierce. New York: Monthly Review Press, 1976.

Anderson, Carol. *Eyes off the Prize: The United Nations and the African American Struggle for Human Rights, 1944–1955*. New York: Cambridge University Press, 2003.

Anderson, Perry. "Internationalism: A Breviary." *New Left Review* 14 (March/April 2002): 5–25.

Anghie, Antony. *Imperialism, Sovereignty and the Making of International Law*. New York: Cambridge University Press, 2005.

———. "Legal Aspects of the New International Economic Order." *Humanity: An International Journal of Human Rights, Humanitarianism, and Development* 6 (Spring 2015): 145–58.

———. "Whose Utopia? Human Rights, Development, and the Third World." *Qui Parle: Critical Humanities and Social Sciences* 22 (Fall/Winter 2013): 63–80.

Arato, Andrew, and Jean Cohen. "Banishing the Sovereign? Internal and External Sovereignty." In *Politics in Dark Times: Encounters with Hannah Arendt*, edited by Seyla Benhabib et al., 137–71. New York: Cambridge University Press, 2010.

Arendt, Hannah. "Karl Jaspers: Citizen of the World?" In *Men in Dark Times*, 81–94. New York: Harcourt, Brace, 1968.

———. *The Origins of Totalitarianism*. 1951. New York: Harcourt Books, 1994.

———. "Rights of Man: What Are They?" *Modern Review* 3 (1949): 25–37.

———. "Thoughts on Politics and Revolution: A Commentary." In *Crises of the Republic*, 199–234. New York: Harcourt, Brace, 1972.

Armitage, David. *The Declaration of Independence: A Global History*. Cambridge, MA: Harvard University Press, 2007.

Arrighi, Giovanni. "The Winding Paths of Capital: Interview by David Harvey." *New Left Review* 56 (March–April 2009): 61–94.

Arrighi, Giovanni, and John Saul. *Essays on the Political Economy of Africa*. New York: Monthly Review Press, 1973.

"The Arusha Initiative: A Call for a United Nations Conference on International Money and Finance." *Development Dialogue* 2 (1980): 10–23.

Asante, S.K.B. *Pan-African Protest: West Africa and the Italo-Ethiopian Crisis, 1934–1941*. London: Longman, 1977.

Ashton, S. R., and David Killingray, eds. *British Documents on the End of Empire*. Series B, vol. 6, *The West Indies*. London: Stationery Office, 1999.

Aydin, Cemil. *The Politics of Anti-Westernism in Asia: Visions of World Order in Pan-Islamic and Pan-Asian Thought*. New York: Columbia University Press, 2007.

Azikiwe, Nnamdi. *The Future of Pan-Africanism*. London: Nigeria High Commission, 1961.

———. *Liberia in World Politics*. London: Arthur H. Stockwell, 1934.

———. *My Odyssey: An Autobiography*. London: C. Hurst, 1970.

———. *Political Blueprint for Nigeria*. Lagos: African Books, 1943.

———. *Renascent Africa*. 1938. London: Frank, Cass, 1968.

———. *Zik: A Selection from the Speeches of Nnamdi Azikiwe*. Cambridge: Cambridge University Press, 1961.

Bain, William. *Between Anarchy and Society: Trusteeship and the Obligations of Power*. New York: Oxford University Press, 2003.

———. "The Political Theory of Trusteeship and the Twilight of International Equality." *International Relations* 17 (March 2003): 59–77.

Bâli, Asli, and Aziz Rana. "Constitutionalism and the American Imperial Imagination." *University of Chicago Law Review*, 85 (March 2018): 257–92.

Beckford, George. *Persistent Poverty: Underdevelopment in Plantation Economies of the Third World*. New York: Oxford University Press, 1972.

Beckles, Hilary McD. *Britain's Black Debt: Reparations for Caribbean Slavery and Genocide*. Kingston: University of West Indies Press, 2013.

Bedjaoui, Mohammed. *Towards a New International Economic Order*. Paris: UNESCO, 1979.

Beitz, Charles. "Justice and International Relations." *Philosophy and Public Affairs* 4 (Summer 1975): 360–89.

———. *Political Theory and International Relations*. Princeton, NJ: Princeton University Press, 1979.

Bell, Duncan. "Beyond the Sovereign State: Isopolitan Citizenship, Race and Anglo-American Union." *Political Studies* 62 (June 2014): 418–34.

———. *The Idea of Greater Britain: Empire and the Future of World Order, 1860–1900*. Princeton, NJ: Princeton University Press, 2007.

———. *Reordering the World: Essays on Liberalism and Empire*. Princeton, NJ: Princeton University Press, 2016.

Benanav, Aaron. "A Global History of Unemployment: Surplus Population in the World Economy, 1949–2010." PhD diss., University of California, Berkeley, 2014.

Benhabib, Seyla. *Another Cosmopolitanism*. With Jeremy Waldron, Bonnie Honig, and Will Kymlicka. Edited by Robert Post. New York: Oxford University Press, 2006.

———. *Critique, Norm, Utopia: A Study of the Foundations of Critical Theory*. New York: Columbia University Press, 1986.

———. *Transformations of Citizenship: Dilemmas of the Nation-State in the Era of Globalization*. Amsterdam: Koninklijke Van Gorcum, 2001.

———. "Twilight of Sovereignty or the Emergence of Cosmopolitan Norms? Rethinking Citizenship in Volatile Times." *Citizenship Studies* 11, no. 1 (2007): 19–36.

Benton, Lauren. *A Search for Sovereignty: Law and Geography in European Empires 1400–1900*. New York: Cambridge University Press, 2010.

Berlin, Isaiah. "Two Concepts of Liberty." In *Liberty: Incorporating Four Essays on Liberty*, edited by Henry Hardy, 166–217. Oxford: Oxford University Press, 2002.

Best, Lloyd. "The Mechanism of Plantation-Type Economies: Outlines of a Model of Pure Plantation Economy." *Social and Economic Studies* 17 (September 1968): 283–326.

Bhagwati, Jagdish. *The New International Economic Order: The North-South Debate*. Cambridge, MA: MIT Press, 1977.

Birch, A. H. *Federalism, Finance and Social Legislation in Canada, Australia and the United States*. Oxford: Clarendon, 1955.

———."Inter-governmental Financial Relations in New Federations." In *Federalism and Economic Growth in Underdeveloped Countries*, edited by Ursula K. Hicks et al., 113–29. London: George Allen and Unwin, 1961.

Bishop, Matthew L., et al. *Caribbean Regional Integration: A Report by the University of West Indies Institute for International Relations*. St. Augustine: Institute for International Relations, 2011.

Blackburn, Robin. *The American Crucible: Slavery, Emancipation and Human Rights*. New York: Verso, 2011.

Bockman, Johanna. "Socialist Globalization against Capitalist Neocolonialism: The Economic Ideas behind the New International Economic Order." *Humanity: An International Journal of Human Rights, Humanitarianism, and Development* 6 (Spring 2015): 109–28.

Borgwardt, Elizabeth. *A New Deal for the World: America's Vision for Human Rights*. Cambridge, MA: Belknap Press of Harvard University Press, 2005.

———. " 'When You State a Moral Principle, You Are Stuck with It': The 1941 Atlantic Charter as a Human Rights Instrument." *Virginia Journal of International Law* 46 (2006): 501–62.

Bradley, Mark. *The World Reimagined: Americans and Human Rights in the Twentieth Century*. New York: Cambridge University Press, 2016.

Buchanan, Allen. "From Nuremberg to Kosovo: The Morality of Illegal International Legal Reform." *Ethics* 111 (July 2001): 673–705.

Buck-Morss, Susan. *Hegel, Haiti, and Universal History*. Pittsburgh: University of Pittsburgh Press, 2009.

Bull, Hedley, and Adam Watson, eds. *The Expansion of International Society*. Oxford: Clarendon, 1984.

Bulmer, Simon, et al. "UK Devolution and the European Union: A Tale of Cooperative Asymmetry?" *Publius: The Journal of Federalism* 36 (Winter 2006): 75–93.

Bunche, Ralph. *A Worldview of Race*. Washington, DC: Associates in Negro Folk Education, 1936.

Burgess, Michael. *Federalism and European Union: The Building of Europe, 1950–2000*. New York: Routledge, 2000.

Burke, Edmund. "Speech on Mr. Fox's East India Bill." In *Select Works of Edmund Burke: Miscellaneous Writings*, 95–191. Indianapolis: Liberty Fund, 1999.

Burke, Roland. *Decolonization and the Evolution of International Human Rights*. Philadelphia: University of Pennsylvania Press, 2010.

Byrne, Jeffrey James. *Mecca of Revolution: Algeria, Decolonization, and the Third World Order*. New York: Oxford University Press, 2016.

Cabral, Amilcar. "Anonymous Soldiers for the United Nations." In *Revolution in Guinea: An African People's Struggle*, 40–41. London: Love and Malcomson, 1969.

Callwell, Colonel C. E. *Small Wars: Their Principles and Practice*. London: Harrison and Sons, 1906.

Campbell, Horace. "The Impact of Walter Rodney and Progressive Scholars on the Dar es Salaam School." *Social and Economic Studies* 40 (June 1991): 99–135.

Canovan, Margaret. *Nationhood and Political Theory*. North Hampton, MA: Edward Elgar, 1996.

Carnegie, Charles. "Garvey and the Black Transnation." *Small Axe* 5 (March 1999): 48–71.

Cassese, Antonio. *International Law*. Oxford: Oxford University Press, 2005.

———. *Self-Determination of Peoples: A Legal Appraisal*. New York: Cambridge University Press, 1995.

Chakrabarty, Dipesh. *Habitations of Modernity: Essays in the Wake of Subaltern Studies*. Chicago: University of Chicago Press, 2002.

———. *Provincializing Europe: Postcolonial Thought and Historical Difference*. Princeton, NJ: Princeton University Press, 2000.

Chatterjee, Deen K., and Don E. Scheid, eds. *Ethics and Foreign Intervention*. New York: Columbia University Press, 2003.

Chatterjee, Partha. *Lineages of Political Society: Studies in Postcolonial Democracy*. New York: Columbia University Press, 2011.

———. *Nationalist Thought and the Colonial World: A Derivative Discourse?* Minneapolis: University of Minnesota Press, 1986.

———. *The Nation and Its Fragments: Colonial and Postcolonial Histories*. Princeton, NJ: Princeton University Press, 1993.

———. *The Politics of the Governed: Reflections on Popular Politics in Most of the World*. New York: Columbia University Press, 2004.

Chowdhury, Subrata Roy. "Legal Status of the Charter of Economic Rights and Duties of States." In *Legal Aspects of the New International Economic Order*, edited by Kamal Hossain, 79–94. 1980. New York: Bloomsbury, 2013.

Clarke, Jane. *The Rise of a New Federalism*. New York: Columbia University Press, 1938.

Cocks, Joan. *Passion and Paradox: Intellectuals Confront the National Question*. Princeton, NJ: Princeton University Press, 2002.

Cohen, Jean. *Globalization and Sovereignty: Rethinking Legality, Legitimacy, and Constitutionalism*. New York: Cambridge University Press, 2012.

———. "A Global State of Emergency or the Further Constitutionalization of International Law: A Pluralist Approach." *Constellations* 15 (December 2008): 456–84.

Colby, Elbridge. "How to Fight Savage Tribes." *American Journal of International Law* 21 (April 1927): 279–88.

Collingwood, R. G. *An Autobiography*. Oxford: Oxford University Press, 1939.

Collins, Michael. "Decolonisation and the 'Federal Moment.'" *Diplomacy and Statecraft* 24 (February 2013): 21–40.

Contee, Clarence G. "Du Bois, the NAACP, and the Pan-African Congress of 1919." *Journal of Negro History* 57 (January 1972): 13–28.

Cooper, Frederick. *Africa since 1940: The Past of the Present*. New York: Cambridge University Press, 2002.

———. *Citizenship between Empire and Nation: Remaking France and French Africa, 1945–1960*. Princeton, NJ: Princeton University Press, 2014.

———. *Colonialism in Question: Theory, Knowledge, History*. Berkeley: University of California Press, 2005.

———. *Decolonization and African Society: The Labor Question in French and British Africa*. New York: Cambridge University Press, 1996.

———. "Possibility and Constraint: African Independence in Historical Perspective." *Journal of African History* 49 (July 2008): 167–96.

Cooper, Frederick, et al., eds. *Beyond Slavery: Explorations of Race, Labor, and Citizenship in Postemancipation Societies*. Chapel Hill: University of North Carolina Press, 2000.

Coulthard, Glen. *Red Skin, White Masks: Rejecting the Colonial Politics of Recognition*. Minneapolis: University of Minnesota Press, 2014.

Currie, David, ed. *Federalism and the New Nations of Africa*. Chicago: University of Chicago Press, 1964.

Curry, W. B. *The Case for Federal Union: A New International Order*. London: Penguin Books, 1939.

Davis, David Brion. *The Problem of Slavery in the Age of Revolution, 1770–1823*. 1975. New York: Oxford University Press, 1999.

"Declaration of the Rights of the Negro People of the World." In *Selected Writings and Speeches of Marcus Garvey*, edited by Bob Blaisdell, 16–24. Mineola, NY: Dover, 2004.

De Wet, Erika. "The International Constitutional Order." *International & Comparative Law Quarterly* 55 (January 2006): 51–76.

Doyle, Michael W. *Empires*. Ithaca, NY: Cornell University Press, 1986.

Du Bois, W.E.B. *Africa, Its Geography, People and Products* and *Africa—Its Place in Modern History*. 1930. Edited by Henry Louis Gates Jr. New York: Oxford University Press, 2007.

———. "The African Roots of War." *Atlantic Monthly* 115 (May 1915): 707–14.

———. *Black Reconstruction in America, 1860–1880*. 1935. New York: Free Press, 1992.

———. "Color and Democracy: Colonies and Peace." In *The World and Africa and Color and Democracy*, edited by Henry Louis Gates Jr., 237–330. New York: Oxford University Press, 2007.

———. *Darkwater: Voices within the Veil*. 1920. Mineola, NY: Dover, 1999.

———. "A Future for Pan-Africa: Freedom, Peace, Socialism." In *The World and Africa and Color and Democracy*, edited by Henry Louis Gates Jr., 187–90. New York: Oxford University Press, 2014.

———. "Inter-racial Implications of the Ethiopian Crisis: A Negro View." *Foreign Affairs* 14 (October 1935): 82–92.

———. "The League of Nations." *Crisis* 18 (May 1919): 10–11.

———. "Let Us Reason Together." *Crisis* 18 (September 1919): 231–35.

———. "Liberia, the League and the United States." *Foreign Affairs* 11 (July 1933): 682–95.

———. "Prospect of a World without Race Conflict." *Journal of American Sociology* 49 (March 1944): 450–56.

———. *The Souls of Black Folk*. 1903. Edited by David W. Blight and Robert Gooding-Williams. Boston: Bedford Books, 1997.

———. "To the Nations of the World." In *W.E.B. Du Bois: A Reader*, edited by David Levering Lewis, 639–41. New York: Henry Holt, 1995.

———. "The World and Africa: An Inquiry into the Part Which Africa Has Played in World History." In *The World and Africa and Color and Democracy*, edited by Henry Louis Gates Jr., xxxv–165. New York: Oxford University Press, 2007.

Dubow, Saul. "Smuts, the United Nations and the Rhetoric of Race and Rights." *Journal of Contemporary History* 43 (January 2008): 45–74.

Eagleton, Clyde. "Excesses of Self-Determination." *Foreign Affairs* 31 (July 1953): 592–604.

Eckel, Jan. "Human Rights and Decolonization: New Perspectives and New Questions." *Humanity: An International Journal of Human Rights, Humanitarianism, and Development* 1 (Fall 2010): 111–35.

Edwards, Brent Hayes. *The Practice of Diaspora: Literature, Translation, and the Rise of Black Internationalism*. Cambridge, MA: Harvard University Press, 2003.

El-Ayouty, Yassin. *The United Nations and Decolonization: The Role of Afro-Asia*. The Hague: Martinus Nijhoff, 1971.

Elazaar, Daniel J. *Exploring Federalism*. Tuscaloosa: University of Alabama Press, 1987.

Emerson, Rupert. "The Fate of Human Rights in the Third World." *World Politics* 27 (January 1975): 201–26.

———. *From Empire to Nation: The Rise to Self-Assertion of Asian and African Peoples*. Cambridge, MA: Harvard University Press, 1960.

———. "Pan-Africanism." *International Organization* 16 (Spring 1962): 275–90.

———. "Self-Determination." *American Journal of International Law* 65 (July 1971): 459–75.

Evans, Gareth, and Mohammed Sahnoun. "The Responsibility to Protect." *Foreign Affairs* 81 (November/December 2002): 99–110.

"Extracts from the Theses on the International Situation and the Policy of the Entente Adopted by the First Comintern Congress." In *The Communist International: 1919–1943 Documents*, edited by Jane Degras, vol. 1, 31–36. New York: Frank Cass, 1917.

Falk, Richard. "The Haiti Intervention: A Dangerous World Order Precedent for the United Nations." *Harvard International Law Journal* 36 (Spring 1995): 341–58.

Fassbender, Bardo. *The United Nations Charter as the Constitution of the International Community*. Boston: Martinus Nijhoff, 2009.

———. " 'We the Peoples of the United Nations': Constituent Power and Constitutional Form in International Law." In *The Paradox of Constitutionalism: Constituent Power and Constitutional Form*, edited by Martin Loughlin and Neil Walker, 247–69. Oxford: Oxford University Press, 2008.

Fassin, Didier. *Humanitarian Reason: A Moral History of the Present*. Berkeley: University of California Press, 2012.

Fisch, Jörg. *The Right of Self-Determination of Peoples: The Domestication of an Illusion*. Translated by Anita Mage. New York: Cambridge University Press, 2015.

Forrester, Katrina. "Reparations, History and the Origins of Global Justice." In *Empire, Race and Global Justice*, edited by Duncan Bell. Cambridge: Cambridge University Press, forthcoming.

Forsyth, Murray. *Union of States: The Theory and Practice of Confederation*. Leicester: Leicester University Press, 1981.

Fox, Gregory. "The Right to Political Participation in International Law." *Yale Journal of International Law* 17 (Summer 1992): 539–607.

Franck, Thomas M. "The Emerging Right to Democratic Governance." *American Journal of International Law* 86 (January 1992): 46–91.

———, ed. *Why Federations Fail: An Inquiry into the Requisites for Successful Federation*. New York: New York University Press, 1968.

Frank, Andre Gunder. "The Development of Underdevelopment." *Monthly Review* 18 (September 1966): 17–31.

Gadamer, Hans. *Truth and Method*. Translated by Joel Weinsheimer and Donald G. Marshall. 1960. New York: Bloomsbury Academic, 2013.

Gädeke, Dorothea. "The Domination of States: Towards an Inclusive Republican Law of Peoples." *Global Justice: Theory Practice Rhetoric* 9, no. 1 (2016): 1–27.

Gaines, Kevin. *American Africans in Ghana: Black Expatriates and the Civil Rights Era*. Chapel Hill: University of North Carolina Press, 2006.

Garavini, Giuliano. *After Empires: European Integration, Decolonization, and the Challenge from the Global South, 1957–1968*. Translated by Richard R. Nybakken. Oxford: Oxford University Press, 2012.

Garvey, Marcus. "The True Solution to the Negro Problem." In *The Philosophy and Opinions of Marcus Garvey; or, Africa for the Africans*, vol. 1, 52–53. Dover, MA: Majority, 1986.

"General Act of the Conference of Berlin concerning the Congo." *American Journal of International Law Supplement: Official Documents* 3 (January 1909): 7–25.

Getachew, Adom. "The Plantation in Comparative Perspective: Toward a Theory of Colonial Modernity." In *The Oxford Handbook of Comparative Political Theory*, edited by Leigh Jenco et al. New York: Oxford University Press, forthcoming.

Gilroy, Paul. *The Black Atlantic: Modernity and Double Consciousness*. Cambridge, MA: Harvard University Press, 1993.

Girvan, Norman, et al. "The Third World and the IMF: The Case of Jamaica, 1974–1980." *Development Dialogue* 2 (1980): 113–65.

Glendon, Mary Ann. *A World Made New: Eleanor Roosevelt and the Universal Declaration of Human Rights*. New York: Random House, 2001.

Goswami, Manu. "Imaginary Futures and Colonial Internationalisms." *American Historical Review* 117 (December 2012): 1461–85.

———. *Producing India: From Colonial Economy to National Space*. Chicago: University of Chicago Press, 2004.

Gould, Eliga H. *Among the Powers of the Earth: The American Revolution and the Making of a New World Empire*. Cambridge, MA: Harvard University Press, 2012.

Gourevitch, Alex. *From Slavery to the Cooperative Commonwealth: Labor and Republican Liberty in the Nineteenth Century*. New York: Cambridge University Press, 2015.

———. "Labor Republicanism and the Transformation of Work." *Political Theory* 41 (August 2013): 591–617.

Government Proposals for a Republican Constitution. Accra: Government Printers, 1960.

Grovogui, Siba N'Zatioula. *Sovereigns, Quasi-sovereigns, and Africans: Race and Self-Determination in International Law*. Minneapolis: University of Minnesota Press, 1996.

Gündoğdu, Ayten. *Rightlessness in the Age of Rights: Hannah Arendt and the Contemporary Struggles of Migrants*. New York: Oxford University Press, 2015.

Habermas, Jürgen. "The Constitutionalization of International Law and the Legitimation Problems of a Constitution for World Society." *Constellations* 15 (December 2008): 444–55.

———. *The Crisis of the European Union: A Response*. Translated by Ciaran Conin. Cambridge: Polity, 2012.

———. *The Divided West*. Edited and translated by Ciaran Cronin. Cambridge: Polity, 2006.

———. *The Inclusion of the Other: Studies in Political Theory*. Edited by Ciaran Cronin and Pablo De Greiff. Cambridge, MA: MIT Press, 1998.

Hall, Catherine. *Civilising Subjects: Metropole and Colony in the English Imagination, 1830–1867*. Chicago: University of Chicago Press, 2002.

Hardt, Michael, and Antonio Negri. *Empire*. Cambridge, MA: Harvard University Press, 2001.

Harris, John. *Dawn in Darkest Africa*. London: Smith, Elder, 1912.

———. *Slavery and the Obligations of the League*. London: Anti-slavery and Aborigines Protection Society, 1922.

Hartman, Saidiya V. *Scenes of Subjection: Terror, Slavery, and Self-Making in Nineteenth-Century America*. New York: Oxford University Press, 1997.

Heerten, Lassie, and A. Dirk Moses. "The Nigeria-Biafra War: Postcolonial Conflict and the Question of Genocide." *Journal of Genocide Research* 16 (August 2014): 169–203.

Held, David. "Democratic Accountability and Political Effectiveness from a Cosmopolitan Perspective." *Government and Opposition* 39 (March 2004): 364–91.

Helman, Gerald B., and Steven R. Ratner. "Saving Failed States." *Foreign Policy* 89 (Winter 1992): 3–20.

Hendrickson, David. "The First Union: Nationalism versus Internationalism in the American Revolution." In *Empire and Nation: The American Revolution in the Atlantic World*, edited by Eliga H. Gould and Peter S. Onuf, 35–53. Baltimore: Johns Hopkins University Press, 2005.

———. *Peace Pact: The Lost World of the American Founding*. Lawrence: University Press of Kansas, 2003.

Henkin, Louis. *The Rights of Man Today*. Boulder, CO: Westview, 1978.

———. "The United Nations and Human Rights." *International Organization* 19 (Summer 1965): 504–17.

Hesse, Barnor. "Escaping Liberty: Western Hegemony, Black Fugitivity." *Political Theory* 42 (June 2014): 288–313.

Hicks, Ursula, et al., eds. *Federalism and Economic Growth in Underdeveloped Countries*. London: George Allen and Unwin, 1961.

Hobson, J. A. *Imperialism: A Study*. 1902. Indianapolis: Liberty Fund, 2004.

Hoffmann, Stefan-Ludwig. "Human Rights and History." *Past and Present* 232 (August 2016): 279–310.

Holzgrefe, J. L. and Robert O. Keohane, eds. *Humanitarian Intervention: Ethical, Legal and Political Dilemmas*. New York: Cambridge University Press, 2003.

Høgsbjerg, Christian. *C.L.R. James in Imperial Britain*. Durham, NC: Duke University Press, 2014.

Holt, Thomas. *The Problem of Freedom: Race, Labor, and Politics in Jamaica and Britain, 1832–1938*. Baltimore: Johns Hopkins University Press, 1992.

Holtom, Duncan. "Reconsidering the Power of IFIs: Tanzania and the World Bank, 1978–1985." *Review of African Political Economy* 32 (December 2005): 549–67.

Hooper, James, and Paul Williams. "Earned Sovereignty: The Political Dimensions." *Denver Journal of International Law and Policy* 31 (Summer 2003): 355–72.

Ibhawoh, Bonny. *Imperialism and Human Rights: Colonial Discourses of Rights and Liberties in African History*. Albany: State University of New York Press, 2007.

Ibhawoh, Bonny, and J. I. Dibua. "Deconstructing Ujamaa: The Legacy of Julius Nyerere in the Quest for Social and Economic Development in Africa." *African Association of Political Science* 8 (January 2003): 59–93.

Ingram, James D. "What Is a 'Right to Have Rights'? Three Images of the Politics of Human Rights." *American Political Science Review* 102 (November 2008): 401–16.

International Commission on Intervention and State Sovereignty. *The Responsibility to Protect: Report of the International Commission on Intervention and State Sovereignty*. Ottawa: International Development Research Centre, 2001.

Irwin, Ryan M. *Gordian Knot: Apartheid and the Unmaking of the Liberal World Order*. New York: Oxford University Press, 2012.

———. "Sovereignty in the Congo Crisis." In *Decolonization and the Cold War: Negotiating Independence*, edited by Leslie James and Elisabeth Leake, 203–18. New York: Bloomsbury, 2015.

Isaac, Jeffrey C. "A New Guarantee on Earth: Hannah Arendt on Human Dignity and the Politics of Human Rights." *American Political Science Review* 90 (March 1996): 61–73.

Isiksel, N. Türküler. *Europe's Functional Constitution: A Theory of Constitutionalism beyond the State*. New York: Oxford University Press, 2016.

———. "On Europe's Functional Constitutionalism: Towards a Constitutional Theory of Specialized International Regimes." *Constellations* 19 (March 2012): 102–20.

Jackson, Ashley. *The British Empire and the Second World War*. London: Hambledon Continuum, 2006.

Jackson, Robert. *Quasi-states: Sovereignty, International Relations and the Third World*. Cambridge: Cambridge University Press, 1990.

James, C.L.R. *At the Rendezvous of Victory: Selected Writings*. London: Allison and Busby, 1984.

———. "*The Black Jacobins* and *Black Reconstruction*: A Comparative Analysis." *Small Axe* 8 (September 2000): 83–98.

———. *The Black Jacobins: Toussaint L'Ouverture and the San Domingo Revolution*. 1938. New York: Vintage, 1989.

———. *Federation—We Failed Miserably: How and Why*. Tunapuna: C.L.R. James, 1961.

———. "Intervening in Abyssinia." *New Leader* 18 (October 1935): http://www.marxists .org/archive/james-clr/works/1935/new-leader.htm.

———. "Lecture: How I Wrote *The Black Jacobins.*" *Small Axe* 8 (September 2000): 65–82.

———. *Nkrumah and the Ghana Revolution.* Westport, CT: L. Hill, 1977.

———. "Slavery Today: A Shocking Exposure." In *Toussaint L'Ouverture: The Story of the Only Successful Slave Revolt in History*, edited by Christian Høgsbjerg, 206–12. Durham, NC: Duke University Press, 2013.

———. *World Revolution, 1917–1936: The Rise and Fall of the Communist International.* London: Martin Secker and Warburg, 1937.

Jensen, Steven L. B. *The Making of International Human Rights: The 1960s, Decolonization and the Reconstruction of Global Values.* New York: Cambridge University Press, 2016.

Johnson, James Weldon. *Self-Determining Haiti.* New York: Nation, 1920.

Kedourie, Elie. *Nationalism.* London: Hutchinson, 1960.

Keene, Edward. *Beyond the Anarchical Society: Grotius, Colonialism and Order in World Politics.* Cambridge: Cambridge University Press, 2002.

Kennedy, Paul. *Parliament of Man: The Past, Present, and Future of the United Nations.* New York: Random House, 2006.

Keynes, John Maynard. *The End of Laissez Faire.* London: Hogarth, 1926.

———. "National Self-Sufficiency." *Studies: An Irish Quarterly Review* 22 (June 1933): 177–93.

Knock, Thomas. *To End All Wars: Woodrow Wilson and the Quest for a New World Order.* New York: Oxford University Press, 1992.

Kohn, Margaret, and Keally McBride. *Political Theories of Decolonization: Postcolonialism and the Problem of Foundations.* New York: Oxford University Press, 2011.

Koskenniemi, Martti. *The Gentle Civilizer of Nations: The Rise and Fall of International Law, 1870–1960.* New York: Cambridge University Press, 2001.

———. "The Police in the Temple Order, Justice and the UN: A Dialectical View." *European Journal of International Law* 6, no. 1 (1995): 325–48.

Krasner, Stephen. "Rethinking the Sovereign State Model." In *Empires, Systems and States: Great Transformations in International Politics*, edited by Michael Cox et al., 17–43. New York: Cambridge University Press, 2001.

Krause, Sharon. "Beyond Non-domination: Agency, Inequality and the Meaning of Freedom." *Philosophy and Social Criticism* 39 (February 2013): 187–208.

Lafont, Cristina. "Sovereignty, Human Rights and the Responsibility to Protect." *Constellations* 22 (March 2015): 68–78.

———. "Sovereignty and the International Protection of Human Rights." *Journal of Political Philosophy* 24 (December 2016): 427–45.

Lake, David. *Hierarchy in International Relations.* Ithaca, NY: Cornell University Press, 2009.

Lake, Marilyn, and Henry Reynolds. *Drawing the Global Colour Line: White Men's Countries and the International Challenge of Racial Equality.* New York: Cambridge University Press, 2008.

Lal, Priya. *African Socialism in Postcolonial Tanzania: Between the Village and the World*. New York: Cambridge University Press, 2015.

Lansing, Robert. *The Peace Negotiations: A Personal Narrative*. Boston: Houghton Mifflin, 1921.

Laski, Harold. "The Obsolescence of Federalism." *New Republic* 98 (May 3, 1939): 367–69.

Lee, Christopher J., ed. *Making a World after Empire: The Bandung Moment and Its Political Afterlives*. Athens: Ohio University Press, 2010.

Lenin, V. I. "Declaration of the Rights of the Working and Exploited People." In *Collected Works of V. I. Lenin*, vol. 26, 423–26. Moscow: Progress, 1964.

———. *Imperialism: The Highest Stage of Capitalism*. 1917. Chippendale, Australia: Resistance Books, 1999.

———. "The Revolutionary Proletariat and the Right of Nations to Self-Determination." Translated and edited by Julius Katzer. In *Collected Works of V. I. Lenin*, vol. 21, 407–14. Moscow: Progress, 1964.

———. "The Right of Nations to Self-Determination." Translated by Bernard Isaacs and Joe Fineberg. Edited by Julius Katzer. In *Collected Works of V. I. Lenin*, vol. 20, 393–454. Moscow: Progress, 1964.

———. "The Socialist Revolution and the Right to Self-Determination." Translated by Yuri Sdobnikov. Edited by George Hanna. In *Collected Works of V. I. Lenin*, vol. 22, 143–56. Moscow: Progress, 1964.

———. "The Tasks of the Proletariat in the Present Revolution." Translated and edited by Bernard Isaacs. In *Collected Works of V. I. Lenin*, vol. 24, 19–33. Moscow: Progress, 1964.

Levi, Darrell E. *Michael Manley: The Making of a Leader*. London: Andre Deutsch, 1989.

Levitt, Kari Polanyi. *The Origins and Consequences of Jamaica's Debt Crisis 1970–1990*. Mona: Consortium Graduate School of the Social Sciences, 1991.

Levitt, Kari Polanyi, and Michael Manley. "The Manley/Levitt Exchange." *Small Axe* 1 (February 1997): 81–115.

Lewis, W. Arthur. *Aspects of Tropical Trade, 1868–1963*. Stockholm: Almqvist and Wicksell, 1969.

———. "Economic Development with Unlimited Supplies of Labor." 1954. In *Selected Economic Writings of W. Arthur Lewis*, 131–91. New York: New York University Press, 1983.

———. *The Evolution of the International Economic Order*. Princeton, NJ: Princeton University Press, 1978.

———. *The Principles of Economic Planning: A Study Prepared for the Fabian Society*. London: D. Dobson, 1949.

———. *Report on Industrialization and the Gold Coast Economy*. Accra: Government Printers, 1953.

Lindqvist, Sven. *"Exterminate All the Brutes": One Man's Odyssey into the Heart of Darkness and the Origins of European Genocide*. Translated by Joan Tate. New York: New Press, 1996.

Link, Arthur S. *Woodrow Wilson: Revolution, War and Peace*. Arlington Heights, IL: AHM, 1979.

Livingston, William S., ed. *Federalism in the Commonwealth: A Bibliographical Commentary*. London: Cassell, 1963.

Locke, Alain. *Race Contacts and Interracial Relations: Lectures on the Theory and Practice of Race*. Edited by Jeffrey Stewart. Washington, DC: Howard University Press, 1992.

Logan, Rayford. *The African Mandates in World Politics*. Washington, DC: Public Affairs, 1948.

Lorca, Arnulf Becker. *Mestizo International Law: A Global Intellectual History, 1842–1933*. Cambridge: Cambridge University Press, 2014.

Louro, Michele. "At Home in the World: Jawaharlal Nehru and Global Anti-imperialism." PhD diss., Temple University, 2011.

Low, D. A. *The Egalitarian Moment: Asia and Africa, 1950–1980*. New York: Cambridge University Press, 1996.

Lowe, Lisa. *The Intimacies of Four Continents*. Durham, NC: Duke University Press, 2015.

Lowenthal, David. "Two Federations." *Social and Economic Studies* 6 (June 1957): 185–96.

Lu, Catherine. "Colonialism as Structural Injustice: Historical Responsibility and Contemporary Redress." *Journal of Political Philosophy* 19 (September 2011): 261–81.

Lugard, Frederick. *The Dual Mandate in British Tropical Africa*. 1922. Hamden: Archon Books, 1965.

Macmahon, Arthur W., ed. *Federalism: Mature and Emergent*. Garden City, NY: Doubleday, 1955.

Mamdani, Mahmood. *Citizen and Subject: Contemporary Africa and the Legacy of Late Colonialism*. Princeton, NJ: Princeton University Press, 1996.

———. *When Victims Become Killers: Colonialism, Nativism, and the Genocide in Rwanda*. Princeton, NJ: Princeton University Press, 2001.

Mandler, Peter. *The English National Character: The History of an Idea from Edmund Burke to Tony Blair*. New Haven, CT: Yale University Press, 2006.

Manela, Erez. *The Wilsonian Moment: Self-Determination and the International Origins of Anticolonial Nationalism*. New York: Oxford University Press, 2007.

Manley, Michael. *Jamaica: Struggle in the Periphery*. London: Third World Media, 1982.

———. "Message from the Prime Minister of Jamaica, Hon. Michael Manley, to the South-North Conference on the International Monetary System and the New International Order." *Development Dialogue* 2 (1980): 5–6.

———. "Overcoming Insularity in Jamaica." *Foreign Affairs* 49 (October 1970): 100–110.

———. *The Politics of Change: A Jamaican Testament*. 1974. Washington, DC: Howard University Press, 1990.

———. *The Poverty of Nations: Reflections on Underdevelopment and the World Economy*. London: Pluto, 1991.

Mantena, Karuna. *Alibis of Empire: Henry Maine and the Ends of Liberal Imperialism*. Princeton, NJ: Princeton University Press, 2010.

———. "Genealogies of Catastrophe: Arendt on the Logic and Legacy of Imperialism." In *Politics in Dark Times: Encounters with Hannah Arendt*, edited by Seyla Benhabib et al., 83–112. New York: Cambridge University Press, 2010.

———. "On Gandhi's Critique of the State: Sources, Contexts, Conjunctures." *Modern Intellectual History* 9 (November 2012): 535–63.

———. "Popular Sovereignty and Anti-colonialism." In *Popular Sovereignty in Historical Perspective*, edited by Richard Bourke and Quentin Skinner, 297–319. New York: Cambridge University Press, 2016.

———. "Review Essay: Fragile Universals and the Politics of Empire." *Polity* 38 (October 2006): 543–55.

Markell, Patchen. "The Insufficiency of Non-domination." *Political Theory* 36 (February 2008): 9–36.

Martin, Jamie. "Gunnar Myrdal and the Failed Promises of the Postwar International Economic Settlement." *Humanity: An International Journal of Human Rights, Humanitarianism, and Development* 8 (Spring 2017): 167–73.

Marx, Karl. *Capital*. Vol. 1, *The Critique of Political Economy*. 1867. London: Penguin Classics, 1976.

Marx, Karl, and Friedrich Engels. *The Communist Manifesto*. 1848. London: Penguin Classics, 2002.

Mayer, Arno J. *Political Origins of the New Diplomacy, 1917–1918*. New Haven, CT: Yale University, 1959.

Mazower, Mark. *Governing the World: The History of an Idea, 1815 to the Present*. New York: Penguin, 2012.

———. *No Enchanted Palace: The End of Empire and the Ideological Origins of the United Nations*. Princeton, NJ: Princeton University Press, 2009.

McFarland, Victor. "The New International Economic Order, Interdependence and Globalization." *Humanity: An International Journal of Human Rights, Humanitarianism, and Development* 6 (Spring 2015): 217–33.

Michelman, Frank I. "Parsing the 'Right to Have Rights.'" *Constellations* 3 (October 1996): 200–208.

Mitchell, Timothy. *Carbon Democracy: Political Power in the Age of Oil*. New York: Verso, 2011.

Molony, Thomas. *Nyerere: The Early Years*. Suffolk: James Currey, 2014.

Mordecai, John. *The West Indies: The Federal Negotiations*. London: George Allen and Unwin, 1968.

Morefield, Jeanne. *Covenants without Swords: Idealist Liberalism and the Spirit of Empire*. Princeton, NJ: Princeton University Press, 2005.

———. *Empires without Imperialism: Anglo-American Decline and the Politics of Deflection*. New York: Oxford University Press, 2014.

Moses, A. Dirk. "*Das römische Gespräch* in a New Key: Hannah Arendt, Genocide, and the Defense of Republican Civilization." *Journal of Modern History* 85 (December 2013): 867–913.

Moyn, Samuel. "Imperialism, Self-Determination, and the Rise of Human Rights." In *The Human Rights Revolution: An International History*, edited by Akira Iriye et al., 159–78. New York: Oxford University Press, 2012.

———. *The Last Utopia: Human Rights in History*. Cambridge, MA: Belknap Press of Harvard University Press, 2010.

———. *Not Enough: Human Rights in an Unequal World*. Cambridge, MA: Harvard University Press, 2018.

———. "The Political Origins of Global Justice." In *The Worlds of American Intellectual History*, edited by Joel Isaac et al., 133–52. New York: Oxford University Press, 2016.

———. "Welfare World." *Humanity: An International Journal of Human Rights, Humanitarianism, and Development* 8 (Spring 2017): 175–83.

Moynihan, Daniel P. "The Politics of Human Rights." *Commentary* 64 (August 1977): https://www.commentarymagazine.com/articles/the-politics-of-human-rights/.

———. "The United States in Opposition." *Commentary* 59 (March 1975): https://www.commentarymagazine.com/articles/the-united-states-in-opposition/.

Muthu, Sankar. *Enlightenment against Empire*. Princeton, NJ: Princeton University Press, 2003.

Myrdal, Gunnar. *Beyond the Welfare State: Economic Planning and Its International Implications*. New Haven, CT: Yale University Press, 1960.

———. *Development and Underdevelopment: A Note on the Mechanism of National and International Economic Equality*. Cairo: National Bank of Egypt, 1956.

———. *Economic Theory and Underdeveloped Regions*. London: Gerald Duckworth, 1957.

———. *An International Economy: Problems and Prospects*. New York: Harper and Row, 1956.

———. *Rich Lands Poor Lands: The Road to World Prosperity*. New York: Harper and Row, 1957.

Nakhimovsky, Isaac. *The Closed Commercial State: Perpetual Peace and Commercial Society from Rousseau to Fichte*. Princeton, NJ: Princeton University Press, 2011.

———. "An International Dilemma: The Postwar Utopianism of Gunnar Myrdal's *Beyond the Welfare State*." *Humanity: An International Journal of Human Rights, Humanitarianism, and Development* 8 (Spring 2017): 185–94.

Nicholadis, Kalypso, and Robert House, eds. *The Federal Vision: Legitimacy and Levels of Governance in the United States and the European Union*. New York: Oxford University Press, 2001.

Nichols, Robert. "Theft Is Property! The Recursive Logic of Dispossession." *Political Theory*, April 2, 2017, https://doi.org/10.1177/0090591717701709.

Nkrumah, Kwame. *12 Key Speeches of Kwame Nkrumah*. London: African Publication Society, 1970.

———. *Africa Must Unite*. New York: International, 1963.

———. *Axioms of Kwame Nkrumah*. London: Thomas Nelson and Sons, 1967.

———. *The Challenge of the Congo: A Case Study of Foreign Pressures in an Independent State*. New York: International, 1967.

———. "Education and Nationalism in Africa." *Education Outlook* 18 (1943): 32–40.

———. *Ghana: The Autobiography of Kwame Nkrumah*. London: Thomas Nelson and Sons, 1957.

———. *I Speak of Freedom: A Statement of African Ideology*. New York: Frederick A. Praeger, 1961.

———. *Neocolonialism: The Last Stage of Imperialism*. New York: International, 1965.

———. *Osagyefo at the United Nations*. Accra: Government Printers, 1960.

———. *Towards Colonial Freedom: Africa in the Struggle against World Imperialism*. 1947. London: Heinemann, 1962.

Noel-Buxton, Lord. "Slavery in Abyssinia." *International Affairs* 11 (July 1932): 512–26.

Nyerere, Julius. "Biafra, Human Rights and Self-determination in Africa." http:// biafrasay.com/p/327314/biafra-human-rights-and-self-determination-in-africa -by-pres#327314, accessed August 10, 2017.

———. *Freedom and a New Economic Order: A Selection from Speeches, 1974–1999*. Dar es Salaam: Oxford University Press, 2011.

———. *Freedom and Development: A Selection from Writings and Speeches, 1968–1973*. Dar es Salaam: Oxford University Press, 1973.

———. *Freedom and Socialism: A Selection from Writings and Speeches 1965–1967*. Dar es Salaam: Oxford University Press, 1968.

———. *Freedom and Unity: A Selection from Writing and Speeches 1952–1965*. Dar es Salaam: Oxford University Press, 1967.

———. *Ujamaa: Essays on Socialism*. London: Oxford University Press, 1968.

O'Brien, Derek. "CARICOM: Regional Integration in a Post-colonial World." *European Law Journal* 17 (September 2011): 630–48.

Ogle, Vanessa. "States' Rights against Private Capital: The 'New International Economic Order' and the Struggle over Aid, Trade, and Foreign Investments, 1962– 1981." *Humanity: An International Journal of Human Rights, Humanitarianism and Development* 5 (Summer 2014): 211–34.

Onuf, Peter, and Nicholas Onuf. *Federal Union, Modern World: The Law of Nations in an Age of Revolutions, 1776–1814*. Madison, WI: Madison House, 1993.

Orford, Anne. *International Authority and the Responsibility to Protect*. Cambridge: Cambridge University Press, 2011.

Özsu, Umut. "Neoliberalism and the New International Economic Order: A History of 'Contemporary Legal Thought.'" In *Searching for Contemporary Legal Thought*, edited by Justin Desautels-Stein and Christopher L. Tomlins, 330–47. Cambridge: Cambridge University Press, 2017.

Padmore, George. *Africa and World Peace*. 1937. London: Frank Cass, 1972.

———. *The Gold Coast Revolution: The Struggle of an African People from Slavery to Freedom*. London: D. Dobson, 1953.

———, ed. *History of the Pan-African Congress: Colonial and Coloured Unity; A Program of Action*. 1947. London: Hammersmith Bookshop, 1963.

———. *How Britain Rules Africa*. London: Wishart Books, 1936.

———. *The Life and Struggle of Negro Toilers*. London: Red International Labor Union Magazine, 1931.

———. "An Open Letter to Earl Browder." *Crisis* 43 (October 1935): 302, 315.

———. *Pan-Africanism or Communism? The Coming Struggle for Africa*. 1956. Garden City, NY: Doubleday, 1971.

Pahuja, Sundhya. *Decolonising International Law: Development, Economic Growth and the Politics of Universality*. New York: Cambridge University Press, 2011.

Parekh, Serena. "A Meaningful Place in the World: Hannah Arendt on the Nature of Human Rights." *Journal of Human Rights* 3 (March 2004): 41–52.

Parfitt, Rose. "*Empire des Nègres Blancs:* The Hybridity of International Personality in the Abyssinia Crisis of 1935–1936." *Leiden Journal of International Law* 24 (December 2011): 849–72.

Parker, Jason C. *Brother's Keeper: The United States, Race, and Empire in the British Caribbean, 1937–1962*. New York: Oxford University Press, 2008.

———. "'Made-in-America Revolutions'? The 'Black University' and the American Role in the Decolonization of the Black Atlantic." *Journal of American History* 96 (December 2009): 727–50.

Pedersen, Susan. *The Guardians: The League of Nations and the Crisis of Empire.* New York: Oxford University Press, 2015.

Pettit, Philip. "The Globalized Republican Ideal." *Global Justice: Theory Practice Rhetoric* 9, no. 1 (2016): 47–68.

———. "A Republican Law of Peoples." *European Journal of Political Theory* 9 (January 2010): 70–94.

———. *Republicanism: A Theory of Freedom and Government.* Oxford: Oxford University Press, 1997.

Philpott, Daniel. *Revolutions in Sovereignty: How Ideas Shaped Modern International Relations.* Princeton, NJ: Princeton University Press, 2001.

Pitts, Jennifer. *Boundaries of the International: Law and Empire.* Cambridge, MA: Harvard University Press, 2018.

———. "Hobson and the Critique of Liberal Empire." *Raritan* 29 (Winter 2010): 8–22.

———. "Intervention and Sovereign Equality: Legacies of Vattel." In *Just and Unjust Military Intervention: European Thinkers from Vitoria to Mill*, edited by Stefano Recchia and Jennifer M. Walsh, 132–53. New York: Cambridge University Press, 2013.

———. *A Turn to Empire: The Rise of Imperial Liberalism in Britain and France.* Princeton, NJ: Princeton University Press, 2005.

Plamenatz, John. *On Alien Rule and Self-Government.* London: Longman's, 1960.

Plischke, Elmer. "Self-Determination: Reflections on a Legacy." *World Affairs* 140 (Summer 1977): 41–57.

Pogge, Thomas. "Achieving Democracy." *Ethics and International Affairs* 15 (March 2001): 3–23.

———. "Cosmopolitanism and Sovereignty." *Ethics* 103 (October 1992): 48–75.

———. "Severe Poverty as a Violation of Negative Duties." *Ethics and International Affairs* 19 (March 2005): 55–83.

———. *World Poverty and Human Rights: Cosmopolitan Responsibilities and Reforms.* Malden, MA: Polity, 2002.

Power, Samantha. *A Problem from Hell: America and the Age of Genocide.* New York: Basic Books, 2002.

Prashad, Vijay. *The Darker Nations: A People's History of the Third World.* New York: New Press, 2007.

———. *The Poorer Nations: A Possible History of the Global South.* New York: Verso, 2012.

Prebisch, Raúl. *Towards a New Trade Policy for Development: Report by the Secretary-General of the United Nations Conference on Trade and Development.* New York: United Nations, 1964.

Price, Theodore H. Theodore Hazeltine Price to Woodrow Wilson, May 9, 1917. In *The Papers of Woodrow Wilson*, edited by Arthur S. Link, vol. 42, 255. Princeton, NJ: Princeton University Press, 1983.

Quaison-Sackey, Alex. *Africa Unbound: Reflections of An African Statesman.* New York: Frederick A. Praeger, 1963.

Rana, Aziz. *The Two Faces of American Freedom.* Cambridge, MA: Harvard University Press, 2010.

Rawls, John. *The Law of Peoples with the Idea of Public Reason Revisited*. Cambridge, MA: Harvard University Press, 2001.

———. *A Theory of Justice*. 1971. Cambridge, MA: Belknap Press of Harvard University, 2003.

Riker, William. *Federalism: Origin, Operation, Significance*. Boston: Little, Brown, 1964.

Robinson, Cedric. "The African Diaspora and the Italo-Ethiopian Crisis." *Race and Class* 27 (Autumn 1985): 51–65.

———. *Black Marxism: The Making of the Black Radical Tradition*. 1983. Chapel Hill: University of North Carolina Press, 2000.

Roberts, Alasdair. *The Logic of Discipline: Global Capitalism and the Architecture of Government*. Oxford: Oxford University Press, 2011.

Roberts, William Clare. *Marx's Inferno: The Political Theory of Capital*. Princeton, NJ: Princeton University Press, 2017.

Rodrik, Dani. *The Globalization Paradox: Democracy and the Future of the World Economy*. New York: W. W. Norton, 2011.

Rodney, Walter. *How Europe Underdeveloped Africa*. London: Bougle-L'Ouverture, 1972.

———. *World War II and the Tanzanian Economy*. Ithaca, NY: Cornell University Press, 1976.

Rodney, Walter, et al., eds. *Migrant Labor in Tanzania during the Colonial Period—Case Studies of Recruitment and Conditions of Labor in the Sisal Industry*. Hamburg: Arbeiten aus dem Institut für Afrika-Kunde, 1983.

Röling, B.V.A. "The History and the Sociological Approach of the NIEO and the Third World." In *North-South Dialogue: A New International Economic Order*, 175–245. Thessaloniki: Institute of International Public Law and International Relations of Thessaloniki, 1982.

Trouillot, Michel-Rolph. "North Atlantic Universals: Analytic Fictions, 1492–1945." *South Atlantic Quarterly* 101 (Fall 2002): 839–58.

Rossiter, Charles R., ed. *The Federalist Papers*. New York: Signet Classics, 2003.

Rostow, Walt W. *The Stages of Economic Growth: A Non-communist Manifesto*. Cambridge: Cambridge University Press, 1960.

Rothchild, Donald. "The Limits of Federalism: An Examination of Political Institutional Transfer in Africa." *Journal of Modern African Studies* 4 (November 1966): 275–93.

Roy, Audrey Jane. "Sovereignty and Decolonization: Realizing Indigenous Self-Determination at the United Nations and in Canada." MA thesis, University of Victoria, 2001.

Ruskola, Teemu. "Raping Like a State." *UCLA Law Review* 57 (June 2010): 1477–536.

Ryan, Selwyn. "East Indians, West Indians and the Quest for Political Unity." *Social and Economic Studies* 48 (December 1999): 151–84.

Salami, Iwa. "Legal and Institutional Challenges of Economic Integration in Africa." *European Law Journal* 17 (September 2011): 667–82.

Sargent, Daniel. "North/South: The United States Responds to the New International Economic Order." *Humanity: An International Journal of Human Rights, Humanitarianism, and Development* 6 (Spring 2015): 201–16.

————. *A Superpower Transformed: The Remaking of American Foreign Relations in the 1970s*. New York: Oxford University Press, 2014.

Sbacchi, Alberto. "Poison Gas and Atrocities in the Italo-Ethiopian War." In *Italian Colonialism*, edited by Ruth Ben-Ghiat and Mia Fuller, 47–56. New York: Palgrave Macmillan, 2005.

Scharf, Michael. "Earned Sovereignty: Juridical Underpinnings." *Denver Journal of International Law and Policy* 31 (Summer 2003): 373–86.

Schaller, Dominik, and Jürgen Zimmerer. "Settlers, Imperialism, Genocide: Seeing the Global without Ignoring the Local—Introduction." *Journal of Genocide Research* 10 (June 2008): 191–99.

Schmidt, Sebastian. "To Order the Minds of Scholars: The Discourse of the Peace of Westphalia in International Relations Literature." *International Studies Quarterly* 55 (September 2011): 601–23.

Schmitt, Carl. *The Nomos of the Earth in the International Law of the Jus Publicum Europaeum*. Translated by G. L. Ulmen. 1950. New York: Telos, 2003.

Scott, David. *Conscripts of Modernity: The Tragedy of Colonial Enlightenment*. Durham, NC: Duke University Press, 2004.

————. "On the Moral Justification of Reparations for New World Slavery." In *Freedom and Democracy in an Imperial Context: Dialogues with James Tully*, edited by Robert Nichols and Jakeet Singh, 100–120. New York: Routledge, 2014.

————. "Preface: Debt, Redress." *Small Axe* 43 (March 2014): vii–x.

————. *Refashioning Futures: Criticism after Post-coloniality*. Princeton, NJ: Princeton University Press, 1999.

————. "The Temporality of Generations: Dialogue, Tradition, Criticism." *New Literary History* 45 (Spring 2014): 157–81.

Scott, James. *Seeing Like a State: How Certain Schemes to Improve the Human Condition Have Failed*. New Haven, CT: Yale University Press, 1998.

Scott, William. "Black Nationalism and the Italo-Ethiopian Conflict 1934–1936." *Journal of Negro History* 63 (April 1978): 118–34.

Second All Russian Congress of Soviets of Workers' and Soldiers' Deputies. "Decree on Peace." Translated by Yuri Sdobnikov and George Hanna. Edited by George Hanna. In *Collected Works of V. I. Lenin*, vol. 26, 249–53. Moscow: Progress, 1964.

Secretary of State to President Wilson, January 2, 1918. In *Papers Relating to the Foreign Relations of the United States: The Lansing Papers; 1914–1920*. Vol. 2. Washington, DC: Government Printing Office, 1940.

Seeley, J. R. *The Expansion of England*. 1883. Cambridge: Cambridge University Press, 2010.

Sherwood, Marika. *Kwame Nkrumah: The Years Abroad 1935–1947*. Legon, Ghana: Freedom, 1996.

————. " 'There Is No New Deal for the Blackman in San Francisco': African Attempts to Influence the Founding Conference of the United Nations, April–July, 1945." *International Journal of African Historical Studies* 29 (April 1996): 71–94.

Shivji, Issa. *The Silent Class Struggle*. Dar es Salaam: Tanzania House, 1974.

Simon, Joshua. *The Ideology of Creole Revolution: Imperialism and Independence in American and Latin American Political Thought*. New York: Cambridge University Press, 2017.

Simpson, Audra. *Mohawk Interruptus: Political Life across the Borders of Settler States*. Durham, NC: Duke University Press, 2014.

Simpson, Brad. "The Biafran Secession and the Limits of Self-Determination." *Journal of Genocide Research* 16 (August 2014): 337–54.

Simpson, Gerry. *Great Powers and Outlaw States: Unequal Sovereigns in the International Legal Order*. Cambridge: Cambridge University Press, 2004.

Sinha, S. Prakash. "Is Self-Determination Passé?" *Columbia Journal of Transnational Law* 12, no. 2 (1973): 260–73.

Skinner, Quentin. *Liberty before Liberalism*. Cambridge: Cambridge University Press, 1998.

———. "On the Slogans of Republican Political Theory." *European Journal of Political Theory* 9 (January 2010): 95–102.

Skowronek, Stephen. "The Reassociation of Ideas and Purposes: Racism, Liberalism, and the American Political Tradition." *American Political Science Review* 100 (August 2006): 385–401.

Slate, Nico. *Colored Cosmopolitanism: The Shared Struggle for Freedom in the United States and India*. Cambridge, MA: Harvard University Press, 2012.

Slaughter, Anne-Marie. *A New World Order*. Princeton, NJ: Princeton University Press, 2004.

———. "The Real New World Order." *Foreign Affairs* 76 (September/October 1997): 183–97.

———. "Security, Solidarity, and Sovereignty: The Grand Themes of UN Reform." *American Journal of International Law* 99 (July 2005): 619–31.

Sloane, Blaine. "The United Nations Charter as a Constitution." *Pace Yearbook of International Law* 1 (September 1989): 61–126.

Slobodian, Quinn. *Globalists: The End of Empire and the Birth of Neoliberalism*. Cambridge, MA: Harvard University Press, 2018.

Sluga, Glenda. *Internationalism in the Age of Nationalism*. Philadelphia: University of Pennsylvania Press, 2013.

Smuts, Jan. *Africa and Some World Problems*. Oxford: Clarendon, 1930.

———. *A League of Nations: A Practical Suggestion*. New York: Nation, 1919.

———. "Speech to the De Beers Consolidated Political and Debating Association in Kimberley." In *Selections from the Smuts Papers*, vol. 1, 80–100. London: Cambridge University Press, 1966.

———. "Speech to the Legislative Council of the Transvaal Colony." In *Selections from the Smuts Papers*, vol. 2, 551–62. London: Cambridge University Press, 1966.

———. *War-Time Speeches: A Compilation of Public Utterances in Great Britain*. London: Hodder and Stoughton, 1917.

Solow, Barbara, and Stanley Engerman, eds. *British Capitalism and Caribbean Slavery: The Legacy of Eric Williams*. New York: Cambridge University Press, 1987.

"Speech by Marcus Garvey, in Philadelphia, PA, October 21, 1919." In *The Marcus Garvey and Universal Negro Improvement Association Papers*, vol. 2, edited by Robert Hill, 89–98. Berkeley: University of California Press, 1983.

Spinelli, Altiero. "The Growth of the European Movement since World War II." In *European Integration*, edited by C. Grove Haines, 37–63. Baltimore: Johns Hopkins University Press, 1957.

Staniland, Martin. *American Intellectuals and African Nationalists, 1955–1970*. New Haven, CT: Yale University Press, 1991.

Stepan, Alfred. "Federalism and Democracy: Beyond the U.S. Model." *Journal of Democracy* 10 (October 1999): 19–34.

Stephens, Michelle Ann. *Black Empire: The Masculine Global Imaginary of Caribbean Intellectuals in the United States, 1914–1962*. Durham, NC: Duke University Press, 2005.

Stilz, Anna. "Decolonization and Self-Determination." *Social Philosophy and Policy* 32 (October 2015): 1–24.

Sundiata, I. K. *Black Scandal: America and the Liberian Labor Crisis, 1929–1936*. Philadelphia: Institute for the Study of Human Issues, 1980.

Szasz, Paul. "The Security Council Starts Legislating." *American Journal of International Law* 96 (October 2002): 901–5.

Talmon, Stefan. "The Security Council as World Legislature." *American Journal of International Law* 99 (January 2005): 175–93.

Tate, Merze. "The War Aims of World War I and II and Their Relation to the Darker Peoples of the World." *Journal of Negro Education* 12 (Summer 1943): 521–32.

Teitel, Ruti. *Humanity's Law*. Oxford: Oxford University Press, 2011.

Terretta, Meredith. "From Below and to the Left? Human Rights and Liberation Politics in Africa's Postcolonial Age." *Journal of World History* 24 (June 2013): 389–416.

Teschke, Benno. *The Myth of 1648: Class, Geopolitics, and the Making of Modern International Relations*. New York: Verso Books, 2003.

Throntveit, Trygve. "The Fable of the Fourteen Points: Woodrow Wilson and National Self-Determination." *Diplomatic History* 35 (June 2011): 445–81.

Tignor, Robert L. *W. Arthur Lewis and the Birth of Development Economics*. Princeton, NJ: Princeton University Press, 2006.

Tooze, Adam. *The Deluge: The Great War, America and the Remaking of the Global Order, 1916–1931*. New York: Viking, 2014.

Trouillot, Michel-Rolph. "North Atlantic Universals: Analytic Fictions, 1492–1945." *South Atlantic Quarterly* 101 (Fall 2002): 839–58.

Tuck, Richard. "Alliances with Infidels in the European Imperial Expansion." In *Empire and Modern Political Thought*, edited by Sankar Muthu, 61–83. New York: Cambridge University Press, 2012.

———. *The Rights of War and Peace: Political Thought and the International Order from Grotius to Kant*. Oxford: Oxford University Press, 1999.

Tucker, Robert. *The Inequality of Nations*. New York: Basic Books, 1977.

Tully, James. *Public Philosophy in a New Key*. Vol. 1, *Democracy and Civic Freedom*. New York: Cambridge University Press, 2008.

———. *Public Philosophy in a New Key*. Vol. 2, *Imperialism and Civic Freedom*. New York: Cambridge University Press, 2008.

———. "'Two Concepts of Liberty' in Context." In *Isaiah Berlin and the Politics of Freedom: "Two Concepts of Liberty" 50 Years Later*, edited by Bruce Baum and Robert Nichols, 23–52. New York: Routledge, 2013.

Turner, W. Burghardt, and Joyce Moore Turner. *Richard B. Moore, Caribbean Militant in Harlem: Collected Writings 1920–1972*. Bloomington: Indiana University Press, 1992.

United Nations Economic Commission for Latin America. *The Economic Development of Latin America and Its Principal Problems*. Lake Success, NY: UN Department of Economic Affairs, 1950.

Urbinati, Nadia. "Competing for Liberty: The Republican Critique of Democracy." *American Political Science Review* 106 (August 2012): 607–21.

Vitalis, Robert. *White World Order, Black Power Politics: The Birth of American International Relations*. Ithaca, NY: Cornell University Press, 2015.

Von Eschen, Penny. *Race against Empire: Black Americans and Anticolonialism, 1937–1957*. Ithaca, NY: Cornell University Press, 1997.

Wallace, Elisabeth. *The British Caribbean: From the Decline of Colonialism to the End of Federation*. Toronto: University of Toronto Press, 1977.

Wallerstein, Immanuel. *Africa, the Politics of Unity: An Analysis of a Contemporary Social Movement*. New York: Vintage Books, 1969.

Waltz, Kenneth. *Theory of International Politics*. London: Addison-Wesley, 1979.

Walzer, Michael. "The European Crisis." *Dissent*, September 2015, https://www.dissentmagazine.org/blog/michael-walzer-european-refugee-crisis.

Ward, Stuart. "The European Provenance of Decolonization." *Past and Present* 230 (February 2016): 227–60.

Watson, Adam. *The Evolution of International Society: A Comparative Historical Analysis*. New York: Routledge, 1992.

Watts, R. L. *New Federations: Experiments in the Commonwealth*. Oxford: Clarendon Press, 1966.

Weisbord, Robert G. "British West Indian Reaction to the Italian-Ethiopian War: An Episode in Pan-Africanism." *Caribbean Studies* 10 (April 1970): 34–41.

Weiss, Holger. *Framing a Radical African Atlantic: African American Agency, West African Intellectuals and the International Trade Union Committee of Negro Workers*. Leiden: Brill, 2014.

Wendt, Alexander, and Michael Barnett. "Dependent State Formation and Third World Militarization." *Review of International Studies* 19 (October 1993): 321–47.

West African Press Delegation. *The Atlantic Charter and British West Africa: Memorandum on Post-war Reconstruction of the Colonies and Protectorates of British West Africa*. London: West Africa Press Delegation to Britain, 1943.

Whatmore, Richard. *Against War and Empire: Geneva, Britain, and France in the Eighteenth Century*. New Haven, CT: Yale University Press, 2012.

Wheare, Kenneth. *Federal Government*. 1946. London: Oxford University Press, 1963.

Whelan, Daniel J. *Indivisible Human Rights: A History*. Philadelphia: University of Pennsylvania Press, 2010.

Wight, Martin. "Why Is There No International Political Theory?" In *Diplomatic Investigations*, edited by Herbert Butterfield and Martin Wight, 17–34. London: George Allen and Unwin, 1966.

Wilde, Ralph. "From Trusteeship to Self-Determination and Back Again: The Role of the Hague Regulations in the Evolution of International Trusteeship, and the Framework of Rights and Duties of Occupying Powers." *Loyola of Los Angeles International and Comparative Law Review* 31 (2009): 85–142.

———. *International Territorial Administration: How Trusteeship and the Civilizing Mission Never Went Away*. Oxford: Oxford University Press, 2008.

Wilder, Gary. *Freedom Time: Negritude, Decolonization, and the Future of the World.* Durham, NC: Duke University Press, 2015.

———. "Untimely Vision: Césaire, Decolonization, Utopia." *Public Culture* 21 (Winter 2009): 101–40.

Williams, Eric. *British Historians and the West Indies.* 1945. New York: Africana, 1972.

———. *Capitalism and Slavery.* 1944. Chapel Hill: University of North Carolina Press, 1994.

———. *Documents of West Indian History: 1492–1655; From the Spanish Discovery to the British Conquest of Jamaica.* Vol. 1. Port-of-Spain: P.N.M., 1963.

———. "The Economic Development of the Caribbean Up to the Present." In *The Economic Future of the Caribbean*, edited by Franklin Frazier and Eric Williams, 19–25. Washington, DC: Howard University Press, 1944.

———. *Federation: Two Public Lectures.* Port-of-Spain: College Press, 1956.

———. *From Columbus to Castro: The History of the Caribbean, 1492–1969.* 1970. New York: Vintage Books, 1984.

———. *Inward Hunger: The Education of a Prime Minister.* London: Andre Deutsch, 1969.

———. *Negro in the Caribbean.* 1942. New York: Negro Universities Press, 1969.

Wilson, Woodrow. "Abraham Lincoln: A Man of the People." In *The Papers of Woodrow Wilson*, edited by Arthur S. Link, vol. 19, 33–47. Princeton, NJ: Princeton University Press, 1975.

———. "Address to a Joint Session of Congress, February 11, 1918." In *The Papers of Woodrow Wilson*, edited by Arthur S. Link, vol. 46, 318–24. Princeton, NJ: Princeton University Press, 1984.

———. "An Address to a Joint Session of Congress, January 8, 1918." In *The Papers of Woodrow Wilson*, edited by Arthur S. Link, vol. 45, 534–39. Princeton, NJ: Princeton University Press, 1984.

———. "An Address to the Senate, January 22, 1917." In *The Papers of Woodrow Wilson*, edited by Arthur S. Link, vol. 40, 533–39. Princeton, NJ: Princeton University Press, 1982.

———. "A Calendar of Great Americans." In *The Papers of Woodrow Wilson*, edited by Arthur S. Link, vol. 8, 368–81. Princeton, NJ: Princeton University Press, 1970.

———. "Character of Democracy in the United States." In *An Old Master and Other Political Writings*. New York: Charles Scribner's Sons, 1893.

———. "Democracy and Efficiency." In *The Papers of Woodrow Wilson*, edited by Arthur S. Link, vol. 12, 6–21. Princeton, NJ: Princeton University Press, 1971.

———. "Edmund Burke: The Man and His Times." In *The Papers of Woodrow Wilson*, edited by Arthur S. Link, vol. 8, 313–43. Princeton, NJ: Princeton University Press, 1970.

———. *History of the American People.* Vol. 5. New York: Harper and Brothers, 1902.

———. "The Ideals of America." In *The Papers of Woodrow Wilson*, edited by Arthur S. Link, vol. 12, 208–27. Princeton, NJ: Princeton University Press, 1972.

———. "Introduction." In *Conciliation with the Colonies: The Speech by Edmund Burke*, edited by Robert Anderson, ix–xxi. Boston: Houghton Mifflin, 1896.

———. "The Reconstruction of the Southern States." In *Woodrow Wilson: Essential Writings and Speeches of the Scholar-President*, edited by Mario Dinunzio. New York: New York University Press, 2006.

———. "Remarks to the Associated Press in New York." In *The Papers of Woodrow Wilson*, edited by Arthur S. Link, vol. 33, 37–41. Princeton, NJ: Princeton University Press, 1980.

Winter, Jay. *Dreams of Peace and Freedom: Utopian Moments in the Twentieth Century*. New Haven, CT: Yale University Press, 2006.

Work, Ernest. *Ethiopia: A Pawn in European Diplomacy*. New York: Macmillan, 1936.

Wright, Quincy. "The Bombardment of Damascus." *American Journal of International Law* 20 (April 1926): 263–80.

Yelvington, Kevin A. "The War in Ethiopia and Trinidad 1935–1936." In *The Colonial Caribbean in Transition: Postemancipation Social and Cultural History*, edited by Bridget Brereton and Kevin A. Yelvington, 189–225. Gainesville: University Press of Florida, 1999.

Yihedgo, Zeray. "The African Union: Founding Principles, Frameworks and Prospects." *European Law Journal* 17 (September 2011): 568–94.

Ypi, Lea. *Global Justice and Avant-Garde Political Agency*. New York: Oxford University Press, 2012.

———. "What's Wrong with Colonialism." *Philosophy and Public Affairs* 41 (Spring 2013): 158–91.

Zimmerman, Andrew. *Alabama in Africa: Booker T. Washington, the German Empire, and the Globalization of the New South*. Princeton, NJ: Princeton University Press, 2010.

A NOTE ON THE TYPE

THIS BOOK has been composed in Miller, a Scotch Roman typeface designed by Matthew Carter and first released by Font Bureau in 1997. It resembles Monticello, the typeface developed for The Papers of Thomas Jefferson in the 1940s by C. H. Griffith and P. J. Conkwright and reinterpreted in digital form by Carter in 2003.

Pleasant Jefferson ("P. J.") Conkwright (1905–1986) was Typographer at Princeton University Press from 1939 to 1970. He was an acclaimed book designer and AIGA Medalist.

The ornament used throughout this book was designed by Pierre Simon Fournier (1712–1768) and was a favorite of Conkwright's, used in his design of the *Princeton University Library Chronicle*.

CPSIA information can be obtained
at www.ICGtesting.com
Printed in the USA
JSHW050149071022
31365JS00002B/2

9 780691 202341